MW01138920

THE HOUSE OF GOLD

Liam O'Flaherty

Preface by Tomás Mac Síomóin

Copyright © 1929 Liam O'Flaherty

All rights reserved. No part of this book may be reproduced in any form or by any means including electronic or mechanical photography, filming, recording or by any information storage and retrieval or video systems without prior permission from the publishers, Nuascéalta Teoranta.

www.nuascealta.com • info@nuascealta.com

Cover Illustration and Design: © Karen Dietrich,2013.

Typesetting: Nuascéalta Teoranta

Preface © Tomás Mac Síomóin, 2013.

ISBN-13:978-1484097496
ISBN-10:1484097491

ACKNOWLEDGMENTS

The publishers would like to thank the family of Liam O'Flaherty, especially Máiréad Ní hEithir, Jenny and Niall Farrell, Cumann Liam agus Thomáis Uí Fhlaithearta (The Liam and Tom O'Flaherty Society), and Antóin Delap for his sage advice.

CONTENTS

This book was originally published in 1929, and represents a reproduction of an important historical work, maintaining as faithfully as possible the same format as the original work. We appreciate your understanding of occasional imperfections, and sincerely hope you enjoy seeing the book back in print.

PREFACE

As W. B. Yeats intimated in *Parnell* (1938), the outcome of the Irish struggle for independence from Britain made little difference to workers:

> *"Parnell came down the road, he said to a cheering man: Ireland shall get her freedom and you still break stone."*

In the mid-1920s, in the aftermath of that independence struggle and Ireland's internecine civil war, Liam O'Flaherty, scarcely out of his twenties, had already come to a similar conclusion: the pre-revolutionary capitalist order remained wholly intact after the departure of the British garrisons. The Irish Free State guaranteed Ireland's pre-revolutionary role as the supplier of agricultural produce and labor to industrial Britain. A form of comprador capitalism, the economic order that so often defines the nexus of mother countries to their ex-colonies, established itself in Britain's Irish ex-colony, to the detriment of the economic development of the latter.

O'Flaherty was acutely aware that the armed revolt that led to the foundation of the Irish Free State, far from constituting a revolution, merely prolonged the old order under the Irish tricolor. The post office boxes were painted green, as James Connolly, the socialist insurrectionary leader who was executed by the British in 1916, had presaged. The old ascendancy saw its influence greatly diminished after the establishment of the new state. But, as *The House of Gold* indicates, they were quickly replaced by an equally oppressive native gombeen ascendency, buttressed by the Catholic Church, symbolized in *The House of Gold* by the avaricious Ramon Mor Costello (Gaelic: Réamon Mór, Big Raymond), the novel's main protagonist. This new oppressor, of peasant stock, based his wealth on exploitation of a largely rural proletariat and sucked dry his area of influence, the fictitious town of Barra and its environs, of its wealth and hopes for the future. Interestingly, this is the only one of O'Flaherty's novels in which a gombeen man figures as the leading character.

O'Flaherty had raised the red flag over Dublin's Rotunda during the Irish Civil War, a few short years before he wrote *The House of Gold*. Thus, almost uniquely among Irish writers of his day, his friend Sean-Phádraic Ó Conaire (mentioned in the novel) and Peadar O'Donnell excepted, he brought a left political perspective to bear on the literary representation of the society he observed about him. This he did, with a unique amalgam of passion, acute observation and formidable literary prowess, in his dissection in *The House of Gold* of the various strata of Barra society. Oliver Goldsmith's famous lines from his poem *The Deserted Village:*

> *"Ill fares the land, to hastening ills a prey,*
> *Where wealth accumulates and men decay ...* "

define both the backdrop and leitmotif of *The House of Gold*. For the houses, pubs and presbyteries of Barra reek of this Goldsmithian decadence.

Such "decay" in the case of the citizens of Barra, apart from their poverty and abject submissiveness, is compounded by their discombobulated behavior and chaotic thinking. Starting with the Costello family, and extending his soundings through most of the population, both clerical and lay, O'Flaherty dissects this eccentricity of character with sympathy and preternatural psychological acuity. The picture he presents is disturbing. No whimsically amusing Irish "house negroes" of the Somerville and Ross *Irish RM* variety, nor of their contemporary equivalents, *Father Ted, etc.*, adorn the pages of *The House of Gold*, but rather representative samples of a broken people, many teetering on the brink of lunacy.

O'Flaherty's no-holds-barred descriptions of the behavior of the inhabitants of Barra correspond to accounts of the common post-colonial complex of other indigenous peoples, such as the Maori and Native Americans, who were traumatized by harsh colonial processes. In Ireland, this process all but destroyed the native language and culture, reducing significant swathes of the population to the cringing obeisant creatures that crowd the pages of *The House of Gold*. The centrality of drink—a frequently resorted -to self-medication of the psychologically damaged—to social intercourse in Barra is but one indicator (others abound in the text of the novel) of the vitality of such a complex in O'Flaherty's Ireland!

Anybody familiar with Galway, the gaelicisms of its speech and with its people will recognize instantly that O'Flaherty's Barra is, in fact, Galway. The character profiles that abound in the turbulent pages of *The House of Gold* are based, undoubtedly, on identifiable inhabitants of that town in the immediate aftermath of the Irish Civil War (1922-23). But Barra is more than just Galway. O'Flaherty tells us that predatory simulacra of Ramon Mor were to be found in every Irish town of the period, with its mandatory class divide, policed, morally, by the Catholic Church. Thus, *The House of Gold,* presents us with an incomparable panorama, from a left perspective, of the dark side of Irish life throughout the early years of the fledgling Irish state.

O'Flaherty's picture of Barra life is, in fact, the quintessential opposite of the rural Irish Catholic idyll, crystallized in the early poems of his fellow Aran islander, Máirtín Ó Direáin, and enshrined by Éamon de Valera in his St. Patrick's day 1943 radio address, in which the latter spoke of a future Ireland as the:

> *"...home of a people who valued material wealth only as a basis of right living, of a people who were satisfied with frugal comfort and devoted their leisure to things of the spirit; a land whose countryside would be bright with cozy homesteads, whose fields and villages would be bright with sounds of industry, the romping of sturdy children, the contests of athletic youths, the laughter of comely maidens; whose firesides would be the forums of serene old age..."*

But the iconoclastic O'Flaherty didn't shrink from describing the tortuous conscience probing of corrupt and lascivious clerics, the passion of adulterous lovers, and the unrequited passions, not exclusively masculine, that center on the story's "Golden Lady",

Ramon's wife, the exotic Anglo-Irish Nora. Barra is nearer to Sodom than to the "heart-warming" confections of the conventional—and uncensored—Irish writers of his epoch. De Valera's "things of the spirit" sought by most of his Barra characters were mainly of the liquid kind, imbibed to great excess in turbulent Hogarthian scenarios. The sordid shenanigans in Barra's brothel, the Glen Tavern, would hardly have jibbed with that "Holy Catholic Ireland" at the heart of Free State ideology. O'Flaherty cultivated a vigorous prose that was programmed to bite! And, although tempered with extraordinarily beautiful and sensitive descriptions of the scenic ambience of Barra, bite it surely does.

Given the deeply conservative neo-Jansenist Catholic climate of the times, it hardly surprises us that O'Flaherty's warts-and-all vision of one turbulent day in Barra so displeased the Irish Free State Censorship of Publications Board in 1929, that it afforded *The House of Gold* the signal honor of being the first book to be banned by that body for sale and distribution in Ireland. The remit of this Board was to prohibit "indecent" or "obscene" books and *The House of Gold* was deemed to be such. This petty act of the censors drove yet another world-class writer out of Ireland, depriving him of the main target readership to which his *The House of Gold* (and four subsequent works) was entitled. Other leading Irish writers, of course, such as George Bernard Shaw, Seán O'Casey, Seán Ó Faoláin, Frank O'Connor etc., etc., as well as a formidable team of non-Irish authors, fell afoul of this narrow-minded literary inquisition whose stultifying effects on the intellectual life of Ireland have yet to fade fully.

The House of Gold is much more than a mere report on the vagaries of one tumultuous fair day in a rural town of the fledgling Irish state. For O'Flaherty digging deep beneath Barra's social surface, transmuted the locus of this extraordinary novel into one of universal significance. This becomes all the more obvious as we attempt to categorize it in the context of world literature. Paradoxically, as an English-language novel, *The House of Gold*, with its pre-emptive toques of magical realism, adheres most closely to a popular category of post-colonial Latin American novel in which caciques, powerful chieftain-like figures, such as Ramon Mor Costello, lord it over cowering largely indigenous populations which depend abjectly upon them.

Thus, in Juan Rulfo's classic *Pedro Páramo* (1955), the brutal rural cacique of that name ruthlessly impoverishes his tenants and neighbors, the inhabitants of the fictitious Mexican town of Comala. As Ramon is obsessed by his wife, the exotic import Nora, the *femme fatale* and *belle dame sans merci* of Barra, Pedro Páramo is hopelessly enamored of his wife, Susana San Juan, a similarly exotic urban import. She, like Nora, denies her spouse a husband's privileges.

Gabriel García Marquez claims to have memorized *Pedro Páramo* before writing his *Cién Años de Soledad* (1967. *One Hundred Years of Solitude*), in which the reign of a succession of Ramon-like caciques of the Buendía family terminates in the destruction of Macondo, the town they parasitize. Among several Nora-like figures who emerge during the reign of the Buendía family in the town appears an exotic outsider, Fernanda del Carpio, daughter of a ruined aristocrat, who—unlike Ramon's Nora, who spends most of her time day-dreaming in her bedroom—manages the Buendía household with an iron hand.

In a radical inversion of the O'Flaherty-Rulfo template, the Venezuelan novel of Rómulo Gallegos, *Doña Bárbara*, published in 1929, the same year as *The House of Gold,* the ruthless scheming female rural cacique of the same name is likewise doomed to suffer an unrequited lust for the city-educated Santos Luzardo, as she disseminates injustice and corruption in the countryside about her demesne. Unlike the case of *The House of Gold,* Gallegos' aim (he was later to be elected President of Venezuela) , was to promote the superior values, as he saw it, of the metropolis above those of a recalcitrant backward rural order, represented by the person of Doña Bárbara.

A well-known extra-literary Latin American clone of Ramon Mor in recent historical times was Juan Peron (1895-1974), the populist political leader who was mandated electorally three times to rule Argentina. Like Ramon Mor, he frequently referred to his humble background; he categorized his enemies as "enemies of the workers" while amassing a huge private fortune. His "Golden Girl" was Evita Peron (Maria Eva Duarte), to whose whims he was more than glad to cater. Not surprisingly, perhaps, a Spanish translation of *The House of Gold, La Casa del Oro,* was published in Buenos Aires in 1949, during Peron's first mandate, 1946-52. Another case of life imitating fiction?

The Barra folk of *The House of Gold* seem doomed to reproduce their form of social life, even, even when Ramon is no more. For the immense wealth—the source of his power in Barra—remains secure in the clutches of the Costello clan. O'Flaherty sees no sign of redemption emerging from a Barra whose population is vitiated by a sense of powerlessness, intellectual confusion and moral cowardice. The hegemony of the *status quo*—both in its clerical and lay aspects—is depicted by him as being far too powerful to allow the underlying sullen resentment of the local population, articulated by a tiny minority of ineffectual and socially marginalized dissidents, to burst into open revolt. O'Flaherty's *métier* is expressed in precisely nuanced forays into the descriptive realm, not into the prescriptive. In this endeavor, as *The House of Gold* abundantly illustrates, he took no hostages and had few equals.

This re-issue of *The House of Gold* by Nuascéalta, the first since 1929, should find particular resonance in a contemporary Ireland where the threatening figure of the local gombeen merchant has been replaced by that of the Troika. An anxious, submissive and debt-ridden citizenry, unjustly beholden to foreign bond-holders, now takes the place of the debt-ridden citizens of 1920's Barra, cowering under the baleful glare of Ramon Mor Costello.

Since such contagion has now infected the entire world of contemporary capitalism, the basic theme of this extraordinary novel is truly universal. If only for its masterly depiction of the vicissitudes of a population deprived of real power, alternative leaders and a sense of direction, Liam Ó Flaherty's *The House of Gold* deserves an honored place in the world canon of socially committed literature.

Tomás Mac Síomóin
Sant Feliu de Guíxols
Bealtaine 2013

Tomás Mac Síomóin is an award-winning Gaelic novelist, storyteller, poet, and journalist. A doctoral graduate of Cornell University, he has lived in Catalonia since 1998. Translations from Spanish and Catalan, including Juan Rulfo's Pedro Páramo *and the poetry of Ernesto Cardinal, figure among his work, along with polemical essays of cultural and political analysis. His short story* Music in the Bone *was selected by The Dalkey Archive Press for inclusion in* Best European Fiction 2013. *An English-language translation based on his award-winning collection of short stories,* Diary of an Ant: Eleven (mainly) Dark Yarns from the Irish Gaelic, *is published by Nuascéalta. and a translation based on his award-winning novel* An Tionscadal, The Cartographer's Apprentice, *is due to be published in 2013 also by Nuascéalta.*

PART I
PASSION

CHAPTER I

ON the summit of the Black Cliff above the town of Barra, Francis O'Neill was waiting for the wife of Ramon Mor Costello. It was now midnight. He had been waiting two hours. He had begun to despair of her coming.

The moon was full. The sky was littered with stars. There were no clouds. The air was warm and still. It was almost as bright as day. For miles all round the cliff the earth was distinct, gleaming in the moonlight, that distorted everything with its sepulchral glow. Upon the sea there was a golden road of moonbeams, stretching from the cliff to the horizon, dividing the smooth, dark water. In the silence the sound of the waves rose mightily into the firmament like a mournful hymn of death and disembodiment. The sound was terrible in the moonlight, the lapping, tumbling, rolling mumble of measureless water, moving endlessly in ignorant haste, lashing the rocks and grinding them to sand, which it hurled in mounds upon the world's shores from its deep bottoms.

Dark mountains, towering high behind the cliff, added to the night's sinister majesty. In front, the land fell steeply to a rolling plain, on whose edge the town lay by the sea, half-concealed within a grey mist. Near by, the rocks gleamed. In the distance, everything was sombre; except where a tree, or a white wall, caught by the glare of the moonbeams, shone brilliantly.

The cliff was five hundred feet high. It rose precipitously from the sea, bulging outwards at the top. From its summit, a slab of stone, ten feet long and three feet wide, stuck out. This hoary, grey stone, spotted with tawny lichen, shone in the moonlight, like a spear pointed at the moon. A stone wall ran along the cliff, about ten feet from the brink, to keep animals from straying into danger. On this space, between the wall and the cliff, the grass was eaten to the roots by rabbits. Here and there they had scratched little holes, trying to make burrows. Along the path they were sitting on their haunches, nibbling at the grass, scratching, scurrying to and fro.

O'Neill lay face downwards on the grass, beneath the wall, watching the path that led downwards along the cliff to her husband's house below. He was perspiring. He was in a fever of desire.

Then, at last, he saw her come. At the foot of the slope where the cliff joined the lowland, there was a beach of yellow sand. The demesne of Ramon Mor's house lay above the beach, to the right. The wall of the demesne was bound by a sandy road that joined the end of the cliff path. Another narrow road ran to the right from this junction, at right angles to the beach, along the second wall of the demesne. Where these roads joined there was a white cottage, on a ledge of rock at the edge of the beach. He saw her, coming towards the path, against the white wall of the cottage. Then she passed out of sight, concealed by the wall that bound the cliff.

When he saw her he uttered a cry of joy and began to tremble. He got. to his feet and stood on his toes, trying to catch another glimpse of her. Then, failing to see her, he again lay down and put his ear near the ground, trying to catch the sound of her steps. He heard a stone dislodged. He. raised his head. Some way down the path a rabbit was sitting on his hind legs, with his head erect, his ears cocked and his fore legs hanging limply, startled by the stone. The rabbit bounded out of sight. She came around a corner, stooping. He heard her pant. He stood up, leaned forward and called out:

"Nora!"

She stood, raised her head, saw him, waved her hat which she carried in her hand and then came forward running. Without speaking he caught her in his arms. He carried her to a spot beneath the wall and laid her down gently on the grass. Then he knelt beside her and began to kiss her hands, passionately whispering words of endearment between his kisses. He kissed all her fingers, her wrists, her palms, and then, leaning forward, he rubbed his cheek against her bosom. Then he lay beside her, encircled her with his arms and kissed her neck, her lips, her hair, her cheeks, her eyes, her ears. She lay in his arms, panting, with her eyes closed, until he ceased, exhausted by his outburst. Then she opened. her eyes, smiled, kissed him rapidly on the lips, took his face between her hands, kissed his forehead, laughed excitedly and sat up, pushing him gently from her. He made an effort to retain her in his embrace, then he desisted, let himself go limp, dropped his head on her bosom and closed his eyes. He trembled. She stroked his hair.

"Let me breathe," she whispered. "I'm exhausted after climbing the hill. I ran nearly all the way."

"I can't help it," he murmured. "I was waiting so long. I thought you wouldn't come."

"Dar-il-ing !"

She uttered the word on a trilling note like a bird, adding a syllable. Then she touched his hair and his forehead gently with her lips. Excited by these caresses, he raised himself and tried to encircle her neck w1th his hands. She resisted him and said hurriedly:

"Let me take off *my* raincoat. I feel hot."

He jumped up and took off his own coat. He. was wearing flannel trousers and a brown, tweed coat, with a belt at the back. He threw his coat, and then his cap, on the grass. He took off his neck-tie and unbuttoned his shirt at the throat. He rolled up his sleeves. She watched him.

"Won't you be cold like that?" she said. He knelt before her and watched her fingers as she undid the belt of her raincoat. He did not reply. He was trembling.

"Let me " she whispered.

She leaned forward and kissed his bare breast, making a little cooing sound, as her lips passed gently over his skin. He closed his eyes. Then she took off her coat, unbuttoned the jacket of her blue suit and spread the coat on the grass. They sat side by side on the coat, took one another's hands and gazed rapturously at one another. The moonlight was shining on her golden hair. Her hair lay in a thick luxuriant mass of curls on her crown. It bunched about her ears and descended in waves along the back of her head to her neck. On her crown it had a reddish tinge. At the back of her head the colour was of a deeper gold and the hairs were more delicate and soft. Her eyes were of a golden colour. They were rather small, with long lashes that were tipped with gold. Her eyebrows were so fair as to be barely visible. Her ears were small and perfectly moulded. Her lips were full and voluptuous. There was a dimple in her chin. Her complexion was of a creamy colour. She had a swanlike neck, that widened to her bust in a perfect curve. She was tall, with long, supple limbs and a slim body on whose chest two breasts, like rimless bowls upturned, strained against her jersey of green silk. Her skirt just reached her knees. Beneath it her legs showed, modelled with the same perfection as her neck, with voluptuous curves.

Her whole body had a golden sheen and, like that precious metal which has aroused the madness of conquest in countess men, her beauty was almost evil in its turbulent influence on the senses. She was terrible in her beauty, like the lovely, golden sea-plants that wind, swaying languidly, around the limbs o£ a white swimmer and drag him down into their bed, caressing him with many twisting arms. Her eyes by their dreamy languor and her limbs by their slow movements inspired desire and frenzy. O'Neill, sitting beside her, watching her greedily, offered a striking contrast to the voluptuous repose of her golden body. Black-haired, with flashing, brown eyes, a dark skin taut upon bony cheeks, his lean body quivered in the excitement of love. He too was physically exciting, but rather by his extreme vitality than by the perfection of his limbs or features. His eyes alone were beautiful.

"Now," she said, after they had gazed in silence for a long time at one another. "Now. I'm really here with you at last. It's hard to realise It. I thought I would never get away. As a rule he is asleep by ten o'clock, but tonight he kept moving about, coming into my room, arguing and saying that I want to kill him. Ugh!

She shuddered and leaned her head against his shoulder.

"He terrifies me," she said. "How awful it is!"

"Forget him," he said, putting his arms about her and kissing the side of her neck.

She began to sob.

"I can't, I can't," she said. "It's too terrible. Tell me. Tell me something."

"What?" he whispered.

"Have you nothing to tell me?"

He leaned over her, crushed her in his arms and began to whisper words of endearment, kissing her while he spoke. Again she closed her eyes and lay limply in his arms.

But when he moved towards a more intimate caress she opened her eyes and slipped from under him with a sudden movement.

"No no! " she said looking aside furtively, down the path that led to her husband's house. " I still feel him watching me. Sit still beside me and put your arms around me. Speak to me. I'm terribly afraid of him God! Supposing he got up and came looking for, me in my room. I locked my bedroom door, but that s no protection. Heavens!"

He shrugged his shoulders. She looked at him and saw that his face was dark with passion. She touched his arm with the tips of her fingers.

"Don't disappoint me," she said softly. "Why are you angry?"

"Can't you see?" he muttered hoarsely. "I'm mad with love for you and you are only playing with me."

"I?" she whispered excitedly. "Playing with you ! How can you say that? Have I not left my house in the middle of the night to come here to you? No. But I want to be sure of you. I want you all. I want to make sure that I'm not a plaything for you."

Then she whispered very softly:

"You see, you are the first man I ever loved."

"You want to be sure of me?" cried O'Neill. "What more do you want? My God! Look at me!"

He struck his breast.

"I came here two months ago from Dublin after that ruffian had absconded to America and my newspaper went smash. I had to come back and humiliate myself still further by going to live on my father. I am now thirty and I have made a mess of my life. Some damnable curse has followed me in everything I ever put my hand to. You don't know all the things I have done or you wouldn't think that I'd broken this resolution, thrown away this last chance, just because I fell madly in love with you..."

"Francis!" she whispered. "Don't be... "

"No," he interrupted excitedly. "You must listen. I have played and I have been a play-boy all my life, but not now. Christ! The first time I saw you I felt dizzy like a drunken man. You can't tell me now that I'm playing with you after I have thrown away my last chance of getting on my feet and forgetting the past. I want to lose that awful shame of being a waster."

"Dar-il-ing !"

"What is the use?" he cried angrily. "You don't really believe me. You don't really want me. I feel it."

"Oh! I do. I do. Don't torture me."

"No, you don't. I'm a cursed fellow. God! When I think of it. Bred like a pauper. Then I'm sent away to school, after my people have starved themselves to collect enough money to make me a priest. I run away from the seminary and become a revolutionary. I'm put in jail. My people are disgraced. My mother died of the disgrace. I believe it. It was that killed her. Since then I have gone from one thing to another. I have even been a secret service man. Then I started a paper with that scoundrel Mullally. He ran away with the funds and the paper went bankrupt. Then I came home with the idea of going to America. My sister gave me the money to go. The money is spent long ago. I'm still here. For two months now, I have thought of nothing night and day but you. Nothing seems to matter but you. The whole world is turned upside down. I have lost all sense of shame. I'm going to do what I have never done before, just because I love you, for it's not for myself I'm going to do it. Yet you think I'm playing with you."

"But sweetheart, don't you understand what I mean? Don't you understand that it's because I want you all to myself that I want you to wait."

"I don't understand," he said. "I have waited two months."

She shuddered.

"No," she said. "While he is down there in that terrible house I couldn't feel happy if I gave myself to you. If you take me now I couldn't leave. I'd want to go away with you at once."

"That's what I want you to do," he said eagerly, leaning towards her.

"No, no," she said. "We mustn't. Then he'd win."

O'Neill drew back.

"What do you mean by saying he'd win?" he whispered.

She did not reply for a few moments. She was looking out over the sea.

"I hate him," she said bitterly.

O'Neill started.

"Then you started an affair with me in order to revenge yourself," he said angrily.

"Now don't get cross," she said softly. "You don't understand. You think I'm cruel, but you don't know what I have suffered. I didn't know you were an admirer of my husband."

"I an admirer of Ramon Mor Costello ! I loathe the man."

"Then why did you say I'm cruel because I hate him?"

"It was you said it yourself."

"Yes, but you changed suddenly just now when I said I hated him and that I mean to win."

"Nora," he said, taking her two hands in his. "Don't let's argue. We have no time. What does he matter?"

She withdrew her hands gently and covered her face with them. She began to sob.

"Nora!" he whispered.

"No, you don't love me," she mumbled through her tears. "You have no pity for me. You only want to amuse yourself. I wish I were dead."

He threw himself on his knees before her and cried :

"Forgive me, Nora. Forgive me."

He laid his head in her lap. She took his head between her hands, raised it and kissed him on the lips.

"Say you love me," she whispered.

"I adore you."

"And you'll protect me."

"Come away with me to-morrow, after I'm through with this business."

She shuddered and said :

"It's impossible. I can't come away with you to-morrow. You don't know him. He's capable of anything."

"How do you mean? I'm not afraid of him!"

"Hush! Don't talk foolishly. I know you are not afraid. But I'm afraid of him. While he lives I cannot escape him. He has told me several times in my room at night that some day he won't be able to keep his hands off me."

"Good God ! The brute! The man is a savage. And to think that that brute has grabbed everything in the town and in the whole countryside! An ignorant, surly bear, with no more feeling in him than a stone!"

"No, no. That's not quite true. He has a terrible personality. He is really terrifying. He is a genius. I always know when he is in the house, even though I don't see him or know that he has come in."

"Genius be damned!" said O'Neill furiously. "If he is a genius then the country is full of them. In every little town in Ireland you will find a man like Ramon Mor, a grabber, who makes his money by worse usury than Shylock ever practised."

"No, no," she said. "There can't be another man like him in Ireland. It is impossible to believe that even in the whole world there is such a man. A monster, but still a genius."

"I'll agree with you that he is a monster," said O'Neill bitterly. "And I have cause to hate him more than you. When I was a child he was the terror of my life. How it used to humiliate me to see my mother bow to him in the street, because we owed him money! I remember the first time I saw him. He came into our village on a side-car to buy pigs from people that owed him money. My mother rushed out of the yard, wiping her hands in her apron. She bowed to him and asked him for a word. He bent down without a smile or a nod of salutation and listened to her. She kept wringing her hands in her apron while she spoke. I hated him for the cool way he listened to her, frowning, with his big lips stuck out, as if she were a block of stone or a slave. When he drove away I asked her who he was and she answered in a terrified voice: 'Hush, darling. That's Ramon Mor. We owe him money. He could come down on us and take everything we have if he wanted to, same as he is doing with the Hernons. But God gave him a kind heart. I know he'll pity my little ones!' How terrible that seemed to me, to be in the power of such a monster And it was still more humiliating, next day, when father brought a sack of flour on our mare from Ramon's shop in the town. I knew that mother had been begging off him. God I When I think of that I feel I could stab him to the heart." ·

Carried away by the hatred of Ramon Mor which she had aroused in him, he had forgotten his desire for her. He sat with his knees drawn up and his arms folded on his chest, looking out at the sea.

"You can't understand that," he added. "You have never suffered hunger."

"There are worse things than hunger," she said softly.

He looked at her gloomily. He suddenly became aware of the perfume with which her body was anointed and of her rich clothes. He was reminded of the riches of the earth which he had never enjoyed and he realised that she was of an alien breed, of a class that had oppressed his own. He momentarily hated her.

"There's nothing worse than hunger," he said fiercely.

"I'm one of the people. I know that. But anyway, we have a clean conscience. That's more than what your people have."

"How do you mean?" she said angrily.

His lips quivered.

"You say you hate him," he whispered. "Then why did you marry him?"

"Because there was no other way out."

"How do you mean?"

"It would take too long to explain, and I can't tell you anything when you speak to me like that."

"I suppose you think I have no right to ask you these things because my father was a peasant and you look on the people as dirt beneath your feet."

"Francis, what on earth are you driving at?"

"You married him for his money."

"You are a beast," she said, making an effort to rise.

With a sudden movement he caught her two arms and held her down. His eyes flashed. With his mouth close to hers he whispered:

" No, you can't go. I have you. Scream if you like. There's nobody to hear you. Nobody will come."

He crushed her in his arms. In the struggle her clothes became disarranged. He could see a little pink band across her breasts. The look of anger left his eyes. She ceased to struggle. Her head fell back. She closed her eyes. He kissed her throat and began to whisper to her. She trembled.

"Do you still want to go?" he said.

She drew him towards her without opening her eyes. "I love you," she whispered. " But you must be kind to me. I love you so much."

Now she did not resist him. While he loved her, she kept crying out that he was wonderful and he repeated her name. Then they lay still in one another's arms. She was the first to move.

"Do you still love me?" she whispered.

He looked at her, laughed aloud and said : "If Christ had known you instead of Magdalen he would never have died on the Cross."

"You say terrible things," she said.

She hugged him and covered his face with kisses. Now they were both exalted by the ecstasy of love. He sang a little love-song to her, with his lips close to hers. When he had finished she said to him:

"That is the most beautiful song I ever heard."

"Come away with me to-morrow, darling," he said, "and I'll sing you thousands of songs."

"I will. I will come with you. But not to-morrow. Not yet."

"Why? Why not?"

"Don't let us talk of that now. You'll get angry again."

"Forgive me. I don't understand. Why can't you?"

"No, no. Don't remind me of that. I want to forget the terrible things you said to me."

"Forgive me, Nora. It was because I loved you and I thought you were playing with me."

"You said I married him for his money."

"Forgive me."

"I forgive you, darling, but you mustn't t believe things like that of me. I didn't marry him for his money, but because there was no other way out."

"What does it matter, anyway?"

"I must tell you. I don't want the slightest thing to be between us."

"All right, then. Tell me. But it doesn't matter to me."

"You won't hate me afterwards?"

"For what?"

"For what I'm going to tell you."

"Why should I?"

"You might."

"Good God I Could anybody hate you after loving you once? Anyway, if it's anything you've done, it would be hard for me to blame anybody for anything after what I've done myself."

"I know, but it's different for a man. Men are forgiven everything."

"Then don't tell me if you are afraid that I might ... "

"But I must. I don't want you to think ... "

"All right. Tell on."

"Hold me tightly in your arms."

"There."

"What do you know of me? Nothing."

"Oh, yes. I know what people have told me around the town. Your father was a landowner from the Midlands. Your mother was English. She ran away with an actor and died in America. Your father gambled away his property on race-horses and then committed suicide by throwing himself in front of a train."

Her lips quivered.

"They say that, do they?" she whispered bitterly.

"In a country town people say any gossip that comes into their heads about anybody who is better off than they are."

"But you believe it."

"It's all the same to me what your people were or did."

"Oh! Well, It's partly true in any case. Only it was not an actor my mother ran away with and father poisoned himself. But ... "

She shuddered and clenched her teeth:

"How I hate these people here I They are venomous."

"It's not you," he said. "They're not bitter against you. It's Ramon Mor they hate."

"No," she said. "They hate me. I see it in their eyes."

He kissed her. She began to cry. Then she dried her eyes and said:

"You said I don't know what suffering is. Isn't that enough, to be left penniless, without a father or mother, at fifteen? I was at school. An aunt took me away and I went to live with her, in a big house near Dublin where she lived with her husband. They were very rich at that time. Her husband owned horses and he was away most of the time, in

England and France and around the country. Sometimes aunt went with him. More often she stayed at home. They were careless, frivolous people and they just let me hang around; not because they were too mean to pay for me at school but just because they wouldn't be bothered. Just let everything go to blazes. With the result that, seeing everybody around me drinking and I was fully grown then, but I knew nothing ... at sixteen I had a child and I didn't know who the father was. God! Those brutes. Aunt was so full of her own affairs that she never noticed or bothered until it was due to come. Then ... "

She stopped to wipe her eyes. He stroked her cheek and said, deeply moved:

"Poor devil! "

"Tell me," she whispered. "Do you hate me now?"

He could not reply because sobs were choking his throat. He kissed her, murmuring that he loved her.

"Aunt was good to me," she continued. "She took me away to France. I don't know what they did to the child. I hated it. I never saw it even. Then she quarrelled with her husband and they were divorced. It was she divorced him but still, when she came back to Dublin, she was quite poor on the alimony and what money she had herself. I know you despise rich people, but in a way it's harder for them when they get poor in their own circle than for people who were never used to having plenty. And she was such a spendthrift. Although she was really fond of me I could see that I was in her way. So I tried to get all sorts of jobs, but I'm not clever, and the sort of thing you need for a job was not what I learned at school. I had admirers, but they weren't the sort that marry a penniless girl. And after my first experience, my heart had hardened too much to allow anything else. Then my husband appeared. He was in Parliament then, you know."

"Yes, I know," said O'Neill. "I was in Dublin. I remember your marriage. Two years ago last May. I remember."

"Yes," she said, with a sigh. "Although I loathe him, I must admit that when I saw him I felt something like love for him. He was so different from all the smelly, unhealthy, ridiculous, shabby people I had been among for years. And then people were quite excited about him in Dublin. You know the way people get excited in the city about anything new. They talked about this picturesque figure, the dour business genius, the ruthless type that was going to put the country on its feet after the revolution. I met him at Phoenix Park races and he proposed at once. He was lost in Dublin society. And then...then of course...it would take more than a night, or a week, to tell you the rest, but I will tell you this much ... "

She paused, caught his arm and said with great vehemence: "I have been faithful to him until now. I was prepared to do my duty by him, although I married him without love. For I admired him. I was mistaken, though. He has driven me to this, with his persecution and his savagery. He has boasted to my face that I'd never inherit a penny of his money. He has shown me the will. After having taken from me my mother's jewels and things my father left to me, he means to leave me penniless. Never mind. It's a fight to the bitter end between us."

She had become so excited that she trembled.

O'Neill drew away from her and covered his face with his hands.

After awhile, she looked at him, started and said in a curious tone :

"What's the matter?"

"Nothing," he muttered. "It's just ... Curse him. You still belong to him. You can't leave him because he has mesmerised you."

"No, it's not that."

"It is. You can't leave him. Then why have you driven me to this if you're not going to leave him? I have done many things, but until now I have kept my hands clean from robbery."

"It's not robbery," she said. "It won't make you a thief. You're not doing it for yourself alone. It's my own money. I tell you that the jewels he took from me are worth much more than what you can take to-morrow. And have I no rights? Has a wife no rights?"

"You can think of nothing but of him," he cried. "Wife! Wife ! I don't want to think of you as his wife. Can't you come away to-morrow ... "

"Are you mad?" she said. "If we went away to-morrow after you had ... had done what you intend, they would immediately know .... "

"Yes, yes," he said, growing calm. "I never thought of that. I must be mad. Then what's the use of it? What's the use of running the risk of being branded as a thief, just for a little money, since I can't have you?""

Are you getting afraid?" she said. " I'm sorry I agreed to let you do it. Only it was you yourself that suggested it in the first place."

"That's not true," he cried. "I'm not afraid. But it was you suggested it. I remember. The very first day I met you at the doctor's house you began on it. You said the people deserved to be slaves, the way they allowed themselves to be robbed without resistance. And all these revolutionaries you said, wandering round the country penniless couldn't be worth much if they allowed themselves to starve instead of helping themselves."

"All right, then," she said. "If you want to back out ... "

"I don't want to back out, but I'm doing it only for one reason, and that is to get enough money to take you away with me. I'll do it for no other reason."

"But I tell you, darling, that I'll come away with you."

"When?"

"When he's dead," she said slowly.

He started. They looked at one another in silence.

"Then you want me to do that too?" he whispered.

"No, no," she said wildly. "Oh! God! No. Not that. It was something else I meant. No, no. You must promise me not to touch him. Promise me that."

"I promise," he said.

Again she became silent. Then she said irrelevantly:

" What do you think of the doctor?"

"Why?" he said. "What has the doctor got to do with it?"

"Oh! Nothing. I just. ... "

His face became flushed. .

"Why can't you be open with me?" he said.

"The doctor is not friendly with my husband, is he?" she whispered.

"That old woman is friendly with nobody," he said angrily.

"Don't speak ill of him," she said. "He's the only person in this terrible place who has been kind to me."

"He's in love with you. That's why."

"And anyway, you must remember, that it was at his house I met you. I thought you were friends with him."

"You're wrong," he said. "I'm not friends with him, but I have him in my power; that's why he has to pretend to be friends with me. It was he wrote the article for my paper describing your husband as 'An Irish Shylock!' He can't turn against me for fear I might expose him to your husband. That's why he receives me at his house. I only went there, though, as it was my only chance of getting to know you."

"I see," she said quietly. "So he is afraid o£ my husband. I know he disapproved of him on social grounds, but he never said anything to me about him. I suppose he thought it would be indelicate."

"He's as delicate as an old maid," said O'Neill.

"Oh! Yes," she said. "He did say something once or twice about my husband's arteries, and that he should get treatment for them. But my husband won't let a doctor near him."

O'Neill started.

"What does that mean?" he said. "The arteries."

"It's something to do with apoplexy," she said. "Any sudden shock is supposed to be fatal to it in certain cases. I don't understand. A man gets sort of run down, exhausted and then ... Of course, if, as you say, the doctor hates my husband and that my husband has got a hold over him, he might ... I mean, it was the doctor told me about the arteries."

"I didn't say the doctor knows your husband has got a hold over him."

"Still," she said, "it's all the same."

She looked at O'Neill in a curious manner.

"I heard him one day," she said, "talking to his mother. The old woman wanted him to go to the doctor and get some medicine for dizziness. He got furious and said the doctor would only be delighted to get a chance of poisoning him."

O'Neill now got terribly excited and his face worked nervously, as if he were trying to unravel an intricate problem.

"There's nothing in that, of course," she said. "It's merely his usual way of exaggerating things. But still ... "

"Now, I see what you mean," cried O'Neill, jumping to his feet.

"What?" she said calmly.

He knelt on one knee and looked into the distance.

"I feel cold," he said, picking up his coat. He buttoned his shirt and put on his necktie. Then he put on his coat and his cap. He sat down beside her and lit a cigarette.

"You think the shock of being robbed will probably kill him," he said coldly.

She did not answer for some time. Then she said in a low voice:

"He is a miser."

He threw the cigarette he had just lit over the edge of the cliff and said:

"It's a cowardly way to commit murder. I'd rather shoot him and be done with it."

They remained silent for a long time, looking out over the cliff.

"Listen," he cried, suddenly turning towards her and gripping her wrists.

"What?" she said dreamily.

"Let's go away now and leave all this. This is terrible. I don't like *it.* I don't hate him that way. Yes. I do. He deserves to die. But will he die? How do you know? That's a cowardly thing. It's too cunning."

"What are you talking about?" she said dreamily.

"I don't like you when you are like that," he said nervously.

"Yes. I'll do it. Everything is arranged for tomorrow. Let it go ahead. If he dies, he deserves it. That house you are living in now once belonged to Sir Michael de Burgo. He was the landowner around here. My uncle shot him the time of the land agitation. He was a tyrant and an enemy of the people. No man's wife or daughter was safe with him, but he was seven times better than the man that's there now, because, after all, it was not his own class or his own flesh he was eating, same as Ramon Mor is doing. His son never came to live in it afterwards. Then in the last rising of the people, I and the like of me put the finishing touches to the landlord class, fighting with the whole country against us, while Ramon Mor lay low, waiting to see how the cat would jump, by God, at the same time, making money out of our blood by selling rations to the soldiers we were fighting. And when it was all over and we won, it was he stole into that empty house and grabbed the land we fought for. My old father is still in his hut on the mountains and I'm penniless without a roof over my head. He deserves to die. And yet ... it's a cowardly way to ... I don't like it."

She remained silent. He still gripped her wrists. She was looking away from him. Suddenly he began to tremble and threw his arms around her.

"I want you, Nora," he cried passionately. "I am mad with love for you. I want you."

She kissed him passionately and said:

"Darling, if you think you'd be sorry afterwards, don't do it. Only I want you, too, and I want to get some money to go away with you. It's my own money really. He has taken everything I had. And it makes me feel a criminal, every fair day, to see all these half-starved people coming into town with their cattle, selling them and giving all the money to him. He is incapable of pity. To-morrow it will be the same thing. And it will go on and on unless ...Anyway ! I can't escape him. He holds me a prisoner. By terror. And I want you, Francis."

"I love you," he murmured. "I love you."

"Dar-il-ing!"

They clasped one another and kissed. Then she said softly:

"Now, darling, you'll be careful, won't you?"

"There's no danger," he said.

" Afterwards, you'll come straight here and wait for me. It's the best place. Nobody comes here. It's supposed to be haunted, isn't it?"

"Yes, I'll come here ! "

"You'll bring the money. Then we can make plans for going away."

"Yes, yes. Soon. Soon. It will be soon, won't it? I can't endure the agony of waiting for you much longer, having you there at his mercy."

"Yes " she said softly. "I feel it will be very soon. This won't go on much longer. "

"Tell me you love me."

" I adore you."

"And to-morrow you'll tell me when we can go away together."

"Yes. To-morrow night I'll be here at nine o'clock. Then I'll tell you. I'll know by then, if everything turns out all right."

"How?"

They looked at one another excitedly. Then they were both taken by a frenzy of passion. For a long time they remained motionless, looking into one another's eyes. Then they united in silence. It was growing cold with the approach of dawn. The moonlight shone upon their enlaced limbs with the sinister yellow glow that candles in the sconces of a bier throw upon an outstretched corpse, decked for the tomb; golden no more, but yellow, the sick colour of corruption.

Suddenly, when they parted, she started up and said:

"Was that a cock that crew?"

He listened.

"No," he said. "It was a dog that barked among the mountains."

"My God!" she said. "It's nearly dawn. I must be going."

She began to hook her skirt.

"No, no," he cried wildly, kissing her knees. "Not yet."

"I must. I must go," she whispered.

But leaving her skirt still unfastened, she threw her arms about him and they kissed one another wildly, murmuring words of love in ecstasy. Now they were both exalted and they said strange things to one another, while the sky rapidly changed colour and the moonbeams faded from the sea. Tears flowed from her eyes with the rapture of love and he kissed them from her cheeks like drops of precious wine. A cold breeze from the mountains passed over them, murmuring softly. The stars began to fade. The moon had become white.

"I must go," she said.

"All right," he said. "You'll come to-night. Here. At nine o'clock."

"Yes, I'll come. At nine o'clock. Be careful."

"There's no danger. It's all arranged. O'Rourke is in with us."

"You won't desert me," she whispered, putting her arms around his neck and kneeling before him.

"I swear by the mother of God," he cried, with tears in his eyes, "that nothing but death can keep me from you. At nine o'clock. You won't be late."

"Yes. At nine o'clock. Oh! Francis, I hope nothing happens to you."

"Don't be afraid. Nothing can happen to me. I told you it's perfectly safe. We have it all arranged."

He gesticulated. He talked wildly, kissing her face and neck while he spoke. With her eyes closed and her head leaning on his shoulder, she kept pressing him with her arms. Then they started, parted and listened. A curlew called in answer to the dawn, afar upon the borders of the sea, a piercing cry that echoed in the vastness of the silent air.

He bowed his head. She caught up her hat and coat.

"Here at nine o'clock," she said.

"Nine o'clock."

"Good-bye, love."

"Good-bye, beloved."

Once more they embraced wildly. Then she ran from his arms down the path. He stood still, looking after her; she turned at every second step and waved to him. The bird flew over him, flying towards the mountains, invisible, uttering its strange cry. Now he could no longer see her golden hair, nor her neck that was so beautiful. He threw himself face downwards on the grass and he began to sob. Something told him to rise, to follow her, not to let her go, to take her away with him at once. He tried to rise, but he sank to the ground exhausted.

For a few moments he had a clear vision of himself, purified and holy, receiving the Blessed Sacrament of the Eucharist. A voice said to him:

"Keep her. She is your salvation."

He tried again to rise. He could not. Something held him down. The feeling of purity left him. His head grew dizzy. He began to fall asleep. As he became unconscious in sleep he had a vision of a woman's arm, rising in a dark place, curving, trying to encircle his neck and to draw him towards an unseen body. Then it desisted, floated upwards and disappeared within a dark cloud. He heard a voice crying in despair for something that was lost.

It was the curlew calling in the mountains to the dawn.

CHAPTER II

SHE ran down the path. She knew that her husband awoke with the light of day and that the first thing he would do would be to enter her room. But it was easier to climb the path than to descend. The slope was extremely steep and the shorn grass was slippery. She had to cling to rocks, to bushes and to the stones of the wall. In places the path was so narrow that she ran a danger of falling over the brink of the cliff. But such was her fear of being caught that she risked the danger, until, rounding a sharp corner, her foot slipped. She stumbled against the wall. She was thrown towards the cliff's edge. In a wild effort to save herself, she threw herself towards the wall, struck her side against it and fell. She was almost knocked unconscious. Her side was bruised. She had to lie for several minutes, panting, before she could continue. Then, shaken by the fall, she was afraid to run. She picked her steps carefully and lost many precious minutes.

In the east, the sky was already beginning to become spotted with light. It was, however, still quite dark within her husband's demesne among the trees. She began to feel safe as she reached the white cottage at the edge of the beach, near the corner of the demesne wall. She had only to go another two hundred yards and enter the demesne through a small door in the wall that ran at right angles to the beach. She had procured the key for this door.

But she suddenly stopped when she was within two hundred yards of the cottage. She had heard a sound within it. Somebody, in fact, was opening the door. Even then, if she had gone on, she would have escaped. But she was so terrified by the unexpected sound that she could not move until it was too late. The door faced the sea. But would he, whoever he was, not hear the sound of her feet if she ran? After meditating for three seconds she determined to chance that, and she was about to take a pace forward on tiptoe when she dropped to the ground instead. She lay still, holding her breath, almost unconscious with fright.

The parish priest, Fr. Michael Considine, had come out of the cottage. He was walking slowly across the little yard towards the sea, almost in her direction. His left shoulder was towards her. He was walking in a strange manner, very stiff and erect, with his arms folded on his bosom. He was staring fixedly straight in front of him. He did not see her. Yet she was only a few yards from him when he reached the end of the yard and halted.

That cottage had long since been uninhabited. The parish priest had recently bought it. It was practically in ruins, but he repaired it and used it as a fishing and bathing lodge. He was often seen going down there in the evening. But what was he doing there at this hour?

He looked distraught.

The tide was almost at its lowest ebb. From the ledge of rock that bound the yard, there was a sloping mound of boulders to the yellow strand. Through the sand, rivulets were flowing from the rocks into the tide, beyond a belt of coloured pebbles. And in the tideway, among the foam of the smooth waves breaking, swishing like silken skirts upon a ballroom floor, dark weeds were floating, studded like nine-tailed switches on the bed-rocks. The sea stretched out, darkening to the horizon from the blue 'long-shore, swaying with the dawn breeze gently.

The priest stood out pitch-black against the horizon. Upon his tall, thin frame his clothes hung loosely, sagging round his legs and rolling round his body, as on an ill-wrought statue. His coat reached far down his thighs. It was buttoned to the collar on his throat. His neck was long and shrivelled. His head was bare. It was beautiful in outline. Perfectly motionless, it was like the head of a statue. Straight black hair lay flat upon his skull, streaming sparsely down his neck and ending abruptly on his forehead like a wig. He had an enormous forehead. His face was deadly pale, indented with deep lines and so thin that the bones stood out clearly beneath the skin. There were vertical furrows on either side of his thin-lipped mouth. His eyes were sunk deeply in their sockets. His dark eyebrows were raised, his eyes stared, his lips were parted, in a gesture of contemplating something terrible.

He held his hands stretched out in front of him, with his elbows to his sides, as if he were saying Mass. But the movement of his hands was unholy. They were long and thin, covered on the back with an intricate labyrinth of pink veins; and with lifeless dark hairs. There were thick bunches of hair between the second and third joints of his long fingers. His thumbs were short and thick. His hands swayed, half-turning and twisting limply on his wrists, resembling the movements of the many-tentacled jelly-fish that float, belly sideways, in the sea, mid-waters, waving their bladdery arms. Their movement was slow and awful, without seeming purpose, unguided by reason, weaving strange patterns, a sorcery beckoning mystically to the waves that rolled in similar undulations to the strand. Protruding, white, from the black sleeves of his priestly coat, they seemed unattached, and with his distraught eyes he seemed to watch their mime in horror.

He stood thus for some time. And she suddenly thought, watching him, that she might be able to crawl past unseen. He seemed in a trance. But just as she moved to rise, he moved and she dropped once more to the ground and lay still. He shuddered and then glanced round him furtively, rubbing his hands together and then folding them on his bosom. He looked first to the right and then to the left, towards her. She held her breath, prepared to shriek when his eyes should fall upon her. But although it seemed certain that his eyes passed over her body, they did not see her. He looked out over the sea and sighed deeply.

Her terror increased. Was he mad?

Then she heard him speak. At first he mumbled. Then he threw out his arms, paused, and raised them upwards to the sky.

"Jesus! My Saviour!" he cried in a loud, fervent voice. He held his arms aloft, motionless, for nearly a minute. Then he lowered them, with the hands again moving, half-turning, slowly. He bowed his head and joined his hands in front of his chest. He began to pray in a loud voice:

"Lord have mercy on me. I am being swallowed in the abyss of lust. My will is weak. Take this apple of evil from my sight. Crush this demon. I am unclean like a leper. I dare not raise my eyes to Thy Holy Face. Save me or I perish."

He shuddered. Then he raised his hands once more to the sky. His body became rigid and he cried in an angry voice:

"Christ! God I Crush this yellow viper. Her arms are about my neck. Crush her or I perish."

As if there were arms about his neck in reality, he put his hands to his throat and he threw back his head. He staggered backwards and coughed as he steadied himself.

She started and raised her head, excited by what he had said. Fear left her eyes. Hatred took its place. She bit her lower lip. Her forehead became furrowed.

The sky began to break in the east.

The priest began to mutter, caressing his hands and trembling violently. His words were indistinct, jumbled together without meaning. He talked of serpents and of golden hair and of a tower of ivory and of a virgin.

Then he suddenly straightened himself, drew his hands down by his sides, threw back his head and cried out in an arrogant voice:

"You are silent. You have no mercy. Then I defy you. I shall taste this fruit."

He glanced to his right furtively, wiped his mouth with the palm of his left hand and turned about hurriedly, as if to run back into the cottage. But when he moved, he staggered and lurched towards her instead of going in the direction of the hut. He was within three yards of her when he steadied himself and halted. He put his hand to his forehead and panted, stooping forward. Then he straightened himself. She raised herself at the same time and covered her breasts with her hands, rigid with fright.

Her eyes met his. She saw them for a moment, glassy and lifeless, of a pale blue colour, with bloodshot rims. He started. He had seen her.

"Great God!" he cried in a hollow voice.

At the same moment she screamed, closed her eyes and threw herself on the ground.

As she became unconscious, she heard him running towards her, and then she smelt his breath as he bent over her and she heard him whispering her name, and she felt his hands moving over her face.

CHAPTER III

RAMON MOR COSTELLO saw, in his sleep, a hunting dog running in a wood after a deer. He distinctly saw the dog's fangs and the foam upon his lolling tongue and the pieces of briar that lay entangled in his shaggy coat. The dog ran in silence. He could smell the beast's loud breath. He could also smell the trees and the undergrowth and the rotting leaves that strewed the puddly ground. He could hear the dog's paws thudding and splashing through the pools.

The deer was indistinct. Its form was vague, as it went crashing through the brambles with a rustling sound of breaking twigs, followed by a shower of leaves shaken from their branches by its quick passage.

Ramon was urging on the dog. He growled in his sleep and tossed about the bed, clutching the clothes, breathless with excitement. Yet the dog could not overtake the deer. Until, at last, when Ramon could endure the suspense no longer and he was at the crisis of his dream, the trees parted, opening on a high precipice. The hunted deer stood on the cliff top, at bay. As the dog jumped for its throat, the deer changed into a woman. The woman shrieked.

He awoke. His hands were about his throat. He was lying on the floor. The bedclothes were bundled about his head. He lay still and listened. The shriek still re-echoed distinctly. At once, he called out:

"Nora! Are you there?"

There was no answer. He still saw the dog, the wood, the flying deer, the falling leaves. He heard a sound, which was at first that of the deer's passage through the brambles; a crashing sound. It then became heavier and more voluminous, like the sound of a mighty river, in flood, rushing through a gorge. He thought this water was rushing through his head. He became afraid that he had died in his sleep and that the shriek had been his own death-rattle. His brain reeled. He tried to move to assure himself that he was not dead. But his limbs were strangely feeble. He just managed to pull the clothes from about his head. He could not rise. The dream vanished. He realised that he lived, but that he was seriously ill. The trouble was in his head. One side of his face was terribly heavy. The right cheek felt numb. And when he tried to raise his right hand to feel the cheek, it would not move. But almost immediately afterward when he felt a sudden dull pain in his heart and he willed his left hand to touch his side over the heart, the left hand moved feebly to the spot whither he directed it. He realised that his right side was paralysed.

Then, without warning, his head fell forward. A great heaviness overspread his whole body. He could feel the numbness spreading through his limbs. The seat of consciousness passed from his brain to the centre of his body. A bright spark, of a red colour, glowed there. He experienced pain nowhere except at the vague spot where the red light glowed. The pain there was like that of an eye being torn from its socket.

That lasted for about fifty seconds. Then gradually the numbness began to leave his body, beginning at his toes and moving upwards. The parts vacated by the numbness ached intensely. At the same time, while the numbness moved upwards, leaving aching life in its passage, a noise became audible to him. It was at :first a buzzing sound that grew louder, until, when his head was cleared of the numbness, the sound became a shriek. It rang piercingly in his ears for a moment and then vanished. At once another sound reached his ears. This sound was the barking of a dog.

Now he was able to sit up, on the floor. He coughed and cleared his throat. His throat seemed to be clogged by some unpleasant matter. But when he spat nothing came forth. His palate, his tongue and his lips were parched. Now he raised his right hand to feel whether his cheek were hard. Now his hand obeyed him, but he withdrew it when it was level with his chin. He did not wish to make certain whether his cheek were hard or not. He felt terribly thirsty. He growled and tried to rise, suddenly angry with whatever disease it was that assailed him. He could not rise. Instead of rising, he fell forward on his hands and knees. He made no further effort to rise, but began to crawl on his hands and knees towards the wash-stand, to get at the water-cooler.

It was pitch-dark in the room. Of late he feared the moonlight and kept his windows heavily curtained. He struck the wall instead of reaching the wash-stand. He started, still more afraid, thinking his brain had ceased to function and that he had lost his sense of direction. He was roused by this fear and succeeded in getting to his feet by clinging to the wall. He groped about the floor, with his hands held out like a blind man. He found the table. There were matches there and a candle. He struck several matches before he could light one. His fingers felt big and quite numb. When he had lit the match he experienced great difficulty in applying it to the wick of the candle. Undoubtedly, he had practically lost his sense of direction.

Then he walked over to the wash-stand and picked up the water-cooler. He filled a glass with the water and was about to raise it to his lips when he saw himself in the swinging mirror that lay on the table. He dropped the glass to the table hurriedly and stepped aside. His face had terrified him. He stood still, looking to one side furtively, and he said in a whisper:

"What is it?"

He picked up the glass of water and drank it. He felt invigorated. Now his mind began to function thoroughly. Like a watch that has been inadvertently stopped by some impediment, halting the hour hand's progress and starts afresh, when released, with seemingly redoubled speed, so his mind seemed to open out all its cells and to thrust ideas into them from the store-room of his memory. He rapidly recovered his strength and shuffled to his bed, completely forgetting his illness and muttering:

"What's this? What's wrong? Where the devil is everybody at this hour of the morning?"

A dog was barking furiously, in the courtyard of the house, just beneath his window. He could hear the rattle of the animal's chain, as it took a run trying to break loose and then a snap and a choking yelp when it was tossed back after the chain went taut. He went to the window, drew aside the heavy curtains and raised the blind. It was dawn. The sun had not yet risen. He raised the lower part of the window and looked out.

He was wearing a nightshirt. It was too short for his massive body and stuck out in an enormous curve about his stomach and chest, like the loose garment worn by a pregnant woman. It was tied at his throat by a red cord with tassels instead of being buttoned. He had used it for years, and in the meantime he had grown corpulent. It strained at his chest. His chest showed through the opening, covered with matted hair. A holy medal of Our Lady of Perpetual Succour hung among the hair from a string.

The dog, seeing him, stopped barking and began to whine, swinging his tail.

"Lie down, Bran," he cried. "Hey! Tom! Tom Patch! Are you in bed yet?"

The yard was square and paved with cobble-stones. It was very large. To the left and in front, there were stables. On the right, there was a tall stone building and a stonewall in which there was a large cavity which had once been an archway, with a gate. Through the cavity, ruined buildings were visible and a paddock with a rick of hay. The paddock was overgrown with thistles. Over the roofs of the stables, he could see, from his window, an orchard, kitchen gardens and beyond, large trees with rich meadowland showing through their green foliage. In the yard there were signs of decay. Grass was growing between the cobbles. The stables were half in ruins. Some of the windows of the stone building were boarded up.

Excited by the barking of the watchdog, other dogs at a distance were also barking. Cocks were crowing. Fowls were cackling. Cows were lowing. In the trees, birds had begun to chatter, uncertain as yet of the dawn and giving voice sleepily. The air was cold. A slight fog was rising from the moist earth.

In answer to his shouting, a window opened above him to the right. A woman thrust out her head and shoulders. It was his sister Mary. She had an old overcoat about her head.

"In the name of God," she said. "What has happened?"

"How do I know?" shouted Ramon at her. "That's what I want to know myself. Didn't you hear the dog?"

"Yes, but ... "

"Devil take it," he cried. "Where is that scoundrel? Is nobody getting up and the morning near spent? Tom ! Tom Patch!"

Mary pulled in her head quickly and lowered her window. Feet came pattering down a stairway within the stone building. Then a door opened with a screeching sound and a man rushed out into the yard, holding a coat in one hand and holding up his trousers with the other. His boots were unlaced. His trousers were unbuttoned and his braces trailed behind him. His shirt was open. He was a little, fat man, with a black beard that encircled his face, showing little more than a short, thick nose, fat red lips and little blue eyes. He was as round as a barrel.

"Ga! Ga!" he cried, looking about him. "What's up?"

He rubbed his eyes.

"I'm asking you what's up?" shouted Ramon. "What's that dog barking for?"

Tom Patch looked up, saw Ramon and started.

"Ga! Ga!" he said. "God bless your honour. I didn't see you. The dog ! Did you say the dog?"

"Yes, the dog," shouted Ramon. "Get around the house, you fool, and see if anything is taken. Devil take it, am I to be plundered by robbers and ye all loafing in yer beds at this hour of the morning? Where is that fool O'Rourke? Is he in bed too?"

"Ga! Ga! Mr. Costello," said Tom, waving his coat. "The stallion. I was up all night with him. He's that bad I had to get O'Rourke out of his bed and the two of us hooked up the poor beast. I just lay down half an hour ago and ... "

"Oh! Blast the stallion," shouted Ramon, banging the window sill. "Do you know it's fair day or is it gone out of your mind you are? Don't mind the stallion. God Almighty! Run, man, don't stand there. Mary! Mary, I say."

The other window opened and Mary stuck out a bare arm, which she waved at her brother, crying:

"I'm pulling on my clothes."

"Call the girl," he said.

Her arm disappeared and her window fell with a clatter.

"Don't bang that window," he roared. "D'ye want to break all the glass in the house?"

Tom Patch ran into the stone building and began to shout up the stairs:

"Larry. Get up. The master is calling ye."

"Huh ! " said Ramon, pulling in his head and lowering his window.

He began to dress himself hastily. He had rolled up his clothes in a bundle and placed the bundle on a chair by the head of his bed; as is customary with poor peasants. There was no underwear among them. He first put on a grey worsted shirt, then brown frieze trousers with whitish spots, then a waistcoat that did not suit the trousers. It was of a dark grey colour and newer. The coat suited the trousers, but it was so much knocked out of shape that it looked quite different. The socks were homespun, of grey thread. His boots were heavy, with elastic sides, after the old fashion.

He pulled on his clothes pell-mell. They were so loose and· shapeless that it would not matter very much if he had put his legs through the sleeves of the coat and his arms through the legs of the trousers. The result could be hardly more extraordinary. He looked like a humpy bag, not very full and yet bulging in places. He took a large silver watch from the chair, wound it in spite of his hurry, and put it in his left waistcoat pocket. He trailed a heavy silver chain across his stomach, through a button of the waistcoat and put the end of the chain, to which he attached a bunch of small keys, in his right pocket. The watch had a celluloid guard on its face.

While he wound and disposed of the watch he strode about the room, blowing out his breath with puffed cheeks, examining the floor. It was a habit he had every morning. He might have mislaid an important paper or a coin during the night. Leaving it about, it might fall into the hands of the maid who cleaned the room. There was nothing. The room was like a cavern. It was very large with a high ceiling, from which the plaster had fallen in spots. It was simply furnished, with the bed, a little table near the bed, a chair and the wash-stand. A small mat was crumpled up among the bedclothes which he had dragged with him to the floor in his nightmare. Otherwise the floor was naked. The wood, that had once been polished, was worm-eaten. The whole room looked withered. There was not a solitary decoration of any kind. The heavy curtains on the windows were really old army blankets that had been manipulated.

He noticed that the candle was still burning on the washstand. He rushed towards it and quenched it greedily; striking his tongue against his palate with a gesture of horror at such waste of wick and tallow in broad daylight. He picked up an old brown velour hat that hung on the support of the mirror on the stand. He crushed it on to his head, moved towards the door, halted, shrugged his shoulders, glanced about him furtively and then seized the mirror with both hands. He looked into it.

"Hal" he said. .

His face had completely recovered from the attack. Delighted, he took off his hat and brushed it on his sleeve, moving his jaws, as if he were munching something. It was a gesture that was typical of him.

He was six feet three inches in height. He weighed a little over sixteen stone. His body was massive. His hands, feet, thighs, shoulders and neck were developed to an extraordinary degree. His shoulders stood out far beyond the line of his body, and it was for this reason that his body, in spite of the size of his chest, stomach and thighs, didn't fill his clothes. His neck was very thick and red. The skin on it was in flakes at the back. It was covered there with tiny undulations, like the neck of a bull. In front, at the throat these undulations were deep waves of loose fat that concealed his chin when he bent his head. He was fifty-two years of age, but his hair was as plentiful and luxuriant as that of a strong young man. It was turning slightly grey. It curled, but it was more matted than curly. It appeared never to have been parted or combed and the hairs were remarkably strong. Owing to the great size of his skull and the additional mop of hair which he refused to crop closely, lest he might waste a part of himself, his hats were always too small for him. There was a ring around his skull, the mark of the hat's rim. The hair, bunched up within this ring, was like a royal crown. At the back of the skull, beneath the mark of the hat, a little row of hair stuck upwards.

The skull was shaped like that of a lion and his countenance bore a striking resemblance to the gloomy majesty of that animal's expression. He had large, bushy eyebrows of a fair colour. His eyes were grey. They were small but very active, placed wide apart, mobile like the eyes of a seagull on the prowl in the wake of a ship. They had long lashes. His ears were large, but beautifully shaped. His nose also was large, with a knob at the end of it and widespread nostrils. He had a wide mouth, with a large thick underlip. His complexion was bronzed. There were unhealthy patches of a yellowish colour on his cheeks. There were pouches under his eyes. He had heavy jaws, that protruded when he held his head erect and that were almost invisible when he stooped, lost in the fleshy folds of his throat.

The impression produced by his extraordinary size and by the curious inhuman expression of his eyes was not unpleasant. But it was terrifying. It inspired curiosity and admiration of a strange beauty; the beauty of uniqueness; the beauty of an aged oak, whose twisted massive branches and naked, scarred roots are full of majesty.

"Ha !" he said again, fixing his hat on his head. He turned up the rim at the back and turned it down in front over his forehead. Then, stooping forward, he rushed out of the room. His heavy steps resounded.

His room opened on to a long corridor on the second floor. The corridor ran the whole length of the house. There was a window at each end. A great stairway led downwards. A narrow stairway led upwards to the top storey. The corridor was bare like his room. The ceiling was broken in places and the walls were stained. It looked desolate, like the corridor of a deserted monastery. He left his room with the intention of going downstairs to examine the house, thinking that the dog's barking had been in answer to the movements of a robber. He bad a mania that people were always waiting to rob him or murder him in his sleep; especially since he came into this house and the peasants had become hostile to him. But after he had taken three steps along the corridor, he gasped and put his hand against the wall to steady himself. A sharp pain had struck him in the head. He glanced around him furtively, to make sure that he was alone and that nobody had seen this sign of his illness. There was nobody. He shuddered, closed his eyes, giving way to the pain. At once he remembered his nightmare and the shriek. His wife? Was it she?

As soon as he thought of her his strength returned, nourished by hatred. He moved forward slowly, almost on tiptoe, until he reached the door of her room. It was the first door on the stairway, on the left. Her room faced the front of the house. He put out his hand to clutch the door handle and then withdrew it. He listened. If there was nothing wrong and he went into her room and awakened her from her sleep and questioned her, she would drive him into a rage by the contemptuous, cold look in her yellow eyes. That might be dangerous in his present state. He always felt ill after a fit of temper.

But the very thought of this had the effect which he feared would be produced by his entering her room without cause. His big lip shot out, his eyes flashed, he. raised his jaws dangling the baggy skin of his throat. Seizing the door handle he turned it violently. He pushed. The door resisted. He stepped back in amazement. It was locked. She had dared to lock her door in his face. His neck became purple. He drew back his hand and struck the door with his palm. It burst from the lock and swung open. Then he put his hands behind his back, stooped his head and entered the room, walking slowly. He stood within the door and looked towards the bed. Then his mouth fell open. He took his hands from behind his back, let them hang limply by his side and began to nod his head. The bed was empty.

Puffing out his cheeks, he walked slowly towards the bed, stood in front of it, touched it with his hand, became excited, searched *it,* tossing the clothes, feeling the sheets and even looking under it. Then he stepped back.

"It's cold," he said aloud. "She's gone."

There was no force in his voice. It was weak. He could not

understand. He had seen her at eleven o'clock lying in her bed, on her left side, with her face to the wall, lying quite still and breathing deeply. When he had spoken to her to find out if she were asleep, she had raised her head slightly, mumbled something with her eyes closed, stretched herself, sighed and went lax, just like a person heavy with sleep. Now she was not there. The bed was cold. She had left it some time ago. How? She always had breakfast in bed. Always.

He turned about slowly, scratching his head. He examined the room. No. She was gone. But she had taken nothing. The room was the same as he had seen it at eleven o'clock. There was the same odour of perfume and of silk that always excited and embarrassed him on entering the room. The door of the wardrobe was ajar. Her clothes were hanging there. Her things lay on the dressing- table. He went over to the table and picked up one tiling after the other. He suddenly dropped the silver case of a manicure set and said aloud:

"She got ill in the night and went up to Mary's room." He was going to leave the room to go to his sister, when he saw her pyjamas on the floor. He stopped.

"Where are her clothes?" he said in a whisper. "They were there on that chair."

He pointed to an armchair by the head of the bed. It was empty. Yet her clothes were there last night, with the underwear on top, in a fluffy heap. He drew himself erect, pulled his hat farther down his forehead and said in a hollow voice :

"She's gone."

He rushed towards the door, buttoning his coat. He went down the stairs, paused at the first landing and looked into the drawing-room and then went down to the hall. He stopped five paces from the hall door. It was locked and chained on the inside. She had not gone out that way. He crossed the hall towards the kitchen quarters. He went through a passage and reached the back entrance. As he passed the kitchen door he heard a sound.

"Who's that?" he shouted.

Somebody dropped a pot into the sink and cried out:

"Great God! You terrified me."

It was his sister Mary.

"It's you, is it?" he shouted. "How did you get here?"

"I just came down," she said. "What's the matter?"

Without answering her, he went to the back door, turned the handle and opened it.

"Ha!" he cried. " It's unlocked. This is the way she went out. Who gave her the key? You?"

He rushed into the kitchen and caught up a big knife as he passed the table. He brandished the knife at his sister. He looked quite mad. She put her hands to her bosom and leaned back against the sink, gaping at him in terror. There were big veins in his neck.

His sister was as lean as he was stout. Her back was slightly curved from stooping constantly over her work. She had long, stringy, black hair that was hanging down her neck in loose plaits. She had not time to dress herself properly. Her face was emaciated. Her complexion was of a sickly yellow colour. Her eyes were blue. They glittered. They had an expression that was a mixture of avarice and idiocy. She had a hooked nose. Her only resemblance to her brother was in her mouth. Her underlip was thick and it had the same nervous habit of continually moving, as if tasting the flavour of something. Her hands were like claws, worn with work. Her clothes were of the poorest stuff. She still wore the black bodice that was fashionable among peasant women in the last generation, high around the neck and buttoned all the way down the front. Her waist was extremely narrow. Although she was seven years younger than Ramon she looked much older. She was withered.

"Are you tongue-tied?" he shouted at her. "Can't you speak?"

"What is it?" she said in a hoarse voice. "I opened the door. Isn't that all right? Don't I do it every morning? I just opened it."

"You're a liar," he said. "Where is the key?"

"There it is," she said, pointing to a bunch of keys that lay on the dresser.

He examined the bunch of keys. The key of the kitchen door was there. He dropped the knife to the floor. He bent his head and frowned.

"Eh?" he said. " You just opened it?"

"Yes, I did. Just a minute ago. What's the matter? Is there something stolen?"

"You just unlocked it?"

"Yes. For God's sake, tell me what's the matter."

"On your soul, you just opened it?" he cried, looking up at her fiercely.

"On my soul, I did," she whispered, crossing herself.

"Can't you tell me what's up?"

"My wife," he shouted, turning towards the door. "She's gone. My curse on her. But I'll find her. She'll not escape me. Call everybody.

Search the house. Find her. Search everywhere."

She followed him into the passage, wringing her hands and crying:

"Is it Nora? God! What has happened to her?"

In a few minutes there was an uproar in the house. Tom Patch, Larry O'Rourke, the housemaid, Mary and Ramon himself were rushing around from room to room, searching. Ramon shouted, telling them to hurry, to search every hole and corner. He was completely beside himself and unable to think; for it was obvious that, if his wife had dressed herself, she had left the house. The servants dared not question him to know what had really happened. They were terrified of him, more terrified than usual, because he had an expression of helplessness on his face and, also, he looked ill. A powerful personality, whom people have learned to fear and feel comforted in a curious way by their fear, causes consternation when anything out of the common happens to him.

At last, Ramon, while wandering around the hall, chanced to go into a room which had remained unused during his occupancy of the house. It opened off the hall, on the right. It had been a gun room in the time of the former owners. It was supposed to be permanently locked up. However, the door opened when he turned the handle and, on entering the room, he found that the shutters had been taken from the window and that the window itself was wide open. It was a French window and it opened on the lawn. One had only to step down about eighteen inches on to the gravel path.

He started. Now everything suddenly became clear to him. An unreasoning fear took possession of him. He realised that she had deliberately got up and left the house for some purpose, having made plans beforehand for her escape. She had not walked in her sleep, as he had been trying to persuade himself that she might have done. Immediately he thought that there was a plot afoot against his life. The ordinary jealousies of a husband were overwhelmed for the moment by a sense of danger to his own safety arising probably from his illness and from the remembrance of the look of absolute hatred in her yellow eyes of late when he gibed at her.

He tried to hide this terror from himself by confusing it with something else. And he muttered aloud :

"The terrible shame and disgrace of it. What will people say? I can't show my face. They'll laugh at me."

He wanted to persuade himself that she had run away from him; but he knew instinctively that she had not; that she would fight him to the end. He raised his two big hands in front of his chest and looked at them, with his underlip thrust out. He thought in agony of his whole life's work brought crashing to imminent ruin by this damned woman, who had cast a spell over him. He could not escape from her. He could not conquer her. She was killing him. Christ!

He lowered his head, clasped his hands behind his back and left the room, walking lifelessly, dragging his feet after him. He met his sister in the hall. He looked at her gloomily and said, pointing to the open door of the gun room:

"She went out that way."

He paused, shook himself and added, munching with his lips:

"She stole out in the night."

"Then we better search the grounds."

"Search where you like," he said.

"But my God, something must have happened to her," said Mary.

"Clear out of my sight," he said angrily. "Go on. Search the grounds. Call everybody out."

They all went out after her, on to the lawn, looking at him cautiously as they passed him. He remained in the hall, staring at the floor, thinking rapidly, getting ready for the struggle that he felt was imminent. It would have to be decided at once, one way or another, this struggle between him and his wife. Then he heard a croaking voice on the stairs behind him. He looked up. His mother was coming down grumbling and coughing, leaning on the banister with one hand and fixing a little shawl about her head with the other.

She was seventy-two years of age and so small that it was hard to believe that she had given birth to such an enormous man. She was little over four feet in height. There was hardly any body to her. Her black skirt was wide, and it came in at the waist so tightly, that her two hands joined could easily encircle her there. A little shawl covered her head, tied beneath her chin. It almost concealed her face, showing only her eyes, her nose and her mouth. Her eyes were very sharp and small. Her nose was hooked. Her mouth seemed to be the central point of her face, for it drew all the skin of her face towards it in a bunch. It was very small and the lips were shrivelled. Her lower lip had the same nervous habit of perpetual movement as both her children had. Like the mouth of a knotted bag, her mouth was the living symbol of avarice.

"What brought you out of bed?" he said.

He addressed her in the brutal manner customary with peasants when speaking to their mothers. Respect for parents is not instinctive in humanity. It is a product of civilisation. Even in civilised society it is largely produced by the fact that old people often hold on to their property until death. But the old woman, herself a peasant, paid no heed to this brutality.

"And what's all the row about?" she said crossly; in a haughty tone, however, showing no fear of her terrible son. "What's all this rushing about for?"

"Oh! leave me alone," he said, turning away from her. "This is not a hag's business."

"A hag, indeed! " she said, reaching the hall and straightening. herself. "Ha! What's up, will ye tell me?"

She strutted forward, with her little wrinkled hands crossed on her bosom. She walked as straight as a soldier and she was just as sprightly in her carriage.

"What's up?" he shouted at her. "What's up? Can nobody say anything but what's up? My wife is gone. That's what's up."

She whistled.

"Your wife is gone," she said, throwing back her head and uttering the last word on a very low key. "Where?"

"How the devil do I know?" he said. "Can't you leave me alone?"

"Huh !" she said, trembling with rage. Her little eyes glittered. She came close to him and shook a little fist in his face. "It's a fine fool you are, Ramon Mor. A fine fool, indeed ! Huh ! Gone indeed ! Where are your wits, child? It's gallivanting she is, or whoring with a lover in the dead of the night."

"Shut up, you hag," he muttered. "Go back to bed."

"Indeed, then," she cried. "I won't go back to bed. It's a long day, it seems, before you can do without the mother that bore you in hardship. And it was a foolish day you got too big for your boots and brought this foreign strip into the country of your ancestors. She came unknown to me and against my will, and the devil a tear will I drop when she goes; if she does go. Gone, indeed ! It's in a ditch she is lying with some blackguard of the town !"

"Woman !" he cried, trying to rouse himself to anger.

But her words had struck deep into him. His stomach was heaving in and out, like an empty sack puffed by the wind.

"Woman, your grandmother !" she said, shrugging herself. "Pruff! Pruff ! There you are now, disgracing yourself in front of all the servants, roaring like a mad bull about the house without your collar and tie. Every drunken ruffian in the town 'll have the bellyache laughing at you before the sun goes down. Mother of God ! If you had taken the stick to her back as I told you and not let her take the bit between her teeth and put the bedsheet between her flesh and yours, you wouldn't be standing there like a fool, with all the world laughing at you. If she's gone let her go, and if she comes back give her the rod. But don't shout. Age has brought you no sense. It's your father's softness that broke out in you when you let that yellow stripach from God knows where put the comether on you. I didn't have a day's peace since she came into the house. She lying in luxury and idleness, while honest people have to work with death whispering in their ears. Pruff !"

"Pruff !" she repeated, strutting around him, fiddling with her little shawl.

He said nothing. He clasped his hands behind his back. His head became dizzy. He wanted to tell his mother that he was ill. But he was too proud to do so. At the same time, his jealousy took a new form, fattening on the suggestions she had made.

Watching him with her piercing little eyes, she noticed the effect her words had on him. She was pleased. She felt that this was her great opportunity for getting rid of her enemy, Nora. She idolised her son, with the avaricious love of a peasant woman. She hated Nora for having come between her and her son. For fifty years Ramon had belonged completely to her. The first time he escaped from her he was captured. If he had only made Nora suffer by ravishing her body, by making it disfigured and gross in the labours of pregnancy, she would have had some compensation for the tortures of jealousy she suffered. But he had not done so. The woman had remained intact and beautiful, like the figure of a beautiful devil, flaunting in idleness the beauty of her sinful body before the shrivelled, withered bodies of the mother and daughter.

"Call them in," she said harshly. "What are they doing out there? Looking for a needle in a haystack. Or do you want the whole town to know that you are put to shame in your own house? Call them in, I say."

"Eh?" he said, drawing in a deep breath. "It's easy for you to talk."

He waved his hand and mumbled something, and he wanted to tell her that passion was more powerful than wisdom, that he had gone too far, that it was now too late to withdraw that he must see it through. But as he did not himself exactly understand his own condition, or what he meant to do and as he was furthermore too proud to expose himself even to his mother, he did not utter his thoughts aloud. Instead he said: "Mind your own business." And he rushed out into the lawn.

She followed him to the door, still talking.

The others were coming up from the direction of the gate lodge and he heard the voice of his steward, Dan Farrelly. He hurried down the drive and saw them when he rounded some shrubberies. Nora was there too. She was being carried by Tom Patch and Larry O'Rourke, who had their hands joined beneath her. Her head was leaning against O'Rourke's shoulder. Her hands hung limply. Her eyes were closed. Mary walked behind, carrying Nora's hat and coat. Farrelly was gesticulating and talking loudly. The maid had her hand to her mouth, in a gesture of vague alarm. When they saw Ramon, they all halted. He motioned them on. Mary said something.

"Take her into the house," he said. "Mary, run in and get things ready. Brandy. Did she faint? Who found her?"

Farrelly touched his cap and said:

"It was me found her, sir."

The others went on. Ramon did not glance at Nora. He beckoned to Farrelly. Farrelly came up, toying with a dead leaf.

He was a nimble little man of middle age with a narrow, long, brown beard. His face had the servile, melancholy expression which is so deceptive among a certain class of peasants. *As* the saying is, "one would think that butter could not melt in their mouths," they look so gentle. They always address a man as "brother," and they scatter prayers through their conversation. Yet they are as sly as foxes. Their tongues are merciless. Like wasps they fatten on all sorts of corruption.

It is also curious that persons of this type are invariably found in the service of men like Ramon Mor. Powerful personalities are always surrounded by knaves.

Farrelly had been a bailiff in charge of the de Burgo estate while it remained unoccupied. When Ramon purchased the estate he retained Farrelly, thereby adding to the unpopularity of his act, for Farrelly was intensely disliked in the district.

He looked at Farrelly in the confidential manner which he always used to disarm the suspicions of people whom he wished to circumvent. It was an attitude of seeming humility and innocence. Under this mask, he was most to be feared.

"What happened?" he whispered.

"It was this way," said Farrelly. "I told my old woman to set the alarm clock, for I'm a terrible sleeper and thunder wouldn't wake me when I'm having a good nod. When she shook me up, she said she heard an awful screech. 'Go out,' says she. 'There's some poor creature in trouble.' Them are the words she said. I just got up and pulled on a few things. Saving your presence, look at the way I am. I didn't take time to button my flap. I ran out from the lodge on to the shore road, and who did I see coming along—it was grey dawn then—but the parish priest."

"Fr. Considine?" said Ramon, starting.

"Himself," said Farrelly, "and he ... he staggering about with ... with excitement on the road."

He spat on to the grass and looked at Ramon knowingly, in order to point out that he knew very well why the priest was staggering, but that he was too decent a man to mention it. Ramon looked at him sternly. Farrelly lowered his eyes meekly.

"He waved his hand to me," he continued, imitating the gesture. "I ran down. There she was, near Jack Geraghty's old house, Lord have mercy on his soul, lying in a dead faint. Fr. Considine and myself brought her over to the lodge between hands and we gave her a drop of brandy. I was just going to run up and warn the house when they came down looking for her."

"Ha!" said Ramon. "Where is Fr. Considine?"

"He had to run off," said Farrelly quietly, again looking at Ramon in a knowing way. "It's his early Mass this morning, I suppose."

"He didn't say how he found her?"

"No, we had only a few words in the excitement. It was all in a rush, God preserve her. I hope she is ... "

"It was how she walked in her sleep," said Ramon.

"Then something must have terrified her. Maybe it's Fr.Considine spoke to her suddenly. It's a dangerous thing. She often does it. Only this is the first time she left the house. A fall she got off a horse when she was a child. She was complaining of a headache last night when she went to bed. But with the help of God she'll be all right after a bit of a rest."

"Amen!" said Farrelly, reverently raising his cap. Ramon glanced sharply at him and saw that he did not believe a word of this rather far-fetched explanation.

"Thanks, Dan," he said. "You've done a good morning's work for yourself, and I'm not the man to forget a thing like this. But ... not a word about Fr. Considine. Ye know what I mean?"

He suddenly looked at Farrelly ferociously and the little man drew back. He wanted to let Farrelly understand that there must be no gossip about this business. Farrelly dropped his eyes and it was hard to say what he was thinking of behind his mask of innocence.

"Hurry now," said Ramon brusquely. "Get the cattle ready for the fair. Sell them through and through for the price I told you last night. Take what you can get for the two strippers, separately. You might as well drive that suck yearling too. He'll do no good in his second year. And keep them well together. Those two heifers are beginning to spring."

"Yes, sir," said Farrelly.

"And ... I'll leave an order in Finnigan's that the men are to get as much porter as they want during the day. Hurry now. It's getting on."

"Yes, sir. Good morning, Mr. Costello."

Farrelly touched his cap and they parted.

The sun was rising. Its rays fell faintly on the grass, giving no warmth. As he walked towards the house, he felt the oppression with which the rising sun inspires the sick and the troubled. A new day for which he had no strength was coming stealthily with its labour. For the first time in his life he looked with longing at a life of obscurity, at the peasant life from which he had dragged himself, goaded by ambition. The silence of the mountains. The sombre quiet of great, uninhabited cliffs. The murmur of summer bees. Village smoke rising straight into an empty sky. The whispering of women huddled by a well at dusk. Silence. Peace. Bowed heads. God.

He saw with distrust and aversion the undulating lawn upon which the sunbeams were gleaming faintly. He saw the trees, the shrubbery, the gravelled carriage way, the high boundary walls, the great house grown old in grandeur, with creepers on its face. He felt that he had been caught in a trap and that he was an alien here. He was shut off from his people. He was deserted, sick, doomed.

But his face, angry and defiant, concealed these thoughts. Just as an old oak-tree, rotting at the core, conceals with its scarred bark, its tangled roots and its knotted limbs the imminence of its fall.

As he entered the hall, Tom Patch and O'Rourke had just descended the stairs and were turning towards the kitchen. He called after them.

"You milk the cows, Tom," he said. "You, Larry, you better get dressed. You may have to go for the doctor. I'll let you know in a minute."

He met the maid on the stairs coming down with a night jar to get hot water into it. He felt that he must stop her also and give her some order; so he told her to make sure that the water was boiling hot. He felt a terrible need for activity, for speech, for directing things, in order to forget the curious dizziness in his head.

He went up to Nora's room. They had just got her into bed. Mary was arranging the clothes about her. His mother was strutting about, muttering.

"This is no place for you," she said to her son. "You'll be only in the way for the present. There's nothing wrong with her."

"Leave my way," he said, going past her to the bed.

"Don't disturb her now," said Mary. "I just poured a little brandy down her throat. She's sleeping. She must have met with some bad hurt. There are marks on her. There's a big bruise on her side and her clothes were torn and dirty. Look at them."

She pointed to the clothes that lay in the armchair. Ramon did not look at them. He stared at Nora. She lay on her back, with the clothes tucked closely about her. She appeared to be asleep. Her face was very pale.

The mother came up to him, looked at him cunningly, and then looked at Nora and smiled.

"Sleep, my grandmother," she said. "It's not sleeping she is."

"Mother, hold your tongue," said Mary sharply. She was sitting on the bed, with her arm across Nora's body.

"I suppose I had better send for the doctor," said Ramon.

"Didn't you send for him yet?" said Mary. "Tell someone at once."

"What are you giving orders for?" said the mother.

"You'll be the next, maybe, to go traipsing in the night. You impudent thing! What does she want the doctor for?"

The maid entered the room without knocking, carrying a night jar.

"This is the hot water, ma'am," she said to the old woman.

"I don't want it," said the old woman.

"Bring it here," said Mary. "Is it hot?"

"Jenny," said Ramon, "tell O'Rourke to saddle the grey mare and to go for the doctor."

"Why send him on the mare?" said Mary. "Wouldn't the car be quicker and handier?"

"None of your impudence," said the old woman.

"Motor-car, indeed! Waste of petrol and extravagance. Aren't we grand?"

"Mother!" said Ramon angrily. "Keep quiet."

"Yes," he continued. "Tell him to take the car instead. I'll want it anyway to go into town early with the accounts."

"Yes, sir," said the maid.

"And bring hot water to your master's room," said the old woman. "Ramon, it's time for you to shave and to put on your front. You'll give scandal going about that way, all untidy."

The maid went out, leaving the door open. The old lady shouted after her:

"Were there no doors where you were raised or was it in a bog you were born?"

"Quiet, mother," said Mary, wringing her hands.

"She won't be quiet," cried Ramon, moving to the door.

"The damned hag will send me to my grave soon. What a house ! What a house!"

"Yes, indeed," said the old woman imperturbably, following him out of the room. "What a house ! "

She looked back from the door and said to Mary:

"I'll leave you with that hussy as you're so anxious about her." Then she banged the door after her. She followed Ramon into his room.

"Now what do you want?" he growled.

"You're not looking well," she said, peering into his face.

He started and put his hand to his right cheek. He looked into the mirror.

"They're noticing me," he thought.

"Pooh!" he said aloud. "I look all right."

"You don't, then," she said, sucking her lips, as if pleased with his bad looks. " I don't like those spots on your face. Be careful, Ramon. Your father went that way."

"What way?" he said, horrified. "What way are you talking about?"

"He was taken suddenly," she said. "The doctor wanted to open him up. But I wouldn't let him be touched. I said he'd go to meet his God with a whole body and not patched like an old trousers."

"What ailed him?" he said.

"They didn't know," she said. "He just went suddenly. It was in his insides the hurt was, whatever it was. Be careful, my son. But if anything happens to you, I'll have her arrested on a charge of murder. 'It's she has brought you to this. I've noticed it coming on you this last two years. Get rid of her. Now is your chance. If you don't she'll drive you to your grave. That's what she's after. She wouldn't stop short of poison. They're up to every trick nowadays. What are you going to do with her now? Call in the priest and send her packing. Her and her powder puffs and her fripperies. Packing."

"Later, later," said Ramon. "We'll deal with that later. You have such a temper. You let your tongue run away with your sense. A man should always look well into a ditch before he crosses it."

He was taking off his coat. He seemed to be talking to himself rather than to her, in a subdued tone.

She suddenly became tender.

"You know better, son," she said, in a cooing voice.

"You haven't gone this far in the world without having a shrewd mind. And indeed, it's I am proud of you. God protect you, son." .

She poured out water into his wash-basin. She arranged a towel, soap and a toothbrush for him. The maid fetched the shaving water. He began to shave. She brushed his clothes. She helped him with his toilet, as if he still were a young boy under her intimate care. She asked him delicate questions about his bodily habits.

"All your troubles," she grumbled, "come from giving up the habit of taking senna once a week. I know it."

Ramon felt comforted by the feeling of security that a son gets from his mother in moments of weakness and trouble. Neither uttered a word of endearment nor made a bodily gesture of affection. But they drew together instinctively, after the manner of peasants, to face the crisis that seemed imminent.

When he had shaved and put on his big starched front, she affixed his tie. It was of blue poplin with white spots. She brushed down the shoulders of his coat, standing on tiptoe to do so. Then she said:

"Hurry now. It's time to be looking after things."

He left the room with her, feeling strong and almost at peace.

Ten minutes later it would be hard to think that anything uncommon had happened in the house. The maid and the old woman were preparing breakfast in the kitchen. Ramon was in the yard superintending the men. Two other workmen had come. Cows were being milked. Fowls were being fed. Stables were being cleaned out. There was a great noise and the feeling of happiness that comes from work early in the morning in the country.

Ramon went into the stable where the stallion was strung up. The sick beast was groaning and trembling along the back. He was dying.

But neither Ramon nor anybody else was affected by the meek beast's struggle with death. Life was so much more manifest all round, leaping and shouting and singing with excess of energy. The earth and sky shone in the merry sunlight and thought was stilled. It was the hour of thoughtless movement, of song, of voluptuous yawning, of feet running on wet grass.

He climbed on a gate, shielded his eyes from the sunlight with his hand and looked down through the trees at his green, rolling meadows.

Farrelly was there, already going among the cattle with a barking dog, rounding them up.

Good! The sky seemed full of glittering white dust.

CHAPTER IV

WHEN she was left alone in the bedroom with Nora, Mary threw herself on her knees by the head of the bed . and whispered:

"Nora, are you asleep?"

Nora did not move. She went on breathing regularly, lying motionless with her eyes closed. Mary shook her gently.

"Nora, wake up," continued Mary. "Tell me what happened. Are you hurt? Speak to me. Oh! Why did you go? They'll find out."

Still Nora made no movement. Mary dropped her head to the bed and burst into tears. Then Nora opened her eyes slightly, turned her head a little and looked at Mary. Then she looked hurriedly around the room and closed her eyes once more. She moved, stretching herself. Mary raised her head. Nora put her hand to her face and brushed her forehead. She sighed and opened her eyes wide, as if startled. She raised herself£ against the pillow. Then she caught Mary excitedly and whispered in a dazed manner:

"Where am I? What has happened?"

Mary jumped up and threw her arms about Nora's neck.

"Lie down," she said. "Don't be afraid. It's only me. They're gone. Don't be afraid. I'm with you ! "

"Oh ! God ! " said Nora.

She lay back limply and closed her eyes. She shuddered. Then she stretched out her hand and muttered :

"Give me some water."

Mary ran across the room to the carafe. Nora looked after her. Her eyes were wide open and cunning. She closed her eyes as soon as Mary turned towards the bed with the water.

"Here, take this," said Mary, putting her arms around Nora's shoulders and raising her.

Nora drained the glass.

"Where is he?" she said excitedly.

"Who?"

"The priest?"

"The priest!"

"Yes. Fr. Considine. God! Where is he?"

"I don't know."

"He's not here?"

"No."

"Thank God!"

She lay back and closed her eyes. Mary stared at her.

"Mother of God!" she said. "Did the priest catch you?"

Nora turned towards her and said fiercely:

"How do you mean?"

Mary shrank backwards. She flushed and dropped her eyes.

"Sure I know where you were," she said humbly. "Why do you always treat me like this? You know I'm fond of you and that I'll stand by you in spite of them all. I don't care what you do, only don't treat me as if I were a stranger."

"How dare you speak to me like that?" cried Nora haughtily. "What do you mean by saying you know where I was? Where was I? Tell me. What do you mean?"

Mary remained silent, standing by the bed, with her curved back, her hooked nose and her skinny face making her look very repulsive. The look of suffering on her countenance did not relieve this repulsion by arousing pity.

Her ugliness placed her beyond pity.

Nora, sitting in the bed, uncovered almost to her waist, looked magnificently beautiful and haughty.

"Why don't you speak?" she said. "I have had enough of your spying. Can't I go for a walk in this house without being spied on and assaulted by a drunken priest?"

"Oh! God forgive you," said Mary, crossing herself. "Don't say a thing like that. I didn't spy on you. You know yourself I have stood by you since you came here. Don't blame me for what the others did. I'm fond of you, Nora. It makes me so happy to have you here, and I do my best to make you comfortable and be friends with you. But you won't let me. I'm worse off than you are. I have nobody and nobody wants me. Why don't you be kind to me?"

"I say you have been spying on me," said Nora furiously. "I suspected it all along. All your pretence of friendship was a blind. I heard what they said just now. I wasn't asleep. Only I kept my eyes closed with shame. They use you just to spy on me."

"That's a lie," said Mary, raising her head. Her eyes gleamed. "That's a lie. How can you say that? I have nearly damned my soul for you and you say that."

Her face quivered.

"What do I care about your soul?" said Nora, trembling with anger. "You are all hateful to me, all of you. I hate you all."

She began to beat the bedclothes with her hands hysterically.

"Well, then!" said Mary, furious in her turn. "You've made your bed and you can lie on it. You'll be sorry for this. I know all about you, so I do."

"What do you know about me?"

"You'll find out what I know about you in good time. You've treated me like a dog, although for two years I've done everything I could for you and ... "

"Go away from me. I detest you."

"No, I'm not going to go," said Mary, speaking with great rapidity. "I'll tell you now all I want to tell you, but it's your own fault if you've made me hate you, with your pride and your ignorance. When you came here I pitied you, on account of the way mother treated you, and because I thought you married my brother just because you were unhappy and didn't know what to do. Then when you wouldn't speak to me or look at me, I forgave you because I thought you were vexed with me on account of mother and ... Then ... God knows you were the first person I ever saw coming into the house that I felt fond of; and I thought if I were friends with you, that you'd get to like me later on. My life has been hard."

She began to cry again.

"I never had anything but work and abuse all my life. Nobody ever loved me. I know I'm ugly. And it made me feel happy to think maybe I could help you. And I've done my best. Now you turn on me."

Suddenly she caught Nora by the hand, kissed the hand, and said, looking at Nora with a hopeless expression in her eyes:

"Won't you be kind to me?"

Nora looked at her, biting her lower lip, with furrows in her forehead, trembling, in doubt how to treat her.

Just then they heard Ramon's voice below, saying: "Who put a dinge in that mudguard? It's not a dinge? Eh? It's dust. What? Weill Why is there dust there? Can't you keep the car clean? Devil take it. Hurry. Hurry, man. Don't stand there looking like a fool. This is not the time to go clean it. Hurry on back. You'll be wanted."

The car moved off.

"Easy on those gears. Oh! God! Look at the way he handles the gears. You're not driving a cart, blast it."

Ramon moved away, crunching the gravel.

Nora shuddered, looked at Mary and said: "Savages! How can I trust one of you?"

Mary stood up and looked at Nora with hatred.

"Savages are we?" she whispered. "Very well, then. I damned my soul on account of you, but I'll have my revenge. Watch out. I know something. It's a nice walk you took. Watch out."

Suddenly she laughed in a strange manner, almost like an idiot. She caressed her bony hands, one with the other. She stopped laughing and her face became serious, fixed in an expression that was intensely melancholic.

She started, drew back her head, sniffed, and then shook her head violently.

"I hate you," she said in a tense whisper.

Then she moved to the door. As she was closing the door behind her, she looked at Nora and grinned again.

"Get out," said Nora contemptuously. "You cripple."

"Maybe you'll be worse shortly," whispered Mary. Then she closed the door. But immediately she put her back to the closed door, threw back her head, closed her eyes and burst into tears. Sobbing, she went down the back stairs towards the kitchen. Half-way down she heard her mother's harsh voice ordering the maid to take the porridge off the stove. She dried her eyes.

As she entered the kitchen she heard her brother's voice in the yard.

"Who let those geese on to the lawn?" he shouted.

She ran out into the yard.

"Are the geese on the lawn?" she said.

"Eh?" he shouted.

Then he came over to her and said in a whisper:

"What way is she now?"

"She's still asleep," she said coldly.

"Did she say anything in her sleep?" he said, looking at her closely.

"No," she said, without looking at him.

He looked at the ground gloomily.

"Later," he said, half to himself, as he moved towards the house. "Go and turn back those geese."

As she ran towards the lawn, she also said, half aloud:

"Later. We'll see."

She turned the geese off the lawn and stuffed with briars the hole in the gate where they had broken through. She returned to the kitchen.

Breakfast was ready. The old woman was serving porridge. The maid was making tea at the range. Ramon was cutting bread on the dresser. Each morning he measured out each person's ration of bread and butter. He cut the loaf, buttered the slices, divided them into heaps and then swept the bread crumbs into his palm. He swallowed the crumbs.

Seeing Mary stand by the table, looking at the floor gloomily, the old woman said:

"Have you strained the milk yet? You're all the morning sitting in that woman's room and the milk is not strained yet."

"All right, mother, don't shout," said Mary, rushing off to the pantry.

"Pruth ! " said the old woman. "Her head'll be turning next. Call in the men, Jenny. You slut, can't you keep your hair off anything you put your hand to? There's a rib of your hair in this porridge."

"Sorry, ma'am, it was how ... "

"Don't you answer me back. Call in the men. Ramon, you have no time. Have you finished the accounts yet? There's always more work than enough on reckoning day. You better sit down to your breakfast at once."

"All right, mother," said Ramon. "Bring me a cup of tea in my room."

"It's not right to work and eat at the same time," said the old woman. "The sand lark, smart as he is, can't serve two strands at once."

"I'm not hungry, anyway," said Ramon. "I've a lot to do. Send on a cup of tea and don't bother me."

"Pruth! Pruth! " said the old woman. "The shameless hussy. It's in a nice state she's got you. Fair day and all, with the doctor coming and the whole house turned upside down. Give me a fine strapping girl with a pair of hips to her."

"Ech!" he growled, going along the passage. "Will your tongue never take a rest? "

The feeling of security and peace had left him. The dizziness had returned to his head. The men came into the kitchen, coughing on their sleeves, looking around them sheepishly. He entered a little room off the hall. He used it as a study. He kept his important papers there, locked in a safe. It was small and dark. There was just a table, a swivel chair, a desk and the safe. He unlocked the safe, took out a bundle of ledgers, re-locked the safe and sat down to the table with the ledgers. He opened one. His eyes became misty. He could not see the writing. His head wanted to drop on to the table. He wanted to sleep. He felt the weariness of exhaustion in all his limbs.

The maid knocked and entered with a cup of tea. He drank the tea and again tried to read. There was still a blur before his eyes. Now he saw strange things passing through his mind, unpleasant figures, as if he were dreaming.

He kept licking his lips with his tongue. They were parched. He was falling into a doze when there was another knock at his door. Mary entered.

"The doctor is here," she said.

"What doctor?" he said, waking up.

"The doctor," she said.

"Oh! Yes," he said. "Bring him up to her room. I'll see him afterwards. I'll go up to the drawing-room, and see him there, afterwards. Tell him."

CHAPTER V

"GOOD MORNING, Dr. Fitzgerald."

"Good morning. Anything serious the matter with Mrs. Costello?"

"I don't think so. She's resting now. You're to come on up. My brother'll see you afterwards in the drawing room. He's working at present. The fair, ye see, is on today and he always ... "

"Yes. Yes. I understand. That's all right."

Mary led the way upstairs. The doctor followed her, coughing and sniffing. He was a very delicately built man. Being roused from his bed at such an early hour caused an attack of catarrh. He smoked too much and he suffered from chronic indigestion. His face bore a settled expression of unhappiness, directly the result of indigestion, indirectly the result of our barbarous provincial life.

For no punishment can be greater for a refined intellect than to be forced to live in an Irish provincial town. Barbarous food, barbarous companionship, an entire lack of social morality, of culture and of intellectual tolerance cause a melancholy that corrupts the strongest mind.

He was thirty-five years of age and he had been four years in the district as medical officer. His face was handsome. It had that distinction which intelligence and culture always give to the human countenance, born of delicacy and spirituality. His features were regular and well moulded, except for his mouth, which was weak. His forehead was high, broad and clear. His eyes were dark. His hair was scant, also of a dark colour. The frame of his body was finely made, but unhealthy habits of life had brought it to a wretched condition. Although he was not very tall, there seemed to be no end to him, as the saying is. And this inability to hold himself well, like his habit of continually smiling in order to hide the quivering of his lips in moments of excitement or embarrassment, was due to the sense of inferiority that was bred in him by the hostility of the people to his ideas.

He was dressed shabbily. He wore a grey tweed suit. His trousers were not creased. His shoes were in a poor condition. The cuffs of his shirt were frayed. His tie needed ironing. He had not yet shaved and his sallow skin drew attention to the growth of his beard. He looked unkempt, almost down at heel. Yet nobody would dream of suspecting that he was not a man of quality. He had an air of genuine worth which was unmistakable.

He carried a little bag and he walked with his head bent, breathing with difficulty. when he got to the second landing, he paused for breath and put his hand on his chest and cleared his throat.

Mary knocked at Nora's door, opened the door and stepped aside to let the doctor pass. She followed him into the room and closed the door behind her. She stood with her back to the door, clasping her wrists.

"How can I tell you? It's so terrible. I'm ashamed. I can't. I can't."

She shuddered and threw herself back on the pillows, gathering the clothes about her. She sobbed hysterically.

"Nora, Nora?" he whispered, "you must tell me. Be calm. Nothing terrible can really have happened. You are all right, aren't you? Let me see, let me feel your pulse."

"No, no," she said hastily, crouching away from him.

"Don't touch me."

"My God!" he muttered to himself, getting to his feet.

"What's the matter with her?" He stood for a few moments, trying to think what he should do. Then he heard steps in the corridor. Nora raised her head and said in a tense whisper:

"Not a word. Don't let her know."

"What?"

"Hush!"

There was a knock at the door. Mary entered, with two cups of tea on a tray.

"Thanks awfully," said the doctor, going to the door. "I'll take them.

It's very good of you."

He took the tray and brought it to the table. Seeing Mary standing by the door, he said to her:

"I'll call you, if, that is, if I want anything. I'll ... "

"Very well," said Mary.

She went out, shutting the door after her very slowly.

The doctor brought Nora a cup of tea. She sat up. He brought a chair to the side of the bed and sat down to sip his tea. She drank her tea at once.

"Thanks," she said, handing him her empty cup.

"Would you mind going to the door again to see if she is there? Thanks."

Again he went to the door.

"No," he said. "She's gone."

He put his own cup, untouched, on the table with her empty cup.

"Now I want to tell you everything," she said. "Sit down here near me. I have borne this for two years without opening my mouth to a soul. But last night's business has made it necessary for me to speak."

He sat down by the bedside.

"Yes, yes," he said. "Well?"

She bent towards him, put her hands on his shoulders and said, looking into his eyes :

"I can rely on you, Jim, can I not? You really like me, don't you. You are the only one here that I respect as a gentleman. That's why I want to ask you to help me. You won't let me down. Tell me."

The doctor flushed and said nothing. He trembled and he had to make an effort to prevent himself throwing his arms around her.

"I have never said a single word to you," she continued, "about what was happening in this house. I have done my best for two years to be a good wife, but I can endure it no longer. So I'm going to tell you everything. Otherwise you wouldn't understand last night's business. And I don't want you to misunderstand me. I want you so much to respect me. Would you hand me my dressing gown?"

He fetched the dressing-gown. As she put it on, he caught another glimpse of her exposed breast and flushed, overcome with shame at the emotion which her beauty inspired in him. Then she settled herself against the pillow and continued :

"I came here as an utter stranger," she said. "I hardly even knew my husband. We were married six weeks after I met him first and I didn't see much of him in that time. You will understand when I tell you that we had not even kissed one another before we were married. It's terrible and shameful telling you this, but I have to explain. Don't despise me, will you? I was ignorant of life and there were reasons which I can't go into now. I was all alone. I mistook his silence and his awkwardness for something else. We were married in Dublin and then we went for our honeymoon to London. London of all places. It turned out that he had important business there. Even then, he... he made no advances. He seemed to be afraid, tongue-tied. But I rather liked that, thinking it was because of his being different from other men, so. big, so strong, and I stood so much in awe of him that it was really something like love. Then he brought me down here. Then everything changed. All his embarrassment disappeared. And I could at once see that his mother hated me. His sister was even worse, peeping from behind doors, grinning like an idiot. She terrified me more by her pretended friendship than the mother's scowls and abuse. Then he ... My God ! It's impossible to tell you about it. It's contemptible on my part to tell you this. Are you ashamed of me? Tell me."

"Go on," he said in a low voice. "Don't be afraid." He leaned his chin on his hands and looked at the floor. He was trembling. Her eyes gleamed as she looked at him. Her cheeks flushed slightly. Then she covered her face with her hands, began to sob and said in a broken voice:

"When he ... when he ... It became terrible. He is impotent and he .... "

"Eh?" said the doctor, sitting up and looking at her with great eagerness. "I beg your pardon. But tell me. I mean, is this true? Of course, but what I mean is this, from a medical point of view ... It's purely that I ...Go on. Don't let me interrupt you. This is truly extraordinary and yet how natural! The instinct of avarice."

He again put his chin in his hands.

"I don't understand what you mean," she said, looking at him with suspicion. "Don't you believe me?"

"Go on," he said, without looking at her. "Forgive my interruption."

She sighed, thought for a few moments and then continued:

"I suffered agonies," she said. "To put it bluntly, though it's awful to talk about it, I suffered actual physical pain from his constant efforts to ... I don't know. He simply made me· suffer for his helplessness. My God! The agony of it. He said I was cold, that I was bloodless, that I lay like a sack under him. Those were his very words.. How awful! His mother said worse things. I remember one awful day when she was alone with me in the house. I had to put my fingers in my ears. She was abusing me for not having a child and she called me the most foul names. What could I say? I was helpless. When I told my husband about it, he just growled and asked me was I going to let him die childless. Then he began to tell me about all the money I cost him and that he got nothing in return, that I had ruined his life and that I was driving him to an early grave. That night I refused to let him into my bedroom, but he broke open the door and attacked me. Is there no law to protect women? Then the priest began to come about it. They probably called him in. "

"No doubt," said the doctor. "How horrible the whole thing is!"

"Fr. Considine was very civil and all that, but his politeness was even more sinister than my husband's brutality. At first he talked about religion and the duties of a married woman, but later on he talked about other things. And the way he touched me with those horrible hands of his was worse than what he actually said."

"You mean to say that he actually ... "

"Just a moment," she said. "All this time, you understand, life became unbearable in several other ways. Since my marriage I have only been away from this house once. That was during the session of Parliament he attended shortly after our marriage. You remember he refused to contest the following election and retired. Even when we did go to Dublin, he only stayed a week there, and most of that time he practically kept me locked up in my hotel. He hardly let me out of his sight. He refused all invitations. He insulted all my old friends that called. He went to bed at nine. One night, they sent several messages for him, telling him he was wanted for an important division. But he refused to go. Jealousy. He suspected even the waiters. He suspects everybody. Here it has been the same. His meanness is even worse than his jealousy. I have to make my own clothes, and I'm nearly at my wits' end now because I have used all the stuff I brought with me. Then lately he has taken to blaming me for his health. He blames me for turning people against him. He says I have brought a curse on him. Not once but several times he has stood in this room and said quite calmly that some day he won't be able to keep his hands off me. He keeps me a prisoner. Worse. A prisoner has some chance of escape. But I have none. And now ...this humiliation. Last night ... but let me tell you. We have separate rooms. That was his own idea at first; after he exhausted himself and fell ill, he let me have my own room. But it's no privacy, for he keeps coming in and coming in, nagging and standing there with a scowl that terrifies me. Then, last night, he was here until eleven o'clock ... My God! Accusing me of trying to murder ...He said I was trying to poison him. I had a headache. When he went to bed, I got up, locked my door and went out."

"You went out?" said the doctor. "You left the house?"

"Yes," she said. "I went out secretly, through a window, for fear he might get to know."

"With what intention?"

"How do you mean?"

"Just why? I mean, in the middle of the night . Had you an idea of running away, I mean, or just going for help or ... "

"No," she said, looking him steadily in the eyes. "I had no idea whatever. I just felt desperate. I felt that if I stayed in the house another minute I'd go mad. I wanted to breathe the fresh air, to feel free for a few minutes, to walk somewhere. I was terrified. Lately, I have become afraid of his strangling me in my sleep. Last night, after he left, I lay awake, thinking every moment I heard him creeping along the corridor."

"Then you went out. Where did you go?"

"I climbed up to the top of the Black Cliff."

"Alone?"

"Alone!" she exclaimed. "Why? What do you mean?"

"I just meant, weren't you afraid at that hour of the night? The place gives me a queer feeling even in daylight. And it's dangerous."

"No," she said sombrely. "I wasn't afraid. As for the danger ... "

She shuddered.

"Perhaps it would be better if I had."

"Had what? What do you mean?"

"Thrown myself down."

"My God!"

"You know that spike that sticks out from the top?"

"Yes."

"I stood there for a long time wondering should I put an end to it."

"Nora," he said, in a broken voice, seizing her hand.

"Let me finish," she said, taking his hand in both her hands. "I was hurrying back in order to get into the house before anybody got up, when I met the parish priest coming out of that little cottage he has down by the shore."

"I know it. Jack Geraghty's old house."

"He assaulted me," she whispered, lowering her eyes.

The doctor jumped to his feet and stared at her in amazement.

"How do you mean?" he said. "He struck you."

"No, I don't mean that," she said slowly. "I mean that he assaulted me in the other sense of the word."

"You mean to say that he ... "

"Yes."

The doctor dropped into his chair and covered his face with his hands.

"Horrible," he muttered. "Degrading. Horrible."

"Look," she whispered excitedly, exposing her shoulder and her neck, where there were bruises.

He raised his head and looked.

"And here," she said, exposing her side and showing a large bruise.

He touched the bruise.

"I remember being thrown down on a sharp stone or something," she said. "I struggled. My clothes are tom. I don't know exactly what happened. He just rushed at me suddenly. He was drunk. I could smell his breath as he stooped over me on the ground."

"You don't know whether he ..."

The doctor gasped and covered her up hurriedly.

"I became unconscious," she said. "I think I screamed, though."

"Good God!"

He took two steps away from the bed and stood with his back to her. She began to sob. He turned around sharply.

"There was nobody there," he said. "You have no witnesses?"

She shook her head and then she began to wring her hands.

"Now, now," he said, bending over the bed and putting his hands on her shoulders. "Don't give way."

"I can't," she mumbled. "I can't remember anything more. What am I to do? Jim, Jim, can't you help me? What am I to do?"

"Trust me," he said. "Calm yourself. This is a serious matter. But we must face it. It must be handled carefully. You know what the power of the Church is in this country, especially in a matter of this sort. The Church is more sacred than the law, and the citizen has very few rights where the clergy are concerned. But we'll see. There is a limit to everything. Have you told your husband?"

"What's the use? I waited for you to come. You're the only one I can trust. Don't fail me, Jim. Promise me."

She caught him round the waist and pulled him towards her. She laid her head against him. Her golden hair was brushing against his face.

He held himself rigid and bit his lower lip.

"Nora!" he muttered.

She shuddered and withdrew her arms slowly. Then she lay back on the pillow and closed her eyes.

"Don't let them keep me a prisoner," she whispered in a weak voice. "Even though you may despise me after what I've told you, pity me as a woman. Don't let them keep me a prisoner. I'll kill myself."

"Yes, yes," he said, raising his right hand. "I'll go at once. I'll go at once to your husband. I'll ... "

"Don't leave me," she cried, sitting up. "I'm terrified. Don't let them keep me a prisoner. I want to get out. I can't breathe here."

"Calm yourself," he said quietly. "You are in no danger. I'll talk to your husband now. Then, I'll see you later. You may be assured."

Suddenly he seized her hand, kissed it and rushed to the door. She called after him. He waved his hand to her without looking at her. Then he came back to the table, grabbed his bag and went to the door without looking at her. She kept whispering to him, asking him to protect her. He went out.

He was startled to find Mary in the corridor. Had she been listening? He suddenly felt afraid of her. She looked at him calmly.

"I want to see your brother," he said to her sternly.

"He's waiting for you in the drawing-room," she said quietly. "He sent me up to see were you ready."

As he followed her down the stairway, his heart began to beat loudly. He became acutely conscious of the emptiness of the great house, its silence, its shabbiness, the musty smell of old mortar, the sinister, bare walls, the gloom.

It was like a prison.

CHAPTER VI

RAMON MOR stood on a black rug in front of the empty fireplace with his. hands behind his back. With the hair of the rug around his boots, he had the appearance of a large animal standing on a grassy place. He was wearing his hat. His head was thrust forward. His baggy throat, pressed upwards by the collar of his starched shirt front, surged about his jaw in folds. His underlip protruded. His little eyes, fixed on the doctor, looked sinister. The row of hair sticking up behind the rim of his hat on the back o£ his skull resembled the raised mane of an animal.

Enormous, shapeless, with protruding massive shoulders, he looked terrifying.

Before him, the doctor stood quivering like a reed.

"Well?" said Ramon, after they had stared at one another without salutation for several seconds.

The doctor came forward and put his bag on the table. Ramon did not salute him or ask him to be seated. The doctor dropped his bag and then, not knowing how to begin, looked around the room, while he took out his handkerchief and wiped his hands.

The drawing-room was very large. It was cluttered with furniture. The furniture did not suit it. Everything lay about pell-mell. Colours contrasted violently. There were too many photographs on the mantelpiece. The walls were covered with pictures that are sold by the dozen in furnishing shops. Over the mantelpiece there hung an enormous portrait of His Holiness The Pope of Rome. The Pope had his hand raised, as if he were blessing Ramon beneath him on the hearth-rug. As this was the room where Ramon received his guests, the parlour of the house, all the heirlooms of the family were therein gathered, including a spinning wheel and the blackthorn stick brought from Dublin by Ramon's father, as a souvenir of Daniel O'Connell's Birth Celebration. The head of O'Connell was carved on the knob of the stick.

The magnificent, polished floor showed through its meagre carpeting, like traces of a great painting showing through the daub superimposed on the canvas by a charlatan. In the same manner, the ironwork of the fireplace, the work of an Italian craftsman of the eighteenth century and the carved ceiling, stylishly ornamented, contrasted sadly with the ugly, paltry furniture.

But Ramon himself, standing on the black rug, stood out, incomparably superior to everything in the room, both to the ancient grandeur and to its present vulgarity. The strange animal magnetism of his personality transcended his environment.

The doctor put his handkerchief into his pocket, folded his arms, coughed and looked Ramon in the eyes with a great effort of will.

"Your wife," he said, very slowly, "has made a very serious statement."

Ramon's lips moved, caressing one another. He remained silent. The doctor dropped his eyes to the floor. He tried to continue, but he could not do so. His lip trembled, feeling Ramon's eyes upon him. The silence lasted for ten seconds. Then Ramon said in a hoarse whisper:

"What did she say?"

"It's very difficult for me to tell you, Mr. Costello," said the doctor. There was a further silence. Suddenly Ramon thrust forward his right foot, raised his head and said :

"Well! Out with it."

Although he spoke in a low voice, the sound of his words was like a shout. Each word was like the tap o£ a sledge and his throat swayed as he spoke. The sound of his voice had a curious effect upon the doctor. He became so terrified that he lost all sense of fear. He raised his eyes, became rigid and began to speak rapidly.

"She has made a very serious complaint," he said, "against Fr. Considine, and against you she has made a complaint that is no less serious in my opinion. I feel it is my duty as a doctor to tell you this, in this blunt manner. Your attitude prevents me from adopting a more civilised manner. I say this. You have by your treatment of your wife, I cannot but believe her, I say you have brought her to such a pass, mentally, that the consequence may be very serious for both of you. For you, too, because I'll not keep silent if you drive her to despair. Already I say you are largely responsible for last night's dreadful affair and ... "

"What affair?" interrupted Ramon in a hoarse whisper.

This time his voice was barely audible. It was like a whistle. His neck had become purple. His cheeks were swollen.

The doctor, startled by the interruption, put up his hand to loosen his collar, which he felt was choking him. He noticed Ramon's swollen face, his purple neck, the quivering of his stomach. A warning voice said to him:

"Beware. You are driving this man into a fit." This thought discomforted him. His eyes became strained. But the next moment his anger welled up, drowning his conscience.

"Your wife," he said, "accuses the parish priest of attempting to rape her."

"Ha!" said Ramon.

He withdrew the foot he had thrust forward. He looked at the floor. Just as suddenly as it had appeared, the swelling left his face.

"Ha!" he said angrily.

Then he laughed harshly in his throat. He glanced at the doctor and said :

"What more did she say?"

"Have I not said enough?" said the doctor.

His nerves were in such a state of tension that he wanted to scream and hurl himself at Ramon.

"You have certainly said a lot," said Ramon calmly. "A lot for a man in your position, I must say. But I want to hear the whole story. I want to get to the bottom of this. Doesn't it occur to you that I have some right to get a full explanation considering I am her husband? Eh? You have a wife. If she left the house in the dead of night and returned with a story of being assaulted by the parish priest ... "

"Your wife left the house," interrupted the doctor, "because she-"

"Don't interrupt me," snapped Ramon.

"I will interrupt you," shouted the doctor. "I say she left the house because your continual persecution almost drove her out of her mind and she is afraid of violence at your hands."

"I see," said Ramon, again becoming calm. "I see. You have told me enough now. That's all I wanted to know. Now I know where I am."

He thrust forward his foot once more and raised his right hand, clenched, before his chest.

"Now I know where I am," he repeated. "And I've got you where I want you, too."

The doctor started and drew back.

"Well," said Ramon. "There are two ways of dealing with you. One is to break every bone in your body and chuck you out the window. The other is to break you in another way. Dr. Fitzgerald, you've done the worst piece of work you ever did in your life this morning. I've been watching you for some time, going about this town and district. By word and example you have stirred up discontent among the people. I know all about you. Don't you forget that. You've been my most bitter enemy since the first day you set foot in the place. I hear everything. But I'm a quiet man. I prefer to let well enough alone. It's a waste of time turning to kick every cur that barks at my heels. I said to myself that a weak creature like you, with the guts of a pet lamb, was harmless. But I was wrong. You are a snake in the grass, a wasp carrying poison from dunghills. You are worse than that braggart O'Neill. You went about with your whispering about religion and politics. Communism, how are you? Every one-lunged poxy cripple in the country becomes a Communist when he can't digest his food. Every damn thing that went wrong, whether it was typhoid, or the failure of the fishing, or an old woman's cow that died, you blamed me for it. I'm the grabber, the exploiter of the people. Don't speak. Don't you dare deny it. Innuendo is always worse than straightforward accusation. If you had the courage of a man and came to me straight and stuck your fist in my mouth and spoke like a man, I'd respect you. I'm prepared to take off my coat any day to any man and take a licking and take off my hat to a better man. But a snake in the grass like you is contemptible. You deny it? Well! Then, can you deny you were the author of a dirty article that appeared in a dirty Dublin paper run by your friend O'Neill, entitled *An Irish Shylock*? Deny that."

The doctor started. His face was wet with perspiration. He waved his hands.

"Deny it then," said Ramon.

"I deny nothing," cried the doctor, "but ... "

"Ugh!" said Ramon. "I can buy any editor in Ireland for a ten-pound note, not to mention sewer sweepers of that type. But I let that go. Then you wormed yourself into my wife's confidence. You turned her against me, with your damned books and ideas. And now you have the devil's own impudence to face me in my own house and call me a wife-beater. You are a liar, you did. And worse than that, you bring a filthy low accusation against a priest of God, against your own parish priest. Great God Almighty!"

Almost in tears, the doctor cried out:

"I'm not afraid of you. I'll do my duty in spite of everything, in spite of your threats. I'll do my duty. I'm a responsible servant of the community and ... "

"Get out!" whispered Ramon. "Get out! There's the door. By the Lord God! You'll rue this day. I'll hound you from the country. Get out!"

Trembling like a leaf, the doctor picked up his bag and walked to the door. Half-way to the door, he halted, turned about and threatened Ramon with his hand. His face was shining with a wild light.

"You have called on your God," he cried, "and you have said you'll hound me from the country. But you'll not live to do it. The hand of my God is already at your throat. The hand of justice. Let it strike. You'll get no help from me."

"You dog!"

Ramon took a pace forward. Then he halted, muttered something and staggered to a chair. Swaying, blinded by a mist that came before his eyes, he sat down.

The doctor had gone.

Ramon sat still for three minutes, half in a swoon, only vaguely conscious of what had happened. There was a great noise in his head.

Still dizzy and only vaguely realising what he was doing, he went to the door, opened it and called down the stairway for his sister. It was the maid that came running in answer to his call.

"Where is Mary?" he said.

"She's gone to Mass," said the maid.

"To Mass?" he said angrily. "What did she ... all right! I have no time. Has O'Rourke come back with the car yet?"

"He's outside waiting for you. The doctor walked back. He said he preferred to walk. O'Rourke is waiting for orders."

"All right! Bring me my ash-plant. It's in the kitchen."

CHAPTER VII

O'NEILL awoke on the cliff-top, roused by the swishing sound of seagulls' wings about his head. The birds had seen him asleep and had come near, thinking he was dead. But when they saw him open his eyes and stretch himself, they flew away slowly, calling to one another on sinister notes, in disappointment. He jumped to his feet.

Now the earth and sea were radiant with sunlight. The sun's disk was blue with a wreath of dazzling white, from which innumerable' rays, like whirling searchlights, were flashing through the sky, filling the air. with a cloud of shining dust. The earth's vapours, rising to the heat, shifted to and fro, slowly, without wind, shot through and through with sunbeams, glittering.

To the east a great plain stretched to the horizon, with long white strands upon its coast. In the clear air its outline was distinct for forty miles. It was dotted with towns. Its roads were like veins. Its woods were like tufts of hair. Its lakes were like daubs of lead. A railway, twisting like the passage of a snake, ran dark across its surface from the horizon to the town, gleaming in places where the sunbeams struck the rails. Afar off, there was a cloud of smoke upon it and the body of a train, quite tiny, moving with the slowness of a snail.

Nearby, at the foot of the slope, the town lay by the sea, grey, built about the half-circle of the harbour. It shone in the sunlight, and the masts of fishing-boats, moored together in a group, were like needles standing on end.

Then the land rose to the cliff, past the great demesne of Ramon Mor Costello, where the roof of a great house showed among the topmost branches of tall trees, becoming steep and rocky, spotted with white houses, from which wisps of curving smoke arose. The white strands became yellow, and then became a cliff that rose terrace upon terrace, increasing in wild majesty and, sweeping past the spot where he stood, rose higher and became great mountains to the west. There the ocean stretched, without limit to the eye's horizon, from the base of enormous headlands. Inland, the mountains towered to the sky, naked of trees, with their topmost crags shining like jewels. Along the mountain slopes there were dark glens, where peasant hamlets lay.

Everything had assumed the significance of beauty. Here, on the cliff, it was the flocks of birds that lay upon the sea cackling. There it was a horse standing by the wall of a field, neighing for water. There it was a red cow grazing, swishing its tail at the flies that hovered round it. There it was a patch of sea moss, bleached white, spread upon the rocks by the shore. And the cries of animals, of fowl, of dogs, of cows, of horses, of sheep, had a sound of extraordinary joy. And above all the singing of countless larks, that soared so high into the sky that they became invisible, was enchantingly beautiful.

But he neither saw nor heard nor understood the beauty of the scene, for as soon as he awoke, he became aware of what he had to do that day and he uttered an oath and ran from the cliff, leaping over the wall on to the crag beyond. He ran through rocky fields, along a path, until he reached a narrow road that led from the mountain villages to the town. There he sat on a wall.

The people were coming down to the fair of Barra. Already a crowd had gone past the spot where he sat. They had rounded a corner of the road. He could still see the heads of the horsemen, bobbing up and down, over the top of the wall, and he heard the rumble of cart-wheels, the clatter of hoofs, the moaning of cattle, the shouts of the drivers, the swishing of ash-plants lashing the haunches of the beasts.

From above the same sounds reached his ears.

The road was very rough. Ruts and holes had been filled with loose stones, some of which were scattered about by the wheels of carts and by the hoofs of cattle. Here the road wound along the brow of an upland, carved from its rocky face. Streams gushed from the rocks and flowed along the side of the road, gurgling. Flowers, cresses and ferns, growing in the mossy pools and in the. crevices of the rocks, made a beautiful border, as in a garden. The air was perfumed with their rich, sweet fragrance. Beyond the road, the heather was in bloom upon the moorlands, where hordes of bees were singing and snipe were on the wing, uttering loud cries. There, too, stray goats stood on eminences, attracted by the tumult of descending cattle. Everything was green, fresh and in flower, and the air was so clear and still that the dew drying off the earth could be seen winding about, in wisps of pale smoke.

Another throng approached him from the mountains. In front, there were three horses, each carrying two riders, trotting on a tight rein. Behind the horses, a crowd of boys came running, some carrying sticks. Cattle came behind the boys, then a group of men and women walking behind the cattle, and in the rear a row of carts.

They were the people of O'Neill's village. They looked like a tribe of nomads on the march, seeking new pastures. With the dark mountains towering behind them and the great plain stretching below, at the bottom of the winding white road, the little procession excited thoughts of romance. There was a blaze of lurid colours, red cattle, black and grey horses, white frieze shirts, women's skirts of flaming red, cashmere shawls with yellow stripes. While all round them, the wild earth was in flower and larks made music for their triumphal march.

The horsemen saw him and shouted, asking him in whose bed he had lain during the night. And as they passed, they invited him to jump upon a horse and ride into the town. They were singing and their eyes were wild, thinking of the day's festival. The boys glanced at him shyly. The cattle passed, snorting, moaning, prancing, climbing on one another's backs, making wild rushes to and fro. He called out to the people:

"God bless you."

"The same to you," they answered him in chorus.

He jumped off the wall and joined the procession beside an old man, who said to him:

" Ha, there you are!"

The old man was his father.

"Where were you last night?" continued the old man, as they walked along.

"I stayed in the town," said the son casually.

"Ha!" said the father. "With your sister?"

"No."

The old man nodded and said no more. But he glanced shyly at his son with pride. The son frowned, looking at the old man as if he were ashamed of him, or of his own conscience.

The old man was a pathetic sight. He was seventy-five years old, not a great age among our mountain peasants. But lack of care and hardship had played havoc with him. He was still erect, he walked with vigour and his eyes were active. His cheeks were red and they shone, freshly shaven, above his white beard. But all over his body there were unpleasant signs of decay. His eyelids, his lips and his ears were withering like the tips of a leaf in early autumn. His neck was assuming the leprous colour of decrepit old age. His fingers were doubling up into his palms. There was a slight indecision in his movements, as in those of a child. There was a look of incipient idiocy in his eyes. He was over-excited, shouting at his beast and dashing after it with his stick raised. He twitched his shoulders spasmodically. He did not smell very clean. Yet he was dressed with great care, in a black coat, grey frieze trousers, a starched linen front with a poplin tie and a wide-brimmed, black, felt hat.

Deserted by all his children, with his wife dead, he lived alone in his cottage among the mountains, tending his beasts and trying to till his patch of land; yet there was no sign of revolt or of discontent in his face. Even on this son, who had deserted him and on whom all the care of the family had been lavished uselessly, who had been educated by the savings of the children in exile in America, in order to make him a priest and raise one of the family above the level of poverty, he looked with pride and love.

"Why don't you sit on one of the carts?" said the son angrily, feeling ashamed of seeing his father chasing his beast and irritated by the glances of disapproval that the other people cast on him. "You'll only make yourself tired, and it's not necessary."

"Ha I" said the old man, twitching his shoulders. "I'm not tired. Sure God knows what would happen to that bullock if I didn't keep an eye on him. You don't know that beast. He's a devil. He has all the tricks in the bag and a few extra that he invented himself."

"Sure one of the others'll keep an eye on him for you."

"Foo!" cried the old man, with pride. "I never in all my life asked anybody to do my work for me. And it's late in the day to begin now."

With that he rushed forward and struck at a heifer that was going to jump up on his bullock.

A dark man said in a low voice:

"It's no use trying to make him rest. You might as well be whistling to hurry the wind. You know yourself as well as I do that he was never an easy man to get on with and he's worse now. Poor old man! He's to be pitied anyway, on the edge of the grave."

"Aye, indeed," said an old woman, "and if the good God put it into your head, Frank, to stay with him till he dies, it would merit Heaven for you. He has no one but your sister, and that poor creature, who has to work hard in her school, has little strength left to trudge back and forth, four long miles each way, from the town, trying to tend to him."

"Yerra!" said a big man. "Hold yer whist, Mary Ryder. What would he stay here for? If I were a young man again, I'd let every one of my relatives die in a ditch with the hunger sooner than I'd stay a day in the place. Who'd stay on these rocks but a lunatic, working for Ramon Mor Costello?"

"Well, sure," said the old woman, in a plaintive tone, "blood is thicker than water, and there are worse places in this dark world than a mountain glen near the graves of your people. Seven beautiful sons came out of my womb on these rocks, and I raised them as straight as the pillars of a church."

"True for you, Mary," said another woman. "True for you. A person's own salt is sweeter than the honey of a stranger."

"Pooh ! " said the old man, suddenly becoming aware of the conversation. "What would he stay here for? If I thought he had that in his mind, I'd brain him with this stick."

He halted and threatened the air with his ash-plant.

"Bravo, Maurice I" said a young woman from the rear. "I wish there were young men of your spunk, and the girls wouldn't have to go to America for want of husbands."

"Begob!" cried the big man, "sure there's nowhere else for them to go but to America. Aren't they flying every day, as if there were a plague in the country? Soon there'll be nobody left. And that miser down there, that grabber Ramon Mor is the cause of it. He has ruined the country. My curse on him."

"God forgive you," said the old woman. "There's many a house would be without flour only for him. Aye, and without a drop of tea. And isn't he one of ourselves, when all is said and done?"

"That's true," said another woman. "We'd often be empty only for him."

"Devil take his flour and his tea," said the big man. "Look at me. I wasn't reared on flour and tea. I was reared on oaten bread, milk, fish, potatoes and butter. Same as everybody was in my young days. And not an ounce or a drop of that food and drink but was come by within a few miles of my father's door, without having to cross the threshold of a shop for it. But all that is changed now, and it's the doing of that skunk from the island of Inismuineach out there."

They had now debouched into an open space of road. The town lay beneath them. They saw the harbour, with fishing boats moored there in a group, their masts like needles standing on end. Beyond the mouth of the harbour, three small islands lay. A fleet of small boats was coming from the islands to the harbour. Some had sails. Others had oars. In the clear light, the oars glittered, as they were raised, wet with brine. The big man pointed to the island farthest to the west.

"That island of Inismuineach," he shouted, "gave birth to the worst scoundrel that ever set foot in the town of Barra. Ramon Mor's father, Michael the Pedlar."

"Stop now," said the old woman. "Respect the dead:"

"By cripes," said the big man, "he doesn't deserve it, and he won't get it from me. He was before my time, but I often heard my father talk of him. You knew him, didn't you, Maurice?"

"Who?" said the old man, starting, as if he had been day-dreaming.

"Michael the Pedlar."

"Oh! Ho! Pooh! Of course I knew him. He'd be ... let me see ... he'd be the same age as ... "

"Begob, I'll bet he'll tell ye the day he was born," cried a young man. "He remembers what happened sixty years ago to the hour, but he won't know whether his hat is on his head or not. I saw him the other day in a field looking for his hat and it on his head all the time."

"Feoch! Feoch!" said the old man, running after his bullock and forgetting what he had been trying to remember.

"The Pedlar," continued the big man, "came here as a tea man after he had come back from the sea, as an agent for an English tea company. It was he brought tea into the place first."

"And the blessing of God on him for it," said the old woman.

"Amen to that," said another woman.

"My curse on him for it," said the big man. "It's tea has been the curse of the country."

"A likely story," said the old woman. "You with your belly always full of drink. It's more likely it's drink has been the curse of the country."

"Faith then," cried the big man, "you are the one yourself that can lower your naggin as well as any man. So don't be talking. My father told me they used to set the dogs after him at first, but he used to watch for the men to leave the house and then he'd run in on top of the women and before they knew where they were he had put the comether on them. He'd leave the pound of tea on the dresser in spite of them, telling them they could give it back to him next time he came round if they didn't want it. Of course, the curiosity of women made them sample it and then the rest was easy. Now you can't get a young fellow out of the house in the morning without his cup. The whole people are demoralised."

"That's true," said the old man. "He'd be two years older than me. The seventeenth of March he died. I was at his funeral. Ramon was ten years old then and Mary would be about three. Ramon is the same age as my Nora that died, Lord have mercy on her."

"I told you he'd remember it," cried a youth. "He has it now. Listen."

"Don't be making fun of old age," said the old woman angrily.

The young people began to laugh.

"Ha! " continued the old man. "The Pedlar was a great fellow surely. He used to say when they asked him about the health of his family: 'They were all right when I saw them last.' He'd be away maybe six months wandering about. At that time there were no railways same as there is now, and he never hired a horse. He just walked everywhere with his pack, buying up everything. He was like a child. He'd pick up a button or a piece of rag and put it in his big pockets. His pockets were like sacks. But he was quiet and good-natured, and there wasn't many a man could wrestle with him. He had an awful appetite. I saw him one day, for a bet, eating a stone weight of bread in Red Farrelly's of Bally.. "

There was a hoarse laugh.

"A stone weight of bread I A stone weight!"

"Devil a word of a lie in it," said the old man.

"Well," said the big man. "His son is too mean to eat a stone weight of bread. Brian Finnigan that used to be in service with him before he went to America told me that Ramon licks up the crumbs of the bread out of his hand. There's a miser for ye, and he having all the gold of the country in the cellars of his house."

"He's fond of the colour of gold," cried a young man who had come up, riding a black horse. "I bet it was the colour of his wife's hair that made him put a ring on her."

"He put a ring on her," shouted the big man, "but he never put a child in her womb."

"Oh! You blackguard," cried the women. "You have no shame."

"Old Johnny Rogers used to say," cried the old man, "that the colour of gold was no good either on a horse or on a woman."

"Blast him for a liar," cried the young man on the black horse. "I'd give my soul for one kiss from her."

He lashed his horse and galloped on, singing at the top of his voice, while the girls called after him crying:

"What about us?"

"No," cried the old man. "I wouldn't listen to a word said against The Pedlar. There was no harm in him, no more than in a child. It was his wife drove him to meanness. I'd swear that."

"She's from the village of Carra by the lake beyond, isn't she?"

"No, she's not," said the old man. "There's a story to that. It was how her father and mother were evicted the time of the famine. They went down to the town and opened a little shop, that same little thatched house ye see now at the corner of the Fish Market and the Lower Quay. It was there her mother was born. The grandfather died shortly after. He used to fish in the long boats. They used to go off in those days after big fish for oil. He was carried overboard while he was throwing a harpoon. I believe he was a strong man. Then the widow lived there, adding one thing to another, she made a little trade, with the fishermen. She had a hand in everything. With the one daughter she was cosy enough. Then when the Pedlar man came along, she hooked him for her daughter. It was nicely done. Begob, it was considered a terrible crime her being done out of her land, but her seed now has a hundred acres to her one and there you are. Feoch!"

"Ah! They were great managers," said the old woman.

"They denied themselves and they have the benefit of it."

"A fine benefit it is," cried the big man, "to be eating their own flesh. Sure there isn't one of us here that will bring back a penny of the price of our beasts, all going into that man's pockets for the debt we owe him. There isn't a little shop all over the district that doesn't belong to him. Half the town is his and he does nothing with it but letting it go to rot and ruin. Blood an ouns!"

Just then they came to a cross-roads on the edge of the plain. Another road joined theirs, coming from the hill country farther inland. And both roads joined the main road that wound along the edge of the plain towards the town. At the junction of the roads, there was a long thatched tavern, with an open space in front of it, where carts were halted. There was a crowd there, drinking and singing songs. Cattle were lowing. Horses were neighing. Pigs, huddled together in the carts, were squealing. People were shouting, trying to separate the different herds of cattle and to drive past. Afar off, the train began to whistle as it approached the town.

Some of the men of O'Neill's village wanted to halt for a drink, but their women urged them on. This was the famous Glen Tavern. It had a bad reputation, as loose women gathered there at night, to please drunken fellows who were returning from the town, or who had come out from the town to enjoy themselves in secret. They passed on.

The road was now almost level. It was wide and smooth. Yet it was packed with cattle; and motor-cars, trying to pass, had to crawl along hooting. The people no longer sang or shouted and the sound of feet and of hoofs was loud, above the rumble of the carts and the continual moaning of the brutes. A cloud hung over the road; dust and smoking sweat.

Farther on they reached the boundary wall of Ramon Mor's demesne. A lane ran beside the wall down to the shore by the yellow strand. To the left of the lane, the land rose in rocky terraces to the Black Cliff and the spike of stone stretching out from the cliff top could be seen above, black beneath the shadows of the mountains. Tall trees lined the wall of the demesne, shutting the house from view. On the other side of the road, there was a row of cottages, some of them empty, the others very dirty and falling into ruin. They had formerly belonged to the farm servants of the great house.

They all looked at the trees of the demesne, with greed in their eyes.

"It's a great change has come over that place," said the old man, "since de Burgo owned it."

"It's a change for the worse," said the big man. "Bad an' all as de Burgo was he gave employment to a couple of hundred men, one way and another."

"What did he give?" cried the old woman, "but some of the people's money he had stolen from them in rack rents? I often saw men drop down with the hunger working on his land for a shilling a week." .

"That's true," cried old O'Neill in sudden anger. "The tyrant. Ha! He's roasting in hell now. That's a comfort."

"Maybe he is," said the big man. "If there is such a place. It's hard to believe. Who's hand and glove with the priests and bishops? Not us, but the rich. People like Ramon Mor. Him and Fr. Considine are as thick as pickpockets. Everything is all wrong. Look at that land there. Five hundred acres of the best in Ireland. Drop your stick there at night on bare ground and it will be hidden with grass in the morning. All going to loss you might say. Raising cattle for export. What do the people gain by that? Nothing. A lawyer from Dublin, a Republican he was, explained it all to me. The cattle are exported. The English eat them. The grazier gets the money and invests it abroad and he gambles the dividends on foreign race-courses. That's what he said, and it's true for him. Instead of that, that demesne, to pick out a case out of many, divided up into farms, could give a livelihood to ... "

"Awl Hold your whisht, Bartly Gogarty," cried the old woman. "You'd be better off if you minded your land and put a stitch on your wife's back, instead of listening to bladherskite spouted by Republicans from Dublin. You're always with your eye on the holes in your neighbour's stocking and snapping at every dog you see with a bone in his mouth. It's the like of you that's ... "

"Hell to your soul," shouted the big man.

The two of them began a fierce altercation at which the others laughed.

They passed along the wall of the demesne until they reached the town. It began with a dirty street of low, cemented houses, some of which were in ruins. At the doors of the houses there were dirty children, nearly all barefooted. Men lounged against the walls of public houses. Women chatted in the doorways. Everybody was idle, watching the spectacle of the peasants coming to the fair. They looked degenerate and demoralised, contrasting strongly with the hardy mountaineers.

Half-way down the street, they reached the main entrance to Ramon Mor's demesne. Beyond an iron gateway, by which there was a lodge, a gravelled path led through the trees in a straight line for over half a mile. Just as they passed the gate, the doctor emerged from it.

"Hal" said the old woman. "Somebody must be sick there."

O'Neill, who had been walking along all the time, wrapt in his thoughts, heedless of the conversation, started when he saw the doctor and heard the old woman's remark. The people saluted the doctor respectfully, raising their hats. O'Neill pressed forward and said:

"Hello!"

The doctor looked at him gloomily, as he fastened the gate.

"Anybody ill?" whispered O'Neill, coming up close.

"Hm ! " said the doctor.

"Who is it?" said O'Neill anxiously.

Suddenly the doctor's face grew dark and he said: "O'Neill, you are a low dog. You are a cur."

And he walked away. O'Neill became rigid with fright.

He thought at once that Nora had been caught and that she had betrayed him. He walked on with the crowd, trembling.

"What did he say?" whispered the old woman, coming up to O'Neill.

"Eh?" said O'Neill, looking at her angrily.

"Did he say somebody was sick, God help us?"

"I don't know what he said," shouted O'Neill angrily.

"Musha, aren't you cross at a civil question?" said the old woman.

Just then the cattle were halted by a large motor lorry turning in the road. O'Neill whispered to his father. The old man went over to a blank wall and bent his head to listen.

"Have you got any money?" whispered O'Neill.

"Sure, sure," said the old man, unbuttoning his waistcoat.

The people watched, nodding to one another. The old man took a cloth purse from the pocket on the inside of his waistcoat. He tried to untie the string, failed and gave it to his son. The son untied it quickly and passed it back. The old man took a small bundle o£ banknotes from the purse. There were six pound notes in the bundle. He gave three to his son, saying:

"Here. Enjoy yourself. Treat the people of our village."

O'Neill grabbed the notes and without uttering a word of thanks rushed off. The old man hurried back to his bullock, smiling happily.

"A man is only young once," he mumbled.

Somebody said:

"Wouldn't that bring a tear from a stone? Eh? There's a ruffian for you!"

They moved on, reached another cross-roads and turned to the right into the Main Street. That street stretched, sloping steeply, to the Market Square. Beyond the square, they could see a schooner's rigged masts, at the bottom of a deep lane that led down to the docks. The square was flat, a terrace between two slopes. Like the bayonets of soldiers massed in ranks, presenting arms, the spokes of upturned carts surmounted the throng of cattle that filled the market-place. The tumult was as the sound of one voice. Nearby, the awnings of shops, the booths of street vendors on the pavements, the piles of merchandise stacked against walls, the red petrol pumps with their nozzled hoses coiled around them, the cattle-buyers running to and fro, waving their sticks, added to the romantic, wild beauty of the scene.

Lo! A miracle had grown out of the silent dawn, bringing the beauty of enchantment to the ugly town. As when, on the desert wastes of Arabia, the caravans encamp and camels kneel upon the burning sands to drop their loads of spices and of silk, and turbaned merchants sit cross-legged on their carpets, and gems are passed from hand to hand and the wild jackals on distant hills gaze in wonder at the strange tournament of man, with his enslaved beasts, bartering.

A cloud of perspiration rose like incense to the blazing sun.

CHAPTER VIII

RAMON Mor drove into the town through the gateway of his demesne. His car was very large. The hood was lowered. He sat in the rear, with his ash-plant between his knees, with his head drooping, moving his big lip, looking very fierce.

His car looked as extraordinary as himself. It was spotlessly clean, but it needed repainting. There were naked spots on the metal. The upholstery was threadbare. The cloth of the hood was patched. The woodwork was dented with wear. The engine was wheezy. The gears jarred. The radiator plug was just a piece of cork that had been improvised to replace the original one. The windscreen was cracked and the glass was soldered with putty. The shaft of the steering-wheel was bent.

O'Rourke, the driver, looked shabby, hungry and discontented. His hair was too long. His thin face was marked with cuts, received while shaving. His finger-nails were dirty. An exceedingly small and slight man, driving that huge, unwieldy car, with the enormous figure of Ramon sitting behind, he looked like a dwarf carrying around a monster for a circus.

The horn tooted, demanding a passage through the press of cattle in the street. The peasants eagerly made way, raising their hats and curtsying to Ramon, who paid no heed to them. They drove their cattle on to the footpaths and into the doorways of houses. They jammed their cart wheels against the pavements. The beasts brushed against the car, flicking Ramon with their swishing tails, dropping spots of foam on the mudguards from their slavering tongues. They moaned into his ears and their warm sweat floated about his head in smoke. But he did not raise his head to look at them, or move aside to avoid their brushing bodies. He sat like a man struck dead in the contemplation of a dreadful thought.

When the car reached the cross-roads, Ramon raised his head, glanced down Main Street and saw the fair, the awnings, the booths, the cattle, the thronged square, the spokes of upturned carts, like bayonets, the schooner's rigging, the smoke rising to the glittering sun. He tapped O'Rourke on the back with his stick and muttered:

"No use going down that way. Keep on straight through Cross Street; then go around by the Upper Quay."

The car moved on, advancing in low gear, tooting, past a horse trough, into a narrow street that was like a ravine descending to the sea, cobbled, with tall, stone house overarching, dark, falling into ruin. Some houses were empty. Others were buttressed. Clothes hung out to dry on ornate balconies. Carved and columned doorways led into shabby hucksters' shops. Steps led down from the pavement into cellars, where old women sat at tables selling pigs' feet and mussels. There were cobwebs on the windows. There was refuse on the street. Dogs lay asleep in doorways. Peasant women, with their aprons doubled round their waists, wandered with their children, back and forth, bargaining in the little shops for spools of thread and balls of twine and sweets and biscuits and holy pictures and tobacco. There was silence there and the musty smell of an old tomb and they gaped in aweful wonder, like people inspecting a place where murder has been done.

The car passed on, rocking from side to side over the tom cobble-stones, with its gloomy passenger, who, like the commander of a besieged town, sees his citizens starving within the walls and yet sees them not, seeing only the necessity to satisfy his pride by resistance, and plunders their resources without mercy, until rank weeds and vermin are sold in the market-place as food.

The car swung round a blank wall and entered a short street that debouched on to the quay. On one side of this street there was a gasworks. On the other there was a coalyard behind a zinc wall. They both belonged to him. A man in shirt-sleeves was walking in the coal-yard, from the office to a heap of coal, where another man was standing with a horsewhip in his hand. There was a horse, with a cart, near the heap of coal. The place was very still.

The car debouched on to the quay. The quay ended about one hundred yards to the left. There were no houses on that side, except the entrance gate of the gasworks. From the end of the quay a sandy road led round the shore, curving outwards to the right, where a rocky headland bound the harbour's mouth, and curving again to the left towards the yellow strand below the house of Ramon Mor. The Black Cliff was visible afar, with its stone snout protruding over the sea. Rows of cottages and little gardens led from the road beyond the gasworks towards the town and on an eminence near the trees of Ramon Mor's demesne, the square, flat-roofed house of the parish priest shone in the sunlight. It had white blinds on its upper windows.

On the horizon, the summits of the mountains were now encircled with little clouds of mist.

In front, the sandy beach curved in a half-circle, ending in the rocky headland. It was now low tide. There was a fringe of yellow moss, growing on smooth bed-rocks, below the sand. Under the sandbank that bound the road, rowboats were beached. Some of them were wrecks. A few were sunk into the sand to their gunwales. Others had been stripped leaving only the skeletons of their frames. At one point, midway in the strand, a solitary rib of a boat stuck up. It was hoary and barnacled with age.

The car turned to the right along the Upper Quay. The cobbled roadway was very wide. There were great cavities between the cobbles. Some of the holes were patched with asphalt. Others were filled with rough sand and sea pebbles. Grass was growing between the blocks that paved the quay wall. The iron mooring-posts were covered with red dust. There were groups of idle men standing about, fishermen, with forlorn faces and ragged clothes. On the right, beyond a torn pavement, there was a row of houses. Some had fallen down, leaving gaps through which goats and asses could be seen feeding on waste plots among heaps of refuse. The slate roofs were full of holes. One shuttered, empty house had the words OCEANIC HOTEL painted in black on its yellow walls. Birds passed in and out through its torn roof. Its iron balconies were speckled with white bird droppings. There were taverns, foul and gloomy. There were stray men drinking within them, supping black beer in silence.

The quay was dead. The desolate human beings that loafed there were like stragglers left from the sacking of a town.

A pier jutted out into the centre of the harbour, dividing the quay into two, almost even, parts. It pointed towards a small sandy islet that lay across the harbour's mouth. There was a lighthouse on the islet. The point of the rocky promontory, curving like a hook across the harbour, came within two hundred yards of the island. On the other side of the island, the shore was distant, curving away from the mainland in sandy beaches to the horizon, glittering in the sun, with a border of shore grass, waving, yellow like ripe corn. A wrecked ship lay off the sands. The low tide had bared its hulk almost to the keel. Its prow was buried in the sand. Its great rump was raised aloft, exposing the fins of the screw that had once propelled it through the ocean.

There was a scum upon the water of the harbour, as if that, too, were rotting, like a duck-pond on a village green.

The boats had now landed from the islands; except two small coracles coming from the far island and a motor launch that had just set out from Inismuineach, making wide, foaming furrows with its rapid prow.

The islanders had moored their boats about the pier. They had landed their cattle, hoisting them with slings and pulleys, like bags. They had driven them up a little way to the Fish Market, a wide space above the pier. There they had halted them and made a fair of their own. With their rare costumes and their wild features they made a strange spectacle. They looked alien. Some of the men wore rawhide shoes and woollen smocks, dyed blue, with white, bone buttons down the front, embroidered at the throat. They wore wide-brimmed black hats or tam-o'-shanter caps. The women all wore red frieze skirts and heavy, cashmere shawls. Some of the little boys were dressed like girls, in red frieze petticoats and little blue waistcoats with bone buttons. All had beautiful, strange faces, with eyes that were the colour of the sea on a wild day-a brilliant blue. But they were very thin, and they had the mournful expression of people that are nearly always hungry and struggling with abject poverty.

Ramon ordered his driver to halt when they reached the corner of the Fish Market. It was impossible to drive the car through that dense crowd.

"Stay here," he said to O'Rourke. "I'll be only a few minutes. Then I'll want you to drive me to ... "

He did not finish the sentence. He was interrupted by an extraordinary man who emerged from the crowd of islanders and approached the car.

This man was called Tommy Derrane, a well-known fellow in the district, because of his strange conversation and his demented wit. He was terrifying in appearance because of his wild, restless eyes, his pale face, his sudden grin, his hunched shoulders, his bobbing chin and the twitching of his limbs. He was dressed in island costume. He was tall, large-boned, lean, terribly vital, a typical islander.

"God bless you, Great Ramon, son of Michael," he cried in Irish, "you are still on your feet and your heart is strong. That is good. Ha! Ha!"

He laughed, raised his hat and made an extraordinary bow. Some other islanders came near, laughing, following the foolish fellow about for their amusement. Ramon frowned and picked up the satchel in which he carried his ledgers. Taking no notice of Derrane, he whispered to O'Rourke:

"Move the car back a bit out of the way."

Then he stood up to leave the car. The fool continued to speak in a loud voice, gesticulating and looking all round him, as if addressing a great audience.

"It is said," he cried, "that God listens to the prayers of the rich. All the power of the world is in service to the rich man. He can fly like a bird or swim under the sea like a fish and all the wise men of the world are working night and day making potions to protect him from disease. But all the same, the worms are waiting for him and the heavy stone will lie on his chest same as it will lie on the chest of the poor. Grass will grow on his grave and birds will make nests in his empty skull. So it's said by the saints, that lived long ago, in their prophecies. Ha! Ha!"

Ramon got out of the car and began to walk away, frowning at the ground. The wild man continued:

"The rich man turns everything into gold, for he is wise and he has no pity for the hunger of an empty stomach. He has no conscience. He doesn't see the misery of the poor, for he has a magic veil over his eyes. He is deaf and blind like God, who made Hell as well as Heaven. Go your way, sir, and turn neither to your right nor to your left. Fools curse you, but I bless you, for it's nothing to me that you sucked the blood of the villages and the islands. It's the nature of a hawk to pounce on a mouse, and for an eagle to steal the lamb from its mother's teat. Take the bread out of our mouth. God bless you. We'll all be equal one day. Death, I say. The Devil is waiting for us all. It's between God and the Devil who'll have us. A man is no more than a cow to be bought and sold at the cross-roads between Heaven and Hell. Ha! Ha ! "

He yelled, threw his cap into the air, caught it, yelled again and walked away, laughing in an insane manner. A crowd followed him.

Ramon walked, stooping, through the crowd. The people saluted him in Irish, saying:

"God salute you, Great Ramon, son of Michael."

The Fish Market was a triangular space lying between the Upper and Lower Quay. From the apex of the triangle a short, wide street, called High Street, led into the Market Square above. From the Market Square, the fair had overflowed into High Street and into the Fish Market. The whole left side of the triangle belonged to Ramon Mor. There were six houses there, of various sizes, with a little thatched cottage at the lower corner, adjoining the Lower Quay. Most of the houses on that Quay also belonged to him, warehouses and stores.

The little thatched cottage, where Ramon had been born and where the fortune of the family had been founded, was now closed and used as a store-room. The windows were boarded and the thatch was sagging inwards. It looked odd between a tall, stone warehouse on its left and a large, two-storeyed, stone house on its right. On a ground-floor window of the stone house was written, R. Costello, Merchant and Contractor. That was Ramon's office. To the right of this house there was a large building that had once been the principal hotel of the town. It was long and three storeys high. It had been rebuilt. A storey had been added to it. The walls were now cemented. The archway in the centre still remained. Just now, carts were passing through the archway going into the courtyard. This building was Ramon's shop. A crowd of people moved about it, going in and out and halted in groups on the pavement.

There was a row of carts, laden with produce, fowls, eggs, butter, oats, packs of wool, hides. Islanders were coming with baskets of dried fish and hampers of bleached sea moss and little wicker baskets of eggs and bundles of frieze cloth.

Right in front of the door, an island woman was milking a cow, crooning, while her little son stood beside her, holding her apron, with a tin mug in his hand, waiting for milk.

A tall man approached Ramon from the office entrance. It was his cousin, Peadar Mor, his agent on the islands. He was almost as big as Ramon, but he was lean, clumsy, of coarser fibre, less dignified. His eyes were shifty. They shook hands, inquired about their respective families and blessed one another. Peadar Mor spoke in English with a foreign accent.

"I was in the office waiting for you," he said. "I wanted a word with you before the parish priest came. There is a small business on hand that might be worth talking about between the two of us."

"Who?" said Ramon. "The parish priest?"

"Fr. Fogarty. There he is now coming in the motor launch."

Ramon looked towards the launch. It was now crossing the lighthouse.

"What's he up to?" growled Ramon.

"It's about the payments," said Peadar Mor. "Maybe we better talk inside."

"Hurry then," said Ramon. "I haven't much time. I have to be off again. He thinks too much of himself, that meddler."

Several women came up trying to whisper something to him, but he waved his hand and said:

"Later on. I'm in a hurry now."

They entered the office building. His office was on the ground-floor to the left of the hallway. The remainder of the building was used as the residence of his manager and as a boarding-house for the apprentices he always used as assistants in his shops, to save money. Formerly he himself had also lived in this house.

A row of people stretched along the hall to the office door, waiting their turn. Nearly all of these people started forward when they saw Ramon, endeavouring to engage him in conversation about their business, but he walked past without paying any heed to them, in through the open door of the office, followed by his cousin. The office was large, but it was packed with people. A counter stretched across the room, surmounted by a grill, behind which five clerks sat at desks, busy in dealing with the people who were talking to them. One of the clerks stood up when Ramon entered. With a pen behind his ear, he came round to meet Ramon, who was moving towards a door that led into his own private office beyond.

"Excuse me, sir," said the clerk in a whisper, " but the captain of the schooner has just been in and he said he is already loaded to capacity. He'll have to leave about twenty ton of the kelp behind. He's sailing to-day."

The clerk's hair was wet with brilliantine. Ramon sniffed and muttered: "What the name o' God do you put that mush in your hair for? It smells like hell. Eh? I can't be bothered with that captain. Tell him he's got to take all the kelp or go to the Devil. It's none of my business if his ship sinks. What do they want me to do? Send it on the railway and pay more than the whole load is worth? If he comes back tell him to wait for me. I'll have to go out again. And say ... Send a man up to

Finnigan's. The men after the cattle are to have all the porter they want. Porter, mind, but no whisky. Here are the accounts. Get to work. Wait a minute. Come inside here."

The clerk followed Ramon and Peadar Mor into the private office. Ramon whispered to the clerk:

"Give no rebate. Mind. To nobody. Stand no nonsense. Go by the accounts."

"Yes, sir."

The clerk went out, closing the door. Ramon sat down in a swivel chair and leaned his arms on the table. The cousin sat on a chair near him.

"Well!" said Ramon. "What's the trouble now? What did you say about Fr. Fogarty?"

"It's this co-operative society he started for the fishermen last spring."

"I know. It's that freak from Dublin that came down. Go on."

"Well! They didn't do much with it. As you know yourself, they have few nets, and they can't renew them under the new Government."

"Why should the Government renew their nets? All they're good for is begging."

"Well! Anyway, Fr. Fogarty went up to Dublin and saw the Minister of Fisheries about it, but it appears he got nothing much, only a promise that the Government would put up so much if the fishermen put up so much. Then Fr. Fogarty came to me and made the suggestion that the people shouldn't be called on this fair to pay for what they had taken on credit during the year, ye see, so as to be able to use the price of their cattle and pigs to buy the nets. So I says to him that it wasn't for me to say yes aye or no in the matter, seeing I'm only acting for you: But I thought it was queer, I told him that, after taking the buying and selling of the fish out of our hands and starting this co-operative society, he should come and ask ... "

"Damned impudence," muttered Ramon."I'd like him to come to me with that story."

"Well, anyway," continued the cousin, "he got high and mighty and he said something about co-operative shops."

"He what?" cried Ramon, leaning across the table and becoming red in the neck.

"Upon my soul, that's what he said. I up and told him that it was to you he should come with that story. Then he grumbled about the price you are giving for the kelp this year, and he hinted that his organisation might spread and take over everything, buying and selling, same as he said some man was doing in the County Donegal."

"What do the people say about this?" said Ramon in a whisper. "Have you heard anything?"

"Well! There's some talk," said Peadar Mor. "There's some discontent. But it's hard to say. Fr. Fogarty's word'll go a long way with them, I think."

Ramon struck the table with the palm of his right hand.

"We'll see," he said, "whether it will or not."

He drew in a deep breath and jumped to his feet.

"He'll be coming here straight. Did you bring your accounts?"

"Yes, I gave them to the clerk."

"Are they all correct?"

"I think so."

"Go out into the office and go over them with the clerk. And mind, there is to be no mercy. If they are going to fight me, then let them know what they have to fight. I'll see you later. I'll attend to this man here."

Peadar Mor got to his feet and walked out of the room slowly. As he was closing the door, Ramon heard a loud voice in the office, saying:

"Is Mr. Costello here?"

It was Fr. Fogarty. With a quick movement, Ramon sat down again in his swivel chair, pulled his hat farther down over his eyes and began to twirl his thumbs. A clerk knocked, entered and announced the priest. The priest entered. The door was closed.

"Good morning, Mr. Costello."

Ramon raised his head and looked at the priest. He did not speak.

The priest was a tall, handsome man of middle age, with fat, pink cheeks and merry eyes. He carried himself well. He was elegantly dressed. Altogether, he had the air of a hearty man of the world. He ungloved his hands slowly, took off his hat and threw it nonchalantly, upside down, on the table. He threw his gloves into the hat, slid his stick on to the table, raised the tails of his coat elegantly and rested his right thigh along the edge of the board. He leaned forward, put his hand on his knee, coughed and said in a drawling voice that was rather contemptuous:

"I came to see you about a small matter. I hope I'm not disturbing you."

Ramon's underlip was the only part of his face that was visible beneath the rim of his hat. Crouching over the table, with his enormous bulk, shapeless within his hairy, brown clothes, without movement, he looked uncouth beside the elegant priest. Then he slowly raised his head, glancing along the priest's legs, up over his body to his face. His own face was masked under an expression of stupid simplicity that peasants often assume, when they are being questioned about something unpleasant.

"And what might that be?" he said in a low voice.

He lowered his head again, glancing slowly down along the priest's body to his feet, sniffing; as if he were smelling the priest. He shrugged his shoulders slightly. The priest coughed on to the back of his hand.

"I was talking to your cousin about it," said the priest quietly, almost contemptuously. "I suppose he has already told you about it. He came in early."

"My cousin?" said Ramon. "I see. I didn't have time this morning to go into the island business. Now, I suppose maybe it's something connected with the church. Repairs you are thinking of making? In that case, of course, you'll have no difficulty as far as I am concerned. My purse is always open in the cause of charity."

He glanced sharply for a moment at the priest. It was a knowing glance and it meant:

"I am willing to pay you to keep quiet."

But the priest just flicked a speck of dust off his coat and said:

"It's more or less a matter of charity, but it has nothing to do with the church. You must know that things are in a bad way on the islands. In fact, they could be no worse; neither famine nor a plague could be worse than the state of terrible apathy and misery people are falling into; all that are left of them, for they are emigrating every day. Something must be done about it. I feel it is my duty to ... "

"Ha!" said Ramon, stiffening his shoulders. "That's funny."

With a sudden movement, he thrust out his chin, shaking the layers of his throat. His little eyes flashed.

"I beg your pardon," said the priest.

"That's the second time this morning I heard that expression. I feel it is my duty. What is your duty, Fr. Fogarty? Damned meddling. I have no time."

He struck the table with the palm of his right hand. The priest drew back and his nonchalant manner changed suddenly. He flushed.

"I can't be bothered with you," snapped Ramon. "I have no time to waste on you. I know your scheme. But I'm telling you as plain as a pikestaff that I allow no man in this town or district to meddle in my business."

"Excuse me," began the priest.

"I won't," said Ramon. "You're an outsider. You've been on the islands four years. But there are seven generations of Costellos buried under one tombstone in the graveyard of Tobbercasla, on the island of Inismuineach. I don't allow any stranger to come between me and my own blood."

The priest got off the table drew himself up and said with great dignity: '

"Restrain yourself. You'll gain nothing by trying to bully me. I'm not in your debt."

Ramon leaned across the table and whispered :

"You're in my power, though."

"I don't understand you," said the priest contemptuously.

"No," said Ramon. "I got curious about you when I heard some time ago you were bitten by this co-operative idea. I said to myself that you were concerned with more things than religion. I know a few priests up and down the country that started schemes like that and made a little out of it. Like yourself, they had remote parishes and people that hadn't much education or knowledge of accounts. And their societies went smash. They had expensive tastes like you, too. They were fond of English seaside resorts for their holidays."

The priest started.

"Don't budge, Fr. Fogarty," said Ramon. "I'm willing to let well enough alone. It's no concern of mine how you conduct yourself when you are on your holidays. I suppose it's the privilege of your cloth."

Then he pushed back his chair and got to his feet. He whispered in a voice that was hoarse with anger:

"I take no holidays. I have been all my life chained to the wheel, slaving to earn my bread. I have built up this business, like my father and mother before me, by hard work and by denying myself every pleasure in life. It's easy for you that never did a day's work in your life to come with freak schemes to rob me of my business and accuse me of ruining the countryside. How did I find the people living? They were living in houses worse than pigsties on bread and salt. They were no better than savages. It's I put them on their feet. Every young boy or girl I found on the islands or in the villages with any sign of intelligence I helped along and put in the way of earning a good living in a good position all over the country. It was I kept the whole countryside from starvation, feeding them on credit in the bad times. Now, when things are different and they have ideas in their heads, they tum on me and call me a grabber and a tyrant. By the Lord God!"

"If I hear any more of your schemes," he whispered. He picked up his ash-plant off the floor and spat on it. He drew himself to his full height. The priest looked a paltry fellow beside him.

"I'll run you out of your parish like a rat. That's my word for you."

The priest trembled with anger, but he made no effort to control it. He slowly picked up his gloves, his hat and his stick.

"That remains to be seen," he said contemptuously. "That remains to be seen."

He walked to the door, opened it and passed out of the room, leaving the door open after him.

"Eh?" said Ramon to himself, amazed by the priest's manner.

Somebody closed the door.

"Eh?" he said again aloud. "What has he up his sleeve?"

He sat down and then got to his feet at once, saying dreamily:

"I must be going."

But he did not move. His head began to nod. His body became very tired. His head became dizzy. He began to mutter.

"What has he in his mind? Did he notice anything?"

He dropped into his chair. A thick cloud seemed to rise up inside his chest. It entered his throat and he gasped for breath. The back of his neck became stiff. He had to close his eyes to dull the pain that struck them. He remained conscious, but his mind began to play strange tricks with him.

He saw an open grave, with men digging in it. They were shovelling out black earth upon the trodden grass. He asked them whose grave they were digging. They smiled strangely and pointed to a boulder at which he looked and saw mounted thereon a horned fellow whom he immediately recognised as the Devil. The Devil had his tail between his teeth. He was winking his left eye and grinning. Terrified, Ramon called on God and raised his eyes to the sky. He saw God there, but God paid no attention to him. God was soaring about through the sky. He had a curly, yellow beard, and he was dressed in a white garment with a golden rope hanging from his stomach. He was making foolish noises and he was trying to lasso little birds with the end of the rope. The Devil pointed his finger at God and nodded in a contemptuous manner. Ramon gave himself up as lost and held out his hands in appeal towards the grinning Devil and towards the sinister fellows who were mechanically shovelling up dark earth from the deepening grave. And then they all said something, which he could not hear, in one voice, and they pointed at the grave.

Then the Devil hopped nimbly off the boulder, picked up his hat, his gloves and his cane, and walked away casually, across the floor, saying in a haughty tone:

"That remains to be seen."

CHAPTER IX

WHEN he had finished breakfast, Fr. Considine went into his library. He was terribly excited. With his hands concealed within the sleeves of his coat, he began to wander around the room, halting suddenly after every third or fourth step and uttering an exclamation. When he halted, he shuddered violently, drew in his breath through his teeth, shut his eyes and then opened his mouth wide, as if yawning, with his head thrown back; the gesture of a highly strung individual recollecting something shameful.

He glanced around him frequently, furtively, as if expecting to find somebody concealed among the books that lined the walls of the room. At times he raised his feet, one after the other, from the carpet and took a step to one side. He would sit down, at one time in the leather-lined armchair by the empty fireplace, at another time in the swivel chair at his writing-desk; but he arose at once, each time, and went, almost running, to the far end of the room. He avoided looking at the window, from which the curtain had been drawn aside and through which the sun was shining brilliantly.

He acted and looked like a man in the first stages of delirium tremens, when remorse of conscience gnaws furiously at the exhausted mind and the nerves, unfed, run wild upon their circuits and the organs are stupefied by the poison they have soaked. His cheeks had red spots on them, and these spots changed when he became possessed by his intermittent fits of terror. At times they darkened. At other times they almost disappeared.

But his lips did not twitch, nor did his eyes have the dazed look of a man upon whom the strange mania of alcoholic hallucinations is growing. Both his eyes and his mouth had a cunning expression, which contrasted strangely with the distraught antics of the rest of his body.

Now, in daylight, his eyes were of a brilliant ·blue colour. They looked feverish and very intense.

The window was raised. A gentle, warm breeze flowed into the room, bearing the fresh, salt smell of the sea and the distant, dulled sounds of the fair, the continual moaning of brutes and the shouting of people. The house was in silence. Outside the window, bees were humming among the flower-beds that lined the gravelled drive leading to the gate. Now and again butterflies flew across the window, outside. Sometimes the inflowing breeze was perfumed with the odour of flowers. At other times the smell of old leather, from the binding of books, stirred by the sweet breeze, floated around the room.

Yet these beautiful, calm sounds and delicious perfumes served merely to add to the sinister aspect of the room; they made more manifest, by their cheerful contrast, the dark colouring of the books, of the furniture, of the pictures on the walls, of the priest himself, with his distraught antics.

Suddenly the gate swung open slowly, with a plaintive, creaking sound. The priest stood still, listened and said aloud:

"Ha! Here he is."

Then he went on tiptoe to the window, stood to one side and looked out cautiously.

"It's not he," he whispered in amazement. "It's his sister."

Mary Costello was coming up the gravelled drive. His eyes gleamed. He stepped back from the window, took his hands from the sleeves of his coat, looked at them and then rubbed them together rapidly, staring at the floor. Then he went to the door that led on to the hallway and opened it cautiously. He peered out into the hall, towards the left, in the direction of the kitchen. There was nobody in sight. There were low voices in the kitchen, and he heard the sound of vessels being washed. He went on tiptoe along the hall to the front door and opened it. Mary was approaching the door, walking hurriedly, with her eyes on the ground. When she heard the door opening, she started. He raised his hat and beckoned to her to come forward. She bowed and entered the hall. She was panting. He closed the door gently, took her arm and led her into the library. He closed the library door.

She also was terribly excited. She was wearing a tweed suit of grey stuff, with a wide skirt. She carried the medal of a Child of Mary on her neck, over a pink jumper. She wore a black straw hat with a wide brim. She carried a pair of gloves in her hands and she kept fidgeting with them. She looked all around the floor, without raising her eyes to the priest.

"Won't you sit down?" he said, coming forward and offering her a chair near the fireplace.

His manner had changed with her arrival. He had become outwardly calm. He watched her eagerly. But his eyes were still unnaturally brilliant.

She was so nervous that she stumbled over a rug as she went to the chair. He sat near her, in the leather-lined armchair. He crossed his legs, lay back, took out his handkerchief and began to wipe his hands with it. Then he started, became excited for a moment, looked at his hands and put the handkerchief in his pocket. He glanced at her to see had she noticed the excitement. She was still looking at the floor, nervously toying with her gloves. He cleared his throat.

She looked up and said in a whisper:

"I've something to tell you, father. I'm not disturbing you, father."

"Not at all," he said very quietly. "What is it?"

Again she dropped her eyes to the floor and began to tremble. She remained silent.

"What is it?" he repeated.

Suddenly she threw herself on her knees at his feet, clasping her hands in the attitude of a person at prayer and muttered:

"Forgive me, father. I have damned my soul. And now she has made terrible accusations against you. It's all my fault."

"Get up off your knees," he said excitedly, drawing back. "Why do you kneel to me that way? What are you talking about?"

"Let me stay on my knees, father," she cried, clasping his knees. "I want to confess."

"Hush," he whispered, glancing about the room, with a look of terror in his eyes. "Don't speak so loud. My God!"

He became rigid. He grasped the elbows of the chair and pressed against the back and tuned his head slightly sideways, with his mouth open. His face was contorted, just as it had been when he was walking about the room, and he halted suddenly, recollecting something shameful.

He began to mutter to himself in prayer. Then he sighed deeply and became calm.

"Do you want to confess?" he whispered softly, "or is it something you want to tell me in the ordinary way?"

Now his face looked cunning.

"I want to confess," she mumbled. "I have damned my soul on account of her."

His face became still more cunning.

"I see," he whispered. "But you said something about an accusation. Is this something I should know in the ordinary way?"

She burst into tears.

"Oh! Father," she mumbled. "Have pity on me. I don't know what I'm doing. I want to confess. I want to tell you that, too, what she said to the doctor, but there are other things I can only tell you in confession."

"To the doctor?" he gasped.

He bent forward, took her by the shoulder and raised her. He looked into her eyes and said:

"Control yourself. What is it?"

"I'm ashamed to tell you this way, father," she moaned. "I want to confess."

"Shame," he said fiercely, "is a temptation of the Devil. If this is something I should know for my own protection you must tell it to me in the ordinary way."

"But you wouldn't understand unless I tell you the whole thing. And I ... "

He raised his right hand over her head and said in a solemn voice :

"What you are going to tell me will remain a secret, just as if you were kneeling in the confession. Have no fear."

"You won't tell my brother."

"Rest assured. I'll only remember what is necessary for me to know. The rest will be known only to God. Later you may approach the sacrament and get forgiven."

He made the sign of the cross over her and murmured a prayer. She bowed low and muttered something, striking her breast. Then she drew in a deep breath and began to speak rapidly. Her cheeks were flushed.

"It all began," she said, "when Nora came to the house. I began to have awful temptations at night."

"In what way."

She shuddered and remained silent.

"Come, come," he whispered. "Can you not tell me?"

She still remained silent, although she struggled to speak.

"You mean to say," he whispered, "that her presence in the house made you want to do a certain thing?"

She nodded her head and shuddered again.

"And in what way did this temptation affect you?"

"I don't understand, father."

"Did you give way to it?"

"Yes, father."

"Alone?"

"Yes, father."

"Thinking of her?"

"Yes, and of my brother, too."

"How?"

"With her."

"And you have kept it secret? You have not confessed?"

"Yes. I confessed. I went to the curate."

They both remained silent for nearly a minute. They were intensely excited. Mary's face was flushed and her bosom heaved. She stared fixedly at the ground. Her eyes shone with passion. The priest seemed to be possessed with the same passion. His eyes had become sleepy. His lips quivered and he breathed deeply, at long intervals. Then, waving his left hand, he continued:

"Did you, in any way, make any, were you inclined to make, when you were near her, in what way did she?"

"I could see she hated me."

"And yet when you were near her you ... "

"She would hardly speak to me."

"But you went on?"

"Yes, father."

"In the same way?"

"No, father. I used to think she was beating me and then I began to want to have somebody ... "

"With her?"

"Yes, father."

"Not your brother?"

"No, father."

"Why?"

"Because he ... "

"Something you heard?"

"I heard my mother talking to him about her. Then he got another room and I used to hear ... "

"You mean you listened at the door?"

"Yes. I hated her not to have somebody. I wanted her to have a child."

"A child?"

"Yes, because she beat me."

"Actually beat you?"

"No, no, but I used to think she did; that it was she was touching me. Then she'd suffer. She damned my soul."

"By having a child."

"She'd suffer that way. Then I'd have some little one to love and look after. And she wouldn't go away. I was always afraid she'd go away, on account of the things my brother and my mother used to say to her. I thought that would be terrible."

"Because you never before had ... "

"No, father."

"And then you . . . "

" Yes. I used to talk to her about ... "

"What?"

"Any man I thought she might ... "

"And she ... ? Did she ... ?"

"She didn't trust me because she thought I was spying on her and that they just sent me to find out if she was ... Although she became friendly with the doctor he was different. He is a good man."

"Hm! A good man."

"Then, when O'Neill came home a few months ago ... "

"Ha! O'Neill!"

Fr. Considine started and looked at her excitedly. She also started and looked at him. They both flushed and looked away.

"Let us forget that," he cried irrelevantly, waving his left hand. "This is another matter. But have you anything definite?"

"About what, father?"

"What did you say at first? You said something about the doctor."

"I heard her tell the doctor that you ... that you ... it was a terrible thing she said. God forgive her. She must be out of her mind."

"Come, come. What did she say?"

"She said you assaulted her down at Jack Geraghty's house. He asked her then was it with a stick you beat her or how and she said ... "

"My God!" gasped the priest, getting to his feet slowly. He stood erect, rigid, with his hands held slightly in front of him, with his elbows to his sides. She was about to rise, too, when he motioned to her abruptly.

"Still," he said. "Tell me the whole business. This is astounding. It's the Devil's work. Witchery, abomination."

His face was deadly pale. There was murder in his eyes.

"This morning," she said, "when I heard my brother shouting, something told me at once what was the matter, but I didn't want to tell him for the reason I told you, because I wanted her to have a child."

"What?" said the priest savagely. "You believe her?"

Mary put her hands to her mouth and ·stared at his terrible face.

"You believe what she said?" he repeated.

She remained silent for a few moments, gaping at him, with her forehead wrinkled, trying to understand his fury. Then she understood and said eagerly:

"No, no father. But I know where she was. I wasn't thinking of what she said about you. That was afterwards."

The priest put his hand to his heart and sat down, gasping.

"Begin at the beginning," he said, "and tell me about ... What has he got to do with it? O'Neill?"

She began to wring her hands and said:

"If I told him, he'd blame me for not having told him before and anyway ... "

"If you told who ... "

"My brother."

He caught her roughly by the shoulder and whispered:

"Tell me about O'Neill. I must know this before he comes. I am expecting your brother. Perhaps it's not too late."

"About two months ago," she said, "when he came back, I used to talk to her about him. He used to be a lovely boy long ago when he was a student and I used to be very fond of him. I used to see him in the town, but I never spoke to him, for at that time he was going to be a priest. I told her about him and all he had done. God forgive him, he has gone to the bad since then. He was led astray by women like her, same as I was. She seemed to take no notice, but one day I met him in the square and I stopped him and spoke to him. I said to him like this ...I forget what way it began."

"It doesn't matter. Go on. What happened? What did you say?"

"I told him she was wild about him."

"Astounding."

"It's because I hated her, father. God forgive me ... I knew he'd make her suffer. But if she had a child, then the little thing would be innocent, and if she went away there would be something. He has made many women suffer."

She sobbed. The priest drew back, looked at her with his eyes wide open and muttered to himself:

"She is an innocent."

"I told him," she continued, "that she used to go to the doctor's house in the afternoon now and again. Then she met him there. Then I knew that she fell in love with him because she would never speak to me about him. She used to say all the other men I talked about were savages and that they never washed themselves, but about him she said nothing, only shrugged her shoulders. And she began to titivate herself and to go to the doctor's every day. Then O'Rourke that used to be in O'Neill's flying column during the war, I saw him one day coming out of Finnigan's with O'Neill. They walked away separate without speaking to each other. Then O'Rourke came to me and said there was to be a party at the Glen Tavern one night and he wanted to go to it, so would I give him the key of the side gate? I knew well he could go out over the side wall same as he always did, when he was going after girls and didn't want to be seen going out the main gates, but I said nothing. I gave him the key. He kept it for four days and whenever I asked him for it, he said he had put it away somewhere and that he was looking for it. Then he gave it to me back."

"Come. Get to the point. Your brother may be here at any moment."

"Yes, father. I know it was the Devil put it into my head. I thought it was how he was going to come into her. He'd do anything. But it was how she went out. But I couldn't be sure until this morning, when we were all searching for her. I was afraid it was how she had gone away altogether and that she ... "

"Be exact. Who was searching for her. How was it discovered that she had gone out?"

"The dog began to bark when she screeched. Farrelly told me that it was her screech he heard, too. I didn't hear it myself."

The priest looked at her malignly.

"Ramon got out of bed," she continued, "and thought somebody was breaking into the house. Then he found out she was gone and he had us all searching the house. I thought he was going into a fit. Lately he is getting very queer and I'm terrified of him."

"Make no excuses," said the priest irrelevantly. "God will decide."

She rummaged in her bosom and took out a crumpled piece of paper. She handed the piece of paper to the priest.

"I went into her room and searched," she said. "I found that in a little silver box where I knew she keeps things."

"What is it?" he said, staring at the piece of paper.

"It's from him," she said. "I know his writing. Read it. It's only signed F., but I know it's him."

He straightened out the piece of paper, and read:

"Dearest Nora. Don't forget. Ten o'clock on the Black Cliff. I have something very important to tell you. I'll kill myself if you don't come. Love, F."

"That's plain enough," he muttered. "It's obviously he. And then? What happened?"

"I said nothing to Ramon about it. I ran out into the grounds with the others. We found her at the lodge. She was in a faint. Anyway, she pretended she was."

"Ha!"

"I thought she was just .... He is terrible, you know, the things people say about him."

"Who?"

"O'Neill."

The priest looked at her in amazement.

"And you thought when you saw her that..."

"Yes, father."

"What?"

"I just thought she'd have a child, so I felt fond of her and sorry to see her that way all worn out and hurt-looking."

"Hurry," he said angrily. "Be quick."

"She is an innocent," he muttered to himself.

"We brought her to her room and I made them send for the doctor for fear he might have hurt her."

"Fool! The doctor!"

"I didn't know, father. Then I tried to be nice to her, but she turned on me. Then I knew I hated her. So when the doctor came I listened at the door to hear what she was up to. When I heard her make that accusation against you, after I knowing where she had gone and I telling her I knew where she was..."

"You told her?"

"I didn't tell her about the letter, but ... "

"Ha! She doesn't know about the letter?"

"No."

"Or that you know about O'Neill?"

"No."

"Then what did you tell her?"

"I just said to her that it was no use pretending to me since I knew where she was. She just turned on me. She thought I was only trying to find out."

"Good."

"I was struck dumb when I heard her make that accusation, and I saw at once what I had done, and that I had damned my soul."

"Did you hear what the doctor said to Ramon?"

"No. I didn't wait, but I know the doctor would do anything she'd ask him, after the way he spoke to her. She can twist him round her fingers. He's a soft-hearted man. All the people make a fool of him. And he is ... "

"You are not an innocent," cried the priest angrily. "Your mind is perverted."

"Oh, father, don't turn on me."

"Silence," he cried. "It's utterly amazing how you could have descended to these low depths of lust and depravity. Listening at doors and scheming in the most despicable way, and then going behind my back to confess to the curate matters that concern the material welfare of those whose interests have been placed under my direct care. Abomination."

She prostrated herself before him and clutched his shoes. He continued to speak, in an exalted voice, waving his left hand and glancing around the room in a distracted manner.

"You have schemed to bring disgrace on your brother's grey hairs, and to place me at the mercy of this viper and of her atheist friends. You have steeped your soul in the most foul sins of perversion and ... I dare not utter its name, that sin from which the Saviour turns away His gentle face in horror, the sin that burned Sodom, the writing on the wall. But arise and be comforted. The Holy Mother has her arms opened wide to the repentant sinner and the sword of Divine vengeance is ever drawn from the scabbard. Repent lest you be dragged down. I will intercede for you. Not at my feet, but at the feet of God."

Suddenly he dropped his hand, he grew calm and said hurriedly:

"Come. Get up. You must go at once. Your brother may be here at any moment. Slip out the back way."

"But, father ... "

"Later. Later. There is no time now. Hurry."

He helped her to rise. Again she tried to speak. .

"Hush," he said excitedly. "He must not find you here. Hal"

Suddenly the gate swung open with a creaking sound. He hurried to the window and looked.

"Goodness me!" he muttered. "Again somebody... What torture!"

It was Fr. Fogarty who was coming slowly up the drive,
twirling his stick.

"Quick," said Fr. Considine. "Compose yourself. Get out by the back. He must not see you, either. Stop rubbing your face."

CHAPTER X

"Come in."

A maid opened the door, entered and said :

"Fr. Fogarty to see you, father."

"Show him in."

She went out and said:

"This way, father."

Fr. Fogarty, carrying his hat, his stick and his gloves in his left hand, entered the library. He was smiling broadly. His red, merry face was perspiring slightly. He advanced, holding out his right hand and saying in a nonchalant, almost contemptuous voice:

"Morning, Michael."

"Good morning," said Fr. Considine. "I'm glad to see you."

They shook hands.

"What a climb! " said Fr. Fogarty, drawing in a deep breath. "I came up the lane from the Fish Market. My goodness! What a hill you chose to build your house upon! Biblical. What? For a thin man like you of course ... By the way, you don't look up to the mark. You look seedy. Hope you don't mind, but I'm taking the liberty of inviting myself to lunch. I'm on my way to Dublin. I'm catching the night mail. How this room smells like a bishop's study! Fine collection of books, but what the deuce is the good of them? Rather have a bag of golf clubs. Books, books. What's on the menu?"

"I'm afraid I ... some fish I think you could have and a ... yes, I saw a lobster brought in and there is, of course, a leg of ... but let me take your ... "

"No, no. I'll be shifting in a few seconds. I just came up to beg a meal. Oh! How hot it is already! It's going to be a scorching day."

He sat down, choosing the most comfortable chair in the room, the leather-lined armchair. He drew it close to the window, in order to get the benefit o£ the slight breeze.

Fr. Considine went to the fireplace, put his hand to the bell, and said :

"Could I offer you something?"

"By heavens, yes. A whisky and soda would save my life. I'm getting into flesh, I'm afraid. It's the islands. There's nothing but fishing and shooting, and I detest both."

Fr. Considine rang the bell. Then he stood with his back to the empty fireplace, caressing his hands behind his back, gloomy, examining his visitor furtively. His shabbiness contrasted strongly with Fr. Fogarty's elegance. The pallor of his emaciated face contrasted still more strongly with the other priest's plumpness and rosy complexion. But what contrasted most was their expressions. One looked smug and contented, genial on the surface, typical of his class, sly. The other looked tormented, uprooted from his groove by an eruption of passion.

Fr. Fogarty took out a silver cigarette case and offered a cigarette to Fr. Considine.

"I only smoke the pipe," said Fr. Considine quietly.

"I can't get used to a pipe," said Fr. Fogarty, tapping the end of his cigarette against the case. " What a pretty view you have from this window! I think that Black Cliff is the most impressive sight in Ireland. More impressive because nobody knows about it and it has the charm of solitude. It's better that way, perhaps. Give Killarney to the tourists and keep the really beautiful places for ourselves. How extraordinary that spike is, sticking out I Didn't somebody commit suicide there?"

"I heard vaguely about an Englishman that ... "

"Everything is vague. That's the curse of us. We have no interest in anything. There you are, Michael, with all these books and ... Ha! Here we are ! "

"Come in," said Fr. Considine in answer to the maid's knock.

He ordered her to bring whisky and a siphon.

"That girl is very pretty," said Fr. Fogarty, when she had gone out. "Tell me, though. What's come over Costello?"

Fr. Considine started.

"Who?" he said.

"Ramon Mor," said Fr. Fogarty. "He seems to have gone out of his mind. I never in all my life saw such a change come over a man. He turned on me just now, in his office, like a wild animal. He tried to bully me as if I were a schoolboy. He threatened to blackmail me, in fact. There must be ... "

"Hush!" said Fr. Considine.

The maid knocked, entered, put her tray on the writing desk at Fr. Considine's direction and left the room, closing the door gently. Fr. Considine's hand trembled as he took up the bottle to pour out the whisky.

"I'll have it nice and strong if you don't mind," said Fr. Fogarty. "Yes. Something serious must have happened to him. By the way, next time you come over to see me, Michael, I have a treat in store for you. Three bottles of Perrse's, no less. I got them from a friend in Dublin. I'm keeping one for the bishop. You are welcome to a glass or two. It's something extraordinary. Hello! What's happening? Am I to drink alone? You've not turned teetotaller, for goodness' sake."

"All right," said Fr. Considine nervously, as he began to squirt soda-water into Fr. Fogarty's glass. "Say when. I'll have a taste just to ... "

"Woa, woa. Enough."

"Just to keep you company. I rarely drink in the morning." He handed the glass to Fr. Fogarty. Then he took the bottle to pour out some whisky for himself. His hand trembled so much that he filled more than one-third of the tumbler. He was standing with his back to Fr. Fogarty, and in order to conceal from his visitor the amount of whisky he was taking, he fiddled with the siphon for a long time, making a gurgling sound with the tap, without squirting any of the soda. Then at last he poured out a little, took up his glass and turned round.

"I can only drink it very weak during the day," he said. "Your health."

They drank. Fr. Fogarty just took a sip. Fr. Considine almost finished his measure. Then he returned to the hearth-rug and stood with his back to the fireplace.

"What's that you were saying about Ramon Mor?" he said.

"Listen," said Fr. Fogarty. "I want to talk to you about that, now that I am here. How refreshing it is to sit at this window I Not bad stuff at all, Michael. The whole thing is this, and it's serious from my point of view. It's a matter that concerns the whole Church. You can't get people to look at it that way, though. And yet the whole system is going to be the ruin of the Church and of the clergy, of course, along with it. I can do very little, stuck out on these wretched islands. But perhaps the example of my success might have an influence if I can get enough publicity for it. Perhaps it's easier there to succeed, as the people are more cut off, and they still are influenced easily by their priests. But ... "

"Let's see," said Fr. Considine, shrugging his shoulders as if he were cold. " You are referring to your cooperative scheme?"

"As a temporary cure, yes, for a certain portion of the disease. But it's more widespread in ... in its ... the trouble this morning arose from my scheme of getting the people to deal with their buying and selling themselves. I say the man is undoubtedly ill, if not deranged. That's certain. But you see, the whole thing is this. The position of the clergy has been entirely changed since the revolution and the ... and the ... er .... disappearance of the landed gentry. A most remarkable man, Canon Farman, it was he that first ... "

"You mean the secretary to Archbishop ... "

"Yes. It was from him I first got the idea of ... "

"A pure faddist. I know. All these ideas are all right for Dublin drawing-rooms, but ... "

"Hold on a minute till I explain the . . . "

"No, no," said Fr. Considine with great heat. "I have no patience with that type of priest. It's Jesuitism. It's all liberalism under the guise of religion. Let things stay as they are. These ideas have no roots in our country. They are foreign. Let the Church hold her ground, in her own sphere, along the old, holy road. She belongs to the things of the spirit, not of the body."

"But listen. Things cannot stay as they are. They are not as they were yesterday and to-morrow they will be different from what they are to-day. Very different indeed and dangerously different unless we, the clergy, wake from our state of stupid inactivity. The fact that we must face is that the peasants are now in power."

"I don't like that word peasants," said Fr. Considine. "I prefer the word people. All this classification of humanity is part of the new craze."

"Well, it doesn't matter, anyway," said Fr. Fogarty, sipping his whisky. "Peasants or people, they suffer from the drawbacks of every new ruling class. They are at the mercy of those who wish to overthrow religion. It is up to the Church to fill the gap and act as the intellectual and social leaders of the community."

"All theory and nonsense."

"It's not nonsense. You are wrapt in these wretched books and antiquities, Michael. You are ignorant of what's happening. Or rather, you close your eyes deliberately and profess not to see it because it's unpleasant. During the last few years, I have watched it coming in all directions, this cult of irreligion, in our literature, in our amusements, in our politics. It's very subtle. Before we know where we are, unless something is done, there will be a further revolution, and this will be a real one, sweeping away the rights of property and Christianity. The more you try to keep things as they are, to repress restlessness by reactionary methods, the more dangerous the situation becomes."

"That's all moonshine."

Fr. Considine got still more excited and drained his glass. Fr. Fogarty took another sip, looked at his host slyly, and continued:

"No, Michael, it's not moonshine. It's reality. Here in Barra, you are too much under the influence of Ramon Mor and ... "

"How do you mean?"

"I don't mean exactly under his influence. I mean you are practically in his power."

Fr. Considine flushed.

"In his power?" he said angrily. "How do you mean?"

"Please! Don't get angry with me!"

He looked at Fr. Considine with surprise; but his surprise was affected. His eyes were subtle. Fr. Considine's face was working nervously; just as when in the middle of the night, the secret agents of the law swoop upon a suspected criminal and drag him from his hiding-place and place him in a dim room and sit about him questioning; with twitching face, gasping for breath, he snarls at their words, defending his secret with the fury of an animal at bay.

" I know you hold strong personal opinions on this matter," continued Fr. Fogarty suavely. "I know you are an admirer of Ramon Mor. So are we all, to a certain extent. A strong personality, a genius if you will, commands admiration. But the system is wrong, Michael. And it must be abolished. It's really extraordinary that it could be found at the present day in any country in the world, this astounding form of usury. Within a radius of twenty miles of Barra, on all sides, he has the people within his power. All the little shops in the country are his property, so that, if the people don't come directly to him, they have to go to his agents. He can charge whatever price he likes, and as the people are always in his debt, he pays what he likes for their produce, as they have to sell to him, since, as I said before, they are in his debt. It is to his advantage to keep them in a state of poverty and to encourage thriftlessness, for his system is only possible among a population degraded by poverty. It's a slavery worse than any practised under the worst feudal system, because there is no elegance. He spends nothing. I believe he doesn't even invest abroad. He just hoards. I have been told that it has become a mania with him, at times, to stuff money into all his pockets and to go about for days with large quantities of it on his person."

"You've been told lies."

"That may be. It doesn't concern me. But look at what is happening. The people are flying to America. Unless something is done, we are soon going to have no congregation. Something must be done. He can only be beaten by means of the co-operative system. Public opinion must step in and defend, in the event of his opposition to my scheme, the non-payment or even the repudiation of debts. The case is desperate. And then, in the matter of amusements... "

He clenched his fists, raised his elbows and then struck his elbows against his sides.

"We must rouse the people from their apathy," he said with great energy. "If we all work together, it's quite simple. Dances, sports, libraries, of proper books, of course, village halls; all under clerical control. You can't realise how terribly melancholy life is on the islands and it's probably as bad in the mountain districts; all over the country, in fact. I see them on Sundays, sitting on the rocks with a vacant look in their eyes, half starved, with everything vast and still, everything grey and desolate and silent, without energy or initiative, incapable even of coherent speech. It breeds moral indifference, fatalism, race suicide. Their only idea is to fly. Otherwise, if they hadn't this means of escape, the catastrophe would arrive at once. Unless something is done at once, regularly, by the Church, it is certain in any case that they will listen to the voice of despair, the doctrine of violent upheaval. The fact is Michael I have definitely decided to fight."

He wheeled round his chair and faced Fr. Considine. Fr. Considine remained perfectly still.

"This is certainly a very fine opening speech for your campaign that you've been rehearsing," he said coldly.

"Never mind about that," said Fr. Fogarty, quite unperturbed by the other's antagonism. "I'm going to break Costello's power on the islands to begin with. I went to him this morning to ask him not to stand in the way of my scheme and to help, in fact, by letting the people keep the price of their cattle and pigs, just for this year. I intended going quietly, if possible. But it can't be done. And diplomacy or kid-glove fighting is a great mistake when violence is needed. He turned on me like a wild animal. I have to fight him with his own weapons. Pride has driven him out of his senses."

"Take care that it does not drive you in the same direction," said Fr. Considine sharply.

"Pride and his wife," said Fr. Fogarty, with sudden slyness. His eyes twinkled. "What do you think, Michael? That wife of his? Eh?"

Fr. Considine started, looked vaguely at his guest and dropped his eyes.

"He threatened to blackmail me," continued Fr. Fogarty, "but that cuts both ways. I know his wife's antecedents, and I have had my eyes open here during the last two years just as well as he. He said he got curious about me when he heard of my scheme. But I have been curious about his wife."

He got to his feet and kicked his legs to arrange the creases in his trousers.

"I have to use his own weapons," he said. "You'll have to help me in this."

"I?" said Fr. Considine in a hollow voice.

"Yes," said Fr. Fogarty, flicking specks of dust off his waistcoat. "You'll have to help me. Conditions are as bad here as on the islands. You must come out and fight him, too. Otherwise people might talk."

"What do you mean?" said Fr. Considine in a whisper.

Fr. Fogarty looked him sternly in the eyes and said:

"Ramon Mor signed his death-warrant when he married Nora Saunders. She is a dangerous woman, Michael. A dangerous woman. You should have put your foot down long ago. She has changed his whole outlook on life. She has driven him out of his senses. The woman has brought a curse on the place. And I believe she'll ruin more than her husband before she stops."

"Fr. Fogarty," whispered Fr. Considine tensely, "you'll burn your fingers."

They stared at one another. Fr. Fogarty's face still looked calm and contemptuous.

"You mean?" he said haughtily.

"I mean that you'll fail," whispered Fr. Considine. "I wash my hands of your scheme. You need not come for help to me. You are an ambitious man. But I warn you that your methods are not those of a Christian priest, this ferreting about."

Again they glared at one another. Fr. Fogarty smiled subtly.

"Michael," he said. "Take care that your interest in the family does not cause a misunderstanding between the Bishop and yourself. You know there are two things he is death against as far as the clergy are concerned. They are drink and ... I suppose you know Mrs. Costello's history?"

"I don't pry."

"No?" said Fr. Fogarty, raising his eyebrows. "Well! Well! I believe one should defend oneself at all costs where the interests of the Church are concerned."

"I'll give no help to dethrone Ramon Mor in order to make you king," said Fr. Considine furiously.

"That means that you'll go on using the altar of your Church in his favour, just like a paid propagandist."

"Ha!" said Fr. Considine, becoming rigid.

Again there was murder in his eyes.

"And further," continued Fr. Fogarty contemptuously, "that you have an especial interest in the ... "

He started and paused as he heard the gate swing open. He looked sharply towards the window and saw Ramon Mor at the gate.

Fr. Considine, transfixed, did not look towards the window. He stared at Fr. Fogarty, with his head a little to one side, as if listening.

"Ha!" said Fr. Fogarty. "I think that your visitor whom I see at the gate would feel more comfortable without my presence. And ... I think I have changed my mind about lunch. I'll lunch instead with Mrs. Fitzpatrick."

As he uttered this name he looked meaningly at Fr. Considine. Fr. Considine started at mention of this name and said in a whisper:

"I see. Fr. Fogarty, you may one day feel sorry for having driven ... "

He did not finish the sentence. For Fr. Fogarty had walked out of the room hurriedly, leaving the door open after him. Fr. Considine stopped speaking and took a pace forward with his hands stretched out in a gesture that was strange; as if they wanted to strangle something. Then he dropped his hands and walked to the window.

He saw Ramon Mor and Fr. Fogarty passing one another on the drive. They did not salute. Fr. Fogarty passed with his head in the air, twirling his stick. Ramon Mor passed, with his ash-plant trailing behind his back. He looked sideways at Fr. Fogarty with his lower lip stuck out.

PART II
DISINTEGRATION

CHAPTER XI

HE went to the writing-desk, picked up the glass he had used and hid it in a corner of the room, behind a wooden stand on which there was a small statue. Then he went to the hearth-rug, folded his arms on his chest, closed his eyes and listened. He trembled when the hall door-bell rang. Then he opened his eyes, threw back his head and said aloud:

"Here he is now?"

Now his eyes were covered with a dull glaze like wet glass. They looked drugged, like those of a boxer who waits in his corner of the ring after many bloody rounds have passed and everything is becoming dim and confused, the whispered counsels of his seconds, his enemy whose thighs and belly are being rubbed, the sawdust stained with gore, the glaring arc-lights, the frantic shouting of the swaying people. From the moment that he heard the door-bell ring until the moment that he heard the voice of Ramon Mor talking to the servant in the hall, his mind ranged the orbit of its consciousness, seeking an exit from the web which evil circumstance had woven about his hapless life. His mind, grasping, with feeble grip, the last shreds of sanity, spun, like a dislodged star, round and round, unable to break its course and fly out of empty chaos, where it revolved on life's axis.

In chaos it remained, but in a chaos already becoming peopled with the changing and dread phantoms that madmen see. There was God, and yet it was not He, for his mind had lost the measurements of God's proportions and God became the Devil, on sight, through the confusion of their dual attributes. Neither was evil, that fish with shining scales and a beak of ivory, more evil than good, which was a toothless woman riding on an ass; nor was good evil, since God and the Devil, joining forces, shovelled all the good and evil in the world into one heap, which changed into grain and was devoured by a horde of birds that blotted out the sky. Nor did his own senses respond to the urge of memory and register fear against danger, joy against satisfaction, enthusiasm against passion, remorse against sin; but instead of moving inwards with their diverse messages to his brain, they shot outwards into chaos that surrounded his whirling mind, and there their fancies became bloated in the airless wastes, so that he wanted, against wise Nature's orders, to embrace danger and to lacerate himself, lest satisfaction might make honey with his sap and to look upon sin as the desirable golden woman who walked naked among the stars, beyond his reach. Until at last, Despair, a hunchback with one eye in the centre of his forehead, carrying a great flail, flogged God and the Devil and sent them shrieking out of sight, and then his mind suddenly stopped revolving, and he determined to plunge headlong towards the attainment of his one desire, heedless of the consequences. Then all his faculties, exhausted by their vain search for peace, rushed to the assistance of this resolution, without questioning its quality; just as a group of soldiers, surrounded by the enemy, despairing of their lives, pursue with enthusiasm some wild mate, who, inspired by the courage of frenzy, charges from the wrecked post, where they have been hidden, straight into the lines of the enemy. He grew cool and cunning and defiant as he saw Ramon enter the room, enormous through the blurred vision of his glazed eyes, with several heads, dizzily intermingling. His eyes cleared, and he said calmly:

"Good morning."

Ramon did not reply. He stood within the door and glanced slowly round the room. He was wearing his hat. He had his hands behind his back, clasping his stick. Then he pointed with his stick at the writing-table, looked at the priest and said in a sneering tone:

"Still at it?"

The priest looked at the whisky bottle, the siphon and the glass that still remained on the writing-table.

"Fr. Fogarty was here," he said calmly. "I know he was here," said Ramon. "I saw him. But where is your glass? Still at the same tricks? Where have you hidden your glass?"

The priest wet his lips with his tongue. He looked steadily at Ramon and remained silent.

"Hm!" said Ramon, walking over towards the window.

"Pardon me," said the priest. "You are wearing your hat."

Ramon paused, looked towards the priest and then continued to the window. He sat down in the armchair, where Fr. Fogarty had been sitting. He placed his stick between his knees, rested his hands on the knob and looked at the priest. His face was strained. From the nervous movements of his face, it was obvious that he was making a great effort to restrain himself from committing a violent act.

"Are you sober now?" he said in a low voice.

"I must remind you again that you are wearing your hat," said the priest quietly.

"What of it?"

"This is my house. I am a priest."

Ramon started slightly. He looked at the priest. This time, the expression of stupidity and ignorance that came into his face was not affected. It was real. Those words, "I am a priest," brought to his mind, in a flash, the vision of the grave being dug, with its attendant mysteries of the celestial harmony thrown into confusion with God rampant among folly and the Devil plotting evil with cynical calm, after an unknown victory over good. Then he thought of the evil that the priest had brought to pass that morning by his drunkenness and the curious accusation his wife had made against the priest, an accusation that might cause further evil. Now that accusation appeared to be definitely true. He understood why he had brought his stick, and why a few moments before he had to restrain himself from committing a violent act. But instead of justifying his anger and inciting his will to the commission of violence, this understanding made him afraid and incapable. It exposed that one weakness that all men have, even Achilles; and which, in Ramon's case, was the weakness of the non-intellectual man when confronted with the problem of universal harmony.

Superstition! Was the priest a humbug? Was he a devil instead of being a god, evil instead of good? Was he himself, groping after earthly powers, trusting a phantom while he trusted this priest to defend him against the mysteries of what was beyond earth, to comfort him against the earthman's fears of Nature's powers, against the fear of death, against those animal fears that make sheep bleat when the sky is curtained with dark mist and make even lions roar with awe in their stark forests threatening, with the sound of their mighty voices, the unexplainable.

They stared at one another in silence, the one apparently calm and powerful, the other terrified.

Then superstition, having gained an entrance, attacked Ramon's mind still more strongly. He thought of the strange and irresistible passion which made him wed and bring home with him a wife who, by her beauty and the impossibility of enjoying her, had gradually sapped his strength until this morning he had been attacked by a strange disease that almost killed him. And the mysterious things that had happened in the night, his wife's disappearance, the priest being in his hut, drunk, the meeting between the priest and his wife, the hurly-burly at the house, his wife's accusation, the appearance of the doctor, who become brave and arrogant! Were all these things themselves the had suddenly outcome of foolish chance, or were they the result of the Devil's plotting? Was he being gradually enmeshed in a "web of destruction, without his knowing it, and pushed towards that deepening grave?

It was hard to say, for his eyes saw nothing in the calm face of the priest, no more than his mind had seen in the grinning face of the imaginary Devil on the boulder. Then his will came to his rescue. He shrugged himself and assumed the same attitude of defiance that the priest had assumed a minute or two before; but with a difference. Despair had inspired the priest. The pride of life inspired Ramon, giving birth to anger.

Away with superstition! Let avarice gobble up all rival passions and lay waste with its golden fires those menacing doubts that drag men from the banquet of desire; that deep, deep drunkenness which is conquered only by the arrow of the burglar death.

"Your house!" he cried. "What impudence! It's my house. It was I built it for you. You are no priest. You are a drunken gambler. I have saved you time after time within the last ten years from becoming an unfrocked priest, a tramp begging from door to door; and you make this return. And now you insult me to my face. What impudence!"

Then the priest burst forth, goaded by the hunchback with the flail.

"You have saved mel" he cried, holding out his hands. "You ! You dare come here and tell me you have saved me?"

"Aye!" cried Ramon, breathing with great difficulty. "I have saved you."

"You have been my curse," cried the priest, striking his breast with both hands. "You have made me your tool. You have made my life a torture."

Again they stared at one another in silence. They were both trembling. They had spoken in strange tones, like voices heard in a dream. Then they began to speak with great rapidity.

"Were it not for me," said Ramon, "you'd be still a curate, shuffled from parish to parish with your trunks full of books and without a penny in your pocket."

"I was happy then," cried the priest vehemently. "It was not for my good that you used your influence with the Bishop to get me this parish."

"Ha! You were glad enough then to have my influence. Your brother came and begged me to say a word to the Bishop."

"My brother was then in your employment. He told me it was you yourself hinted to him that you'd like to have me here."

"What are you driving at? Why should I want to have you here any more than any other priest?"

"Because you knew that you could use me more easily."

"I use you?" cried Ramon furiously. "I have put thousands in your pockets. I have set your brother up in business. I have put all your relatives on their feet."

"In return for what?" whispered the priest, white at the lips.

"Yes," snarled Ramon, stretching out his hands and dropping his stick to the floor. "In return for this, that you turn against me at this hour, that you ... "

"I'll tell you," interrupted the priest wildly, "what my return was."

"You became a drunkard and a gambler. You came into my house and ... "

"You made me your tool. Just as you hurried Fr. O'Rourke to his grave by making his old age a torture by your complaints, so you destroyed my innocence by your flattery."

"You are very clever, Fr. Considine. You are trying to wriggle out of the corner you find yourself in. But I'll hold you to it now. No more fooling with me."

"I have been many years cornered by you, but now, at least, I have the courage to tell you ... "

"You'll tell me what I want to know and that quickly."

"I know what you want to know and I'll tell you that, too. But I'm first going to tell you that I owe you nothing. I tell you that, instead of having done me a favour, you have been my deadliest enemy ever since I came into this parish."

"Ha! A cur bites the hand that fed him. True for the old saying, 'To help a mean man is to make an enemy.'"

"It's also true that a priest's greatest danger are his poor relations. It was because they struggled to make me a priest and expected a return for the money they had spent that I fell into your clutches."

"My clutches ! God Almighty ! "

"I wasn't two months in the parish when you came to me and asked me to preach from the altar in your interest."

"It's a lie. I didn't."

"You did. And I consented. You were too clever for me. You flattered me first on my preaching, then on my knowledge. I remember your pretended ignorance, going around my library looking at my books and asking me what they were about and who wrote them. Afterwards I found out it was all pretence. For you have knowledge that a man can't get from books."

"None of this. Don't you try to wriggle out of it. I have no time to waste."

"You won't silence me," cried the priest with great dignity. "Hear now what I have not had the courage to tell you when I should have told you. I did your bidding. You didn't ask me directly. You were too cunning, I say. But my pride and my ignorance drove me to it, because I was seduced by your flattery. I preached from the altar in defence of your usury."

"Usury! You told the people they should pay their just debts. Isn't that your duty as a priest?"

"They were not just debts. You were evicting starving people from their homes and seizing their cattle. They would have risen against you but for me."

"Whoever rises against me," cried Ramon, "is going to go down damned quickly, then or now. I don't need your help. I never needed it."

"You needed it then. You paid me for it, too."

"I gave you some money because I pitied you. You hadn't a shirt to your back. Every penny you got out of the parish was begged off you by those hungry hawks of relatives you have. I pitied you, but pity is wasted on you."

"Once I had taken your first bribe," cried the priest, speaking in an exalted voice and looking at the wall, "I changed, as if I had contracted a leprosy of the soul."

"Great God! Listen to him. A bribe!"

"You became a hero in my eyes."

"You came with tears in your eyes to thank me."

"It seemed to me that instead of starting my ruin you had paved the way for allowing me to fulfil my ambition. That damned philosophy!"

"Curse now. It comes well from a priest's mouth!"

"I was damned from that moment," cried the priest, trembling from head to foot, "for after three months on my book, I had a few hours when the grace of God made a last effort to save me and cleared the demon from my mind, and I read what I had done and burned it in terror. It was the sin against the Holy Ghost. Then I began to drink."

"Ha! I didn't know that. You hid it well."

"Then you had me," he whispered tensely, turning towards Ramon. "Instead of writing further I inspired you with my ideas."

Ramon drew back and started. His eyes had a terrified look in them. The priest's eyes had again grown dim, as if they were covered with a glaze.

"You talked of building this house for me," whispered the priest in a strange tone, "and of putting thousands of pounds in my pocket. But what have I put in yours? I told you all I knew. Driven on by the devilish pride I took in your avarice and in your brutal lust for power, I not only kept the people from rising against you but I showed you how to extend your power."

Ramon's lower lip dropped and his eyes began to blink."

"It was I suggested your going into politics. It was I planned your campaign for you. It was I protected you during the revolution. I even became your accomplice in murder."

"Eh?" cried Ramon, stooping for his stick.

He picked up the stick, grasped it in his right hand and began to tremble. The priest shuddered for a moment and looked at the stick. Then he took a short step backwards, leaned forward and folded his arms on his chest.

"Don't you remember," he said in a low voice, "when that ship was wrecked on the sands? You bought the wreck. It had a cargo of grain on board. You sold the rotten grain and made thousands of pounds on it. It lay there for months, while the people took away the grain. The stench of that rotten grain brought a fever to the town. Twenty people died in the fishermen's quarter. I defended you at the inquiry. I perjured myself. It was perjury. It was murder. Murder!"

"Murder!" said Ramon in a voice that was almost inaudible.

"Yes," said the priest. "It was murder."

Now his eyes glittered.

"You are beginning to see what you have done," he continued. "Your conscience is hurting you. For my soul is not the only one you have damned."

"Damned! You! Good God!"

Ramon wiped his forehead with his sleeve.

"And then," cried the priest, raising his voice, "you turned on yourself. The years had brought silver to your hair, but alas, they had not emptied the chalice of your lust. Alas, I say. There was still hope. There is always hope while the soul is free from that sin. There is always hope of repentance. The arms of the Holy Church are open wide for every other sinner. But for Sodom there is no mercy."

He was now beside himself.

"She began by robbing you of your strength. Then she ... "

"Ha!" cried Ramon. "Now I see your dodge."

His eyes hardened. He ceased to tremble. He wet his lower lip with his tongue. The priest's face lost its distracted expression. There was silence.

"All this preaching has been a trick," said Ramon at length.

He had spoken in a low voice, almost to himself. Anger was again coming to his assistance, to overcome the superstitious fears that had been almost brought to life by the priest's accusations.

"You did it," he said in a louder voice. "Now I'm certain of it. I see it in your face."

"What?" said the priest.

"I threatened to break every bone in the doctor's body for daring to say what he said to me; but now I see he spoke the truth. My curse on the lot of you. You all turned me against her. Now I see why."

"What do you see?" whispered the priest.

Ramon raised his shoulders and spat on his stick. The priest started and cried out, raising his right hand:

"One moment."

Ramon looked at him.

"Let me tell you," said the priest, "that I know everything that happened at your house this morning."

Ramon drew back. He looked aside for a moment, towards the writing-table, as if looking for something. He was trying to think what further trick the priest was planning.

"Ha! " he said. "You've been up to the house since I left."

He spoke calmly, because it suddenly occurred to him that he might after all be mistaken; that he might be adopting the wrong attitude towards the priest; that now was not the time to make an enemy of an important ally; that it might really be a trick of his wife and of the doctor to turn him against the priest. If the priest had been up to the house to explain things, perhaps he was innocent of the charge brought against him.

But the priest said sombrely:

"No, I have not been to your house."

He appeared so sure of himself that Ramon wondered still more and was still more discomfited. What was he planning? Ramon took some time to ask the next question:

"The doctor has been here already?"

"No," said the priest in the same manner.

"Then who has been here?" cried Ramon, losing control of himself. "Speak up."

The priest's eyes grew cunning, and he took a long time to answer.

Then he said slowly:

"Your sister has been here."

"My sister!" said Ramon, starting violently.

He sank back into his chair and again dropped his stick to the floor.

"What did she come here for?" he said in a listless voice.

The priest opened his mouth to speak, but said nothing. There were suddenly many voices whispering in his mind, giving him advice. Some counselled silence, saying that he must no longer hope for escape from damnation, except by carrying out his resolution, by his own hand. Others counselled speech, saying there was still hope if Ramon were driven by knowledge of her sin to send her away, or even to take her punishment in his own hands. Then Ramon looked up and the sight of his face made the priest want to have satisfaction by making that face suffer.

"She told me," he said, "why your wife left your house last night."

"And why did she leave the house?"

"To meet her lover."

Ramon's body quivered as if struck by an arrow.

"Who is he?" he muttered.

"Francis O'Neill," said the priest.

"That's good," said Ramon.

He began to breathe rapidly. His head swayed. His eyes, although they were fixed on the priest's face, seemed to be looking at something vague and distant. He appeared to be indifferent to what the priest had said, but to be suffering from a stupor, caused by a pain within himself.

"She gave me this note," continued the priest, taking the piece of crumpled paper from his pocket.

"Give it to me here," muttered Ramon.

He read the note. Then it fell from his limp fingers to the floor.

"Where did you get this?" said Ramon.

The priest told him.

"Good!" said Ramon quietly.

His head still swayed back and forth. The priest watched him fixedly.

"Good," said Ramon again.

His eyes were now fixed on the note that had fallen to the floor. He put out his foot and stamped on the note with great force.

"I have her now," he growled.

The priest started, looked at the far wall and thought:

"He mustn't do it. I must prevent him."

Then Ramon raised his head and cried in a furious voice:

"It's a lie."

"What?"

"It's a lie. You concocted that."

He turned his heel back and forth on the note. His eyes gleamed.

The priest thrust out his hands and cried:

"I swear to you ... "

"You'll swear me nothing. You can't escape me with an oath."

"You mean?"

"Sit down. You get on my nerves standing there. Sit down in front of me. Ha ! You are afraid of me, and well you may be. You have cause. But there are more important things to do."

The priest sat down at the writing-table, facing Ramon.

Now Ramon was possessed of all his strength, and his face, distorted by passion, was terrible.

"I had put my trust in you," he cried, "and all this time you hated me like the rest. It was I asked you to come and talk to her, still thinking you were a holy priest of God; although you drank and gambled I still believed a priest is a priest and holy, no matter what his sins may be. But you were a devil and not a priest. I see now. All this time you've been suggesting to me that I should send her away. Silence!"

The priest had tried to speak, to say that he wanted her sent away because he felt himself falling into the abyss.

"But all the time," continued Ramon, "it was how you. Great God!"

He put his two hands to his face and stroked his cheeks and then looked at the priest and said with horror in his voice:

"A priest I You! You went there .... you took that cottage ... you ... Great God! Is the world at an end? My wife! You! You!"

He shuddered. The priest was spellbound. He kept glancing towards Ramon's limp hands from time to time, quickly, to make sure they were not becoming rigid, ready to pounce on him.

Then Ramon, exhausted by his outburst, dropped his head on his chest. "It's a lie," he muttered. "You and Fr. Fogarty concocted it just now. It's easy for you to work on my sister. Oh! I wish I had my strength left to me to deal with the lot of you. You all hate me. That's why you tried to turn me against her. But now my eyes are opened. Look out, all of you. What I have I hold."

He raised his head and shouted:

"You schemed all this with Fr. Fogarty before I came in. What hold has he over you? You're deserting me for him. But I tell you to look out for yourself. I'm cornered now. I'm sick. But I'm telling you I'm soon going to strike out."

You're mad," cried the priest suddenly in a shrill voice. "Fr. Fogarty said you had gone mad. He's right. You have gone mad."

"Mad," cried Ramon, looking up.

The priest stood up and walked back to the mat, in front of the empty fireplace. He could not keep still, but kept shifting his feet and looking hither and thither, at Ramon, at the door, at the window, at the wall in front of him, at the empty fireplace behind him. This erratic movement of his limbs was the counterpart of the confused working of his mind, because the resolution had just vanished, leaving him a prey to uncertainty, which was a man's head, with a pale, bearded face, that kept changing, at one time the face of Christ, at another time his own face, with startling eyes. The one looked sad and reproachful; the other looked terrified. Now the consciousness of his mind became curtailed, bound by experiences that were so closely connected as to be laced like thread to a piece of cloth. Now it did not move in a circle, along the vault beyond earth, where intellect soars in order to get a sufficiently wide field for its battle with philosophy. It moved on a flat surface hither and thither, and life became extremely sweet and security became necessary at all costs. His senses became normally active and varied passions created pleasant images, which were the outcome of their future satisfaction. God and the soul became of no consequence, as compared to the necessity for winning Ramon to his side and going on living as he had been; but without the plague of lust. She must go. She must be sent away. He said with cunning:

"I have made an enemy of Fr. Fogarty, because I refused to join in the plot against you, and yet you accuse me of scheming against you. You are deliberately ruining yourself. That's what I mean. You must be mad."

"He's trying to fool me," thought Ramon, looking suspiciously at the priest.

"What plot?" he said aloud.

"If you listen quietly and not insult me like a ... "

"Be quick."

"He came here and told me about his visit to your office. Then he tried to persuade me to join him. He's going to launch a campaign against you. He is supported by certain clerical organisations in Dublin. His plan is sure to succeed unless you listen to reason. It's not yet too late."

"What has he got up his sleeve?" thought Ramon.

"And why did you refuse?" he said aloud. "After what you told me just now it wasn't for love of me. That is, if you did refuse."

The priest wet his lips and remained silent. His mind had not been prepared for this question. Again the strange images passed back and forth, now without title or personality, offering no advice. His eyes blazed and his emaciated body trembled within the sagging folds of his shabby garments. He looked pitiable, like some poor, sick fanatic in a desert, who, nearing his death, loses faith in the phantom he has pursued and threatens the empty vault of heaven with his paltry hands, cursing uninhabited chaos.

"Speak," shouted Ramon.

"Yes," cried the priest, suddenly finding an excuse. "I refused because I can't ... I can't turn back. He knows that I gamble and that I drink."

"Ha!" said Ramon suspiciously. "And doesn't everybody in the parish know that?"

"Yes," said the priest feebly. "That's why I refused. I had to borrow money in Dublin one time from Mrs. Fitzpatrick. I lost the first day at the Curragh races. We were both staying at Jury's Hotel. I went to her and borrowed twenty pounds. Then I lost that next day and I had to borrow my fare home from her. She saw me at the races the second day. Fr. Fogarty is a friend of hers. He has just gone to lunch there."

"The solicitor's wife?" said Ramon.

"Yes."

"What has that got to do with it?" said Ramon. "Are you the only priest in Ireland that gambles? Eh? The Bishop himself knows you gamble. Didn't I speak to him for you when he ... "

"And I tell you another thing," cried the priest excitedly. "He is going to use your wife as a means of ruining you."

"He's going to use my wife?" whispered Ramon. "In what way?"

"He told me he has found out something about her antecedents in Dublin. They are the words he used."

"Ah-h-h-h !"

Ramon dragged out this exclamation to a great length. Then he began to nod his head.

"I warned you," said the priest, "that it would be discovered sooner or later."

"Eh ?" said Ramon listlessly.

Staring at the floor, he thought:

"The first time in my life I made a mistake. They'll ruin me."

Delighted at the effect that his words had on Ramon, the priest went on:

"When that woman came to blackmail you last year, I warned you that it was dangerous to treat her with contempt. She has proofs that the child is your wife's. Mrs. Barker, your wife's aunt, was paying for it until your wife got married. Fr. Fogarty must have paid the woman for the information. Why he didn't strike sooner I don't know. I suppose he was waiting for the right moment."

"Fool! Fool!" said Ramon. "If I had only taken her out and drowned her the night I met her it would have been better for both of us. But I loved her. Yet there was no more softness in her heart than in a stone."

"Then why do you insist on letting her ... "

"Silence!" whispered Ramon hoarsely. "She is my wife."

The priest drew back, amazed. He thought he had won. Ramon scowled and then raised his heel off the piece of crushed paper.

"I wonder is it true?" he thought.

He got to his feet and put his hands behind his back.

"I refuse to believe it," he said. "What I have I hold."

"Poison." cried the priest, suddenly losing control of himself. ~

He made a gesture with his hands as if he were holding them over a chalice at Mass.

"It's a poison you want to drink," cried Ramon, moving as if to attack the priest.

But instead, he uttered a groan and moved back in his chair, into which he threw hin1self. He put his hands to his head, pushed off his hat and clutched his hair.

"This is terrible, terrible," he muttered. "My God! This is no time for abuse. How she has destroyed me! What a fool I have been! Yet even now ... "

He looked up, opened his mouth and stared at the priest vacantly.

"It's no use twisting and turning," he said quietly. "They have me cornered. If it's not Fr. Fogarty it's the doctor. They are all waiting. It's just chance which of them will jump on me first. And I'm sick. But ... rather than let her go I'd strangle her. Do you understand that?"

"I see," said the priest.

Ramon picked up his hat and put it on his head.

"Then you refuse my advice," said the priest.

"I don't believe it," cried Ramon savagely. "I believe nothing. It's a plot. It's a concoction. Damn them. They can't beat me."

"I'm lost," thought the priest.

"It's too late now," cried Ramon. Although he spoke aloud he appeared to be talking to himself. "They'd only laugh at me now. And anyway ... do I still love her or is it how I always hated her? Now I see she always hated me. It was my money she was after. Every word she uttered was a lie."

"Listen," said the priest.

"You turned her against me," cried Ramon, shaking his fist at the priest.

The priest was staring fixedly at the wall. His arms were folded on his chest. Beads of perspiration stood out on his pallid forehead. His black, straight hair, like a wig, was moist.

Ramon looked at the wall. Then he looked at the priest.

"What are you looking at?" he said.

Now the hunchback with the flail had again appeared in the priest's vision.

"Don't ask me what I am looking at," he cried. " The woman is cursed. She has ruined more than you. She has ruined me, too. Why should I hide it from you? What is my shame is yours, for you brought me to her feet. Your sister, too, came here to tell me that she had fallen. We are all contaminated. There is something here beyond the understanding. Something devilish. What blasphemy to think that I could help you win her love! To preach divine love to a woman capable only of ruin."

"Ha! " said Ramon. "Then you ... "

"I did," cried the priest.

"I knew it. Ha!"

The priest staggered to the writing-desk, sat down and said:

"I must go to the doctor and stop him from ... "

He stopped suddenly and covered his face with his hands. Ramon stared at him.

"This is the man," he thought, "that I trusted. Now I am alone."

He stood up and began to walk towards the door.

"Where are you going?" cried the priest.

Ramon halted and then turned back towards the window. He sat down again. He began to tap the floor with his stick.

"I have that man in my power," he said.

"Who?" said the priest.

"The doctor," said Ramon. "Let me see. You go to him and tell him that I hold him in the hollow of my hand. I'll bring a libel action against him and win it, if it costs me ten thousand pounds. I'll break him unless he keeps his mouth shut. You tell him that. I'll clear him out of this town. This is my town. I'm going to show them what I can do when I set my mind to it. I've been biding my time. Ha! that sly ferret, Fr. Fogarty! I'll show him, too. He may have the whole Church, from the Pope of Rome to the parish sexton, behind him. I don't give a damn for his Church. I've finished with that, too. You opened my eyes for me. You are only a gang of beggars and humbugs, I warn you, Fr. Considine. You leave my wife alone. Leave her alone, the lot of you."

He suddenly jumped to his feet and looked furtively at Fr. Considine. He put his hand to his cheek. A look of fear came into his eyes. Feeling a pain in his neck, he had seen the open grave, with the men digging in it. Then he shrugged himself, conquered his fear and continued, striding around the floor while he spoke :

"I'll cut the ground from under their feet. I'll get that saw-mills going. I'll put a fleet of steam-trawlers on the harbour. I'll build a big hotel over there near the golf course. I'll bring tourists to the town. I have had all these schemes in my mind for some time, but other worries kept me from working on them. Now I'm going to surprise these gentlemen. If he goes ahead with his co-operative scheme, I'll have every one of his managers bought over in a month, and if I can't buy them I'll undersell them, even if I have to give goods away for nothing. They might as well try to fight the bank at Monte Carlo as fight me. And I tell you, too, that you are going to go the same road as Fr. O'Rourke unless you watch yourself. Rather than ... what are you looking at me like that for? What are you looking at?"

He halted and gaped at Fr. Considine. Fr. Considine had arisen. He was leaning over the writing-desk, staring at Ramon, who had halted on the opposite side of the desk. He had one leg thrust forward. The thumb and four fingers of each hand touched the desk, as if he were going to spring. The hunchback with the flail had come up to him, after having flogged everything out of chaos. The hunchback was grinning and making signs with his flail, to point out that he wanted something else to flog. The priest had snatched the flail from the hunchback's hands and hidden it upon his own person. Now he was definitely going to use it unless Ramon followed his advice. He had also borrowed the hunchback's expression. His eyes were those of a madman.

Ramon had halted sideways. He had been walking in a crouching position with his legs wide apart, staggering with excess of emotion. Now he halted in that attitude, with his head turned. The expression of the priest's face gave him a shock that routed from his mind both the subconscious vision of the grave and the schemes about which he had been talking. He saw in the priest's white lips and in his dilated, gleaming eyes a hatred that was murderous. He immediately thought of his wife and saw that she was necessary for his existence. All doubt vanished.

"Do you still want to go on torturing me?" whispered the priest.

Ramon stood erect. He shuddered. He felt cold and strong like a man who has plunged into an ice-cold bath on a sultry day. Everything appeared futile and meaningless except his wife's beauty, her throat, her golden hair, her yellow eyes, the form of her body, the sound of her voice, the roundness of her breasts, the excitement of holding her in his arms, the intoxication of desiring her, the joy of having her near him. He raised his stick and menaced the priest with it. The priest drew back, saying something which Ramon did not hear. The priest's words were meaningless. Neither did he see the priest any longer. He only saw his wife in all her beauty. He grovelled before her, offering her gifts, all his wealth, the earth and heaven, as a reward for the pleasure of being near her.

It seemed that many veils were tom from his mind, and as each veil was drawn aside, he receded farther and farther from reality, as into the barbarous consciousness of an animal, which is terrified of understanding and sharpens the instincts into an acute cunning, which, laying hold of one vision with terrible power, feeds it on all its strength and looks upon manifold reality with scorn, although reality approaches on all sides with drawn daggers and in a moment the animal's blood is pouring forth.

Now he was still more sick, and his face had become mottled like a rotten apple. His enormous body was a heaving mass, struggling for breath. There was folly in his wandering eyes. But at the core of his being his energy had gathered, deserting the outposts, where it had been shouting at his enemies.

"You leave her alone," he growled. "I warn you. You dare to talk to me of lust? Leave her alone."

The priest dropped into the chair and spread out his hands over the desk.

"You still love her?" he said.

"I still love her," said Ramon. "What of it?"

"Then you are lost," said the priest.

Ramon turned away and walked slowly to the door.

"Wait !" cried the priest, again jumping to his feet.

Ramon paused for a moment at the door. The priest stretched out his hand and said :

"Where are you going?"

Ramon looked at him malignantly for a long time. Then, without speaking, he opened the door and went out.

The priest began to laugh. Then he sat down, stretched out his hands along the ·desk and began to turn them back and forth slowly. He heard Ramon close the hall-door behind him. He looked towards the window. His hands still turned back and forth slowly. He saw Ramon walking down the drive hurriedly and he heard the heavy, crunching thuds of his feet on the gravel.

"Jesus have mercy on me," he said fervently.

CHAPTER XII

THE fair was at its height. People were clapping hands in bargaining, gesticulating, rushing to and fro, arguing excitedly. The beasts were silent. They no longer moaned. They stood in groups, with their heads to the ground, hiding their eyes from the sun's hot light. Exhausted pigs lay stretched asleep in carts, their limbs and heads entwined in stupid helplessness. Flocks of mountain sheep stood with their heads together, making a circle with their rumps, in which briars and pellets of dirt were sticking among the hairy wool. Terrified by their strange environment and the presence of so many people, they stood without sound or movement, except the heaving of their sides and the confused murmur of their rapid, asthmatic breathing.

Now all these beasts, that had come cantering wildly at dawn from the green mountain glens, from the slopes where purple heather bloomed, from the rolling plains of clover grass, had all become unclean. Their sleek and sweet-smelling bodies were fouled with mud and sweat. They were silent as if they smelt the slaughter-house.

The people's eyes looked greedy.

Goaded by the flies, a group of cattle tried to stampede from the middle of the square towards High Street, up which a fresh breeze was blowing from the sea. But immediately the drivers, who had been listening open-mouthed to the bargaining, went among them with sticks, shouting, lashing, throwing their caps. For a moment the cattle bellowed excitedly and a heavy murmur of beasts passed through the square, a bleating, a grunting, a lowing; all roused by the wild dash for freedom and by the fresh, salt breeze that came blowing from the sea. There was a clashing of horns and a rushing of hoofs. Then all the brutes stood still, panting, shuddering.

A heifer's head stuck up above the press of red, perspiring bodies. She moaned, unable to withdraw her head from the glare of the sun. She closed her eyes. She slowly moved her horns and her flabby ears. She licked her slavering jaws with her coarse, pale tongue.

Two Civic guards stood outside the bank, watching. People were going in and out of the bank. Jobbers were paying the peasants for the cattle they had bought. A peasant leaned against a lamp-post counting his money. His face was furrowed and he had his tongue stuck out, counting. He was worried, fearing that he had been cheated. His wife stood beside him, watching the money. She had her shawl far out over her head and her underlip trembled and there were deep lines in her forehead.

"You should have held out longer," she whimpered. "You'd have got that extra half-crown."

"You're wrong," said the peasant. "They're falling already. Twenty-four. Twenty-five and ... "

"Hurry on now," she said. "We'll go over and pay Ramon Mor. Then we'll go home in the cart with the mongeray. Let there be no drinking."

"I'll have to stand a round first," he said, "to the men that gave me a hand with the beasts."

"Oh! Virgin Mary!" she cried. "Is it into Finnigan's you're going?"

"Hell to your soul ! " he said. "Do ye want to disgrace me?"

He moved off across the square, crookedly, because of his heavy boots and his limbs being twisted by ploughing. She followed him, complaining.

District Superintendent Hennessy came out of the police barracks, drawing on a pair of motoring gloves. Sergeant Turley followed him. On the pavement, as he was going to step into his motor-car, the superintendent said to the sergeant:

"Tell McMenamin to go round to Finnigan's and to keep an eye on O'Neill He's up to some mischief. That old pal of his has come in from Tallyfarnan in a Ford car. Keep an eye on the car too. That's a fellow from Dublin that's driving it. Mind now, if Fr. Fogarty and Mr. Fitzpatrick hold this meeting, all the men must be very careful not to get mixed up in any trouble. It's our business to keep order and to be strictly impartial. As far as we are concerned, we have to keep the peace. That's all. There have been complaints going up to Dublin that the police here are in the pay of Ramon Mor. You have to be very careful."

"Yes, sir."

The sergeant saluted. The superintendent drove off around the square towards Main Street.

A group of young girls, arm in arm, entered the square from Main Street, eating sweets from a paper bag which one held in her hand. They were singing a popular dance tune. One said to the others :

"Let's walk on down past Finnigan's and watch the jobbers going in to eat. We might pick up something good for the dance tonight."

A crowd of small boys began to run from all directions towards High Street. A bullock had gone mad with the heat and was dashing down that way towards the Fish Market, excited by the smell of the fresh breeze that was blowing from the sea. Two men were hanging on to his tail. He was dragging the men after him. Another man rushed forward and threw his overcoat over the animal's head. Then they caught him by the horns. Somebody put his fingers into the beast's nostrils.

Fr. Fogarty came out of the office of Mr. James Fitzpatrick, solicitor and commissioner for oaths. He went towards the post office, twirling his stick and slightly raising his hat to a crowd of peasants, who stood on the steps of the court-house, waiting for the arrival of the doctor, whose dispensary was in the court-house building.

"What in the name of God is keeping the doctor till this hour?" said one of them.

"I'll go round to his house," said another, "and stir him up."

"In bed he is," said another. "They say he was over at Ramon Mor's house all night. It's how Ramon Mor's wife is confined, they say."

"No," said another. "It's more likely about that stallion that's sick."

"Sure ye wouldn't bring a doctor to a stallion, ye heathen," said another.

"And why not? Isn't he a thoroughbred?"

Mr. Fitzpatrick himself came out of his office, looking very excited. He went off hurriedly towards Railway Street, looking at his watch and settling his raincoat on his right shoulder.

There was a cloud of dust in the square. The ground was spotted with dung. The motor-cars that were parked along the pavements were white with dust. Three young men, dressed in very ragged clothes, stood in a row outside the Railway Hotel, playing three banjos.

Somebody ran out of the hotel bar, threw them a coin and said in an angry voice, gesticulating:

"For God's sake, get to hell out of here. Play outside the barracks."

Still playing, the three ragged young men moved off and began to sing as they played:

"Yes, sir, that's my baby."

Mr. Lawrence Finnigan, the proprietor of the Railway Hotel, came out of the Railway Street entrance to his property, yawning and stretching his arms above his head. Hearing the three ragged banjo players sing, he also sang in a low, sleepy voice:

"Yes, sir, that's my baby."

Then he stooped, put his hands into his trousers' pockets and spat into the gutter. As soon as he was seen standing on the pavement, he was hailed from all sides by friends. Even the group of girls, who were going past, nudged one another and giggled, trying to attract his attention.

Mr. Lawrence Finnigan, proprietor of the Railway Hotel, chairman of the local branch of the Gaelic Athletic Association, member of the Barra Golf Club Committee, chairman of the local branch of the Licensed Vintners' Association, member of the Third Order of Saint Francis, and formerly handball (soft) champion of the county, was the leader of local society since the revolution.

Thus, although he was only twenty-nine years of age, the effort to maintain his position had corrupted his body to such an extent that he had the appearance of an unhealthy man of thirty-five; since a leader of Barra society must be able to drink as much as the strongest. He looked precociously sinful. He was very short and stout. He had scarcely any neck and his head was large. His face was colourless and quite flat. His thick black hair, swept straight back from his forehead, shone with oil. He was in his shirt-sleeves. His shirt was of pink silk, and the sleeves were puffed out, held by elastic bands above the elbows. He wore a coloured waistcoat with little white buttons all along the front at very short intervals. He wore a pin, shaped like a horseshoe, in a brilliant necktie. His flannel trousers were perfectly creased. His shoes, quite as small as those of a young girl, were of black, patent leather.

His hotel, facing both Railway Street and the square, was a pink building, three storeys high. The hotel entrance was in Railway Street. The bar entrance was in the square. The bar window was very large, and it was adorned with a brass rail. In the centre of the window hung a large portrait of Guinness's Brown Label, surrounded by posters announcing football matches, dances, auctions and the coming of a circus, which owned the largest rat in the world, recently caught in a Liverpool warehouse. Mr. Fitzpatrick, the solicitor, on his way to his house in Railway Street, saw Mr. Finnigan and saluted him.

"Hello, Jack," said Finnigan. "What's the news?"

Mr. Fitzpatrick was a thin little fellow with a sharp nose and a prominent Adam's apple. Always in a state of nervous excitement, owing to the impossibility of dealing, at once, with the number of ambitious schemes he had in mind, he was now more excited than usual, because Fr. Fogarty had assured him that his seat in Parliament at the next election was assured, if the campaign against Ramon Mor should prove to be a success. He caught Finnigan by the arm. Finnigan lowered his head to listen.

"We're going to start the ball rolling this afternoon," said the solicitor.

"Yes," said Finnigan. "What about?"

"We're going to hold a meeting."

"Who?"

"All of us, I hope."

"How do ye mean? All of who?"

" Now don't pretend to be stupid. You promised me your support the other day."

"Oh! I see," said Finnigan, raising his head. "I forgot that. You're going to attack the big fellow."

"Why?" said the solicitor nervously. "Aren't you going to stand in with us?"

"Well! " said Finnigan. "Ye see, Jack, it's like this. You have my moral support all right, but my position in the town is a peculiar one. I'm above politics. Il you know what I mean."

The solicitor's jaw dropped.

"I meant to ask you to act as chairman for the meeting," he said.

"Listen," said Finnigan. "You'd much better leave me in the background."

"Oh! Hang that."

"Listen. Wait till I tell ye. Yer going the wrong way about it. Listen to what I'm going to tell ye."

"What?"

"I've a piece of information for ye that's worth more than yer meeting."

The solicitor looked around him cautiously.

"Step into the bar," said Finnigan. "Farrelly is in there. He's dead drunk, and he's blowing the gaff on what happened last night up at the Big House."

The solicitor looked at Finnigan cunningly. Then he looked at his watch.

"Go ahead," said Finnigan. "I'll be in after ye."

The solicitor hurried into the hotel.

Across the street, bordering on the square, there was a jeweller's shop, which was also a garage, a motor repairs' works, a grocery store and a hardware store. The proprietor, Thomas Mooney, appeared at the door, with his spectacles raised on his forehead. In one hand he held a watch which he was repairing. In the other hand he held a magnifying glass, with which he was examining the watch. Finnigan noticed him. He beckoned to Finnigan. Finnigan went across.

"What's skinny Jack after now?" said Mooney.

"Oh! leave me alone," said Finnigan. "That old codger gives me a pain. He is going to hold a meeting this afternoon."

"Ha!" said Mooney, lowering his spectacles and glancing around the square. "I saw Fr. Fogarty coming out of his office. They're going to launch their campaign against the big fellow."

"And I say the big fellow is going to give them socks if they're going to tackle him that way. I'm no admirer of Ramon Mor, but I know this much. There isn't a man in the town is able to stand up to him. I was just telling Fitz about Farrelly. I wouldn't say a word to that gaum, but I wanted to put him off. He wanted me to act as chairman for his meeting."

"Hey, Larry!"

A motor lorry, which was passing towards Railway Street, halted. A man, wearing a bowler hat and black leggings, leaned out of the driver's seat.

"Hello, Dan," said Finnigan.

"Listen," said the man in the bowler hat. " Would ye buy a good greyhound? He's by Commandant Pierce out of ... "

"Oh I For God's sake," said Finnigan, "take him away. I wouldn't buy a greyhound this minute if he was by Master McGrath."

"But listen. This bloke has won a couple of races at Shelbourne Park."

"I'll buy yer sister, if ye like," said Finnigan.

The man drove off, laughing.

"What were ye saying about Farrelly?" said Mooney.

"Ye mean Ramon Mor's steward, don't ye?"

"Yes," said Finnigan. "The same man. He has a fool's jag on him. Ramon Mor gave him a permit to drink all he wants, him and his men. He sold the cattle right away, and then he began to drink it in bucketfuls. Now he is blathering for all he is worth."

"What about?"

"It appears he heard a yell this morning, before daylight, and he ran out of his lodge. Who did he meet coming along the shore road, there at the yellow strand, but Fr. Considine."

"Ha!"

"He went off with the priest, who by the way, so he says, was staggering, over to Jack Geraghty's cottage, and there was Ramon Mor's wife, lying in a fit."

"Ha! Ha! Ha!" said Mooney. "Then what happened?"

"They brought her along to the lodge. Then the whole house came down looking for her. Ramon Mor told him it was how she walked in her sleep."

"The doctor was up there," said Mooney.

"There's something fishy about it," said Finnigan. "But for God's sake don't say a word to anyone."

"Oh! Good God, no," said Mooney. "The tighter a man keeps his mouth shut *in* this town the better. But isn't it a scandal?"

"You're going to see trouble *in* this town," said Finnigan.

"You are," said Mooney vehemently. "It's heading that way, and it's about time. It's all a scandal. Business is no more. It's dead. Only for that petrol pump "-he tapped a red petrol pump that stood beside him-" I'd have to shut my doors. The jewellery business in this town is dead. It pays about as well as selling matches. And I remember the time when fishermen, after a week's catch, could pay as much as fifteen pounds for a wedding ring. And watches! They'd clean a shelf of watches in a week. There's nothing doing. Now I'm just a huckster. Everything from a needle to an anchor. Every shop in the town is the same. All the shops in Main Street are only dodging the black list by the skin of their teeth. Then all this business going on without let or hindrance. Fr. Considine standing up for every crime and extortion that man commits, instead of defending the poor. If what they say is true, it's no wonder he was staggering, God forgive me, for it's funny people that are wearing a priest's collar nowadays, gambling and drinking and then preaching sermons at honest people, threatening them with hell's fire and damnation."

"It's a fact," said Finnigan. "There isn't a thing that's started in the town for amusement but Fr. Considine jumps on. Dances. We tried to get a few books and papers into the Foresters' Hall, and begob he threatened to burn them if we got them. Immoral literature, he said. Yet he can go and ... "

"Oh! It's shocking," said Mooney. "And look at that woman. With her nose stuck in the air, she won't recognise a soul in the town. We're dirt under her feet. Who is she? Where is she from? The daughter of a suicide and an adulteress and God knows what else. She should be run out of the place. Wandering in the middle of the night ... Good God!"

"Still," said Finnigan cautiously, "a man doesn't know who he is talking to in this town."

Mooney looked about him furtively and whispered:

"You're right there. The town is full of spies. They all run to Ramon Mor. Oh! yes. A tight lip. I'm telling ye."

He dashed into his shop to tell his wife what Farrelly had been saying.

"Hey, Frank ! " cried Finnigan. "Where the devil is your hurry taking you? "

He hurried across the road, having seen Francis O'Neill rounding the corner of the hotel, going in the direction of Railway Street.

O'Neill halted with a start, looked around him furtively, saw Finnigan and smiled. His face was shining. He had just come from the barber's shop. His eyes were slightly bloodshot and there were two vertical furrows between his eyes. His eyes looked worried. In spite of the heat he was wearing a light raincoat. He wore it loose, unbuttoned. He had his hands in the pockets of his trousers.

"Where did ye blow off to last night?" said Finnigan. "Blast it! Ye missed a good thing."

O'Neill started again, disturbed by the question.

"Why? What's the matter?" said Finnigan. "You seem to be in trouble."

"No," said O'Neill, with a forced laugh. "It's just ... I had a long argument with my sister about ... " he drew in his breath through his teeth ... "I'm fed up. Why? What happened last night after I left?"

"The Liverpool lassie turned up," said Finnigan, "and she ... "

"What? The married one?" said O'Neill with affected interest, at the same time glancing round him furtively, with anxious eyes.

"Yes," said Finnigan. "Boys, but she was good. A corker! She had another lassie with her, a little, round, fair-haired totty. You could have had her. Timmins, the excise man, came along with her. We took them in the car as far as Tullyfarnan. Don't be talking! Where the blazes did you go off to?"

"I had to go off," said O'Neill. "I had no money."

"That be damned," said Finnigan. "Will you have an eye-opener?"

"No, not now," said O'Neill. "I'm going home to see the doctor. I'll be back, though, in a few minutes."

"No, come on in," said Finnigan, taking O'Neill by the arm. "I promise you some fun. Farrelly is in there as drunk as a lord. He may be gone by the time you get back. Come on in and listen to him."

O'Neill started.

"Who?" he said. "Dan Farrelly?"

"Yes. He has something in his bonnet. Something that happened up at the Big House last night. Wait, though, till ye hear it from himself."

"Yes," said O'Neill, "I think I will have a drink, now that I come to think of it."

They entered the hotel. There was a crowd of people in the hallway. They were cattle-dealers, nearly all fat, red-faced men, wearing brown leggings and raincoats. They came from all over the country, and they had that cheerful sanguine manner which is characteristic of all men that roam about, gambling with fortune, eating and drinking heavily, indifferent to serious ideas about life, as coarse in their manners and morality as the brutes in which they traffic and yet imbued with the romance that always attaches itself to the plunderer and the vagrant. They filled the hallway with the sound of their rich, deep voices and with the earth smell of their bodies.

One enormous man, standing on widespread legs in the middle of the hallway, blocking the passage, was eating a beef sandwich, which contained nearly half a loaf and half a pound of meat. He tore his meat like an animal. His fingers, as thick as large cigars, were black with dirt. His neck overflowed the collar of his raincoat. While he ate, he gurgled with laughter.

"Done well, Timoney?" said Finnigan to this giant.

The giant stepped aside and looked at Finnigan.

"Stand me half a gallon of porter, blast yer sowl," he said.

"You owe it to me off a bet I had with you last month."

"What about?" said Finnigan.

"Blood an' ouns!" said Timoney. "He pretends not to remember it. It was about that litter of pigs ye bought from Toomey."

"God! Yer right," said Finnigan. "Come on into the snug."

"Go ahead," said Timoney. "I'll be in later."

A deer's antlers surmounted the mirror in the hall. There was also a picture of the Barra otterhounds, led by the late Sir Michael de Burgo. Now, of course, there were no otterhounds and no De Burgos. There were pictures of hurling teams and football teams. There was a picture of The Wild Man from Borneo, that had won the Grand National. There was a picture of Finnigan himself, in shorts, being presented with a medal for handball, by a gentleman who wore thick black moustaches.

The dining-room opened off the hall to the right. It was crowded. People of all classes were there, eating ham and eggs and drinking tea. Each table was occupied. Other people stood about, waiting their turn. Tea was spilt on the tablecloths. Pats of butter had fallen on the floor; everybody seemed to be calling the waitresses, who dashed to and fro in a frenzied way. There was a musty smell.

At the end of the hall, under the stairs, people were standing around a little porthole in the rear wall of the bar. Measures of drink were pushed through the porthole. Waitresses were going upstairs with trays of drink to people who were in the billiard-room. People were standing along the stairway, drinking and arguing.

Finnigan, followed by O'Neill, entered the smoke-room, which lay to the left o£ the hall. Strange to say, in spite of the crowd everywhere else, the smoke-room contained only one solitary individual, a gentleman with a fat stomach. He was fast asleep. His bowler hat covered the upper part of his face to the tip of his nose. There was an unlighted cigarette between his lips. His right foot lay on his left knee. His hands were clasped on his stomach.

"Do you know him?" said Finnigan to O'Neill. "That's Doyle, the commercial traveller. Wait till you see me wake him up. You watch. This is comic."

He walked up on tiptoe to the sleeper, bent forward and whispered in the man's ear, in a loud voice:

"Mutton chop."

The man jumped up at once, rubbed his eyes, looked at his watch and said in a drunken voice:

"Gosh Awrnighty! Is it that time? Gimme dobba Scosh."

"Hurry up, man," said Finnigan. "Your chop is ready in the dining-room."

The man stared vacantly at Finnigan and then staggered out of the room into the hall.

"Come on into the snug," said Finnigan.

They passed through the smoke-room into a passage that led into the public bar. Between the smoke-room and the public bar there was a small room, cut off from the public bar by a wooden partition. This room was called the snug.

The tumult was loudest in the public bar. There, peasants who had sold their cattle were treating one another and drinking luck-penny with the buyers. There were also townspeople with the peasants, receiving drinks for some service they had rendered in the past or might render in the future. On fair days it is customary for peasants to treat people who have done them small services. These people were not yet drunk, but they were in that state of enthusiasm which precedes drunkenness and which is very enjoyable, when the whole world is beautiful and feats of strength, beautiful horses, great fighters, pretty women and all other things that give pleasure to the mind or body are discussed. The eyes gleam. Words flow swiftly from tongues. Energy is unbound. The bar-room floor becomes an arena, on which all the human virtues and the dreams of humanity come to life and joust in merry conflict. The women who stood by the door and made occasional raids, trying to drag away their husbands, made this merry tournament more real.

They entered the snug. Farrelly was there, sitting at a small table. He was very drunk. He sprawled over the board, with his arms stretched out and his head hanging limply. His beard was stained with the foam of beer. His eyes had become fixed and glassy. The solicitor sat near him, watching him eagerly.

When Farrelly saw Finnigan and O'Neill he leaned back in his chair and raised his right hand in salutation. His chair reeled, swayed and would have fallen backwards, had not Finnigan caught it and put it safely on its four legs.

"Safe in port again," said Farrelly. "Damn near foundered that time."

O'Neill nodded to the solicitor. The solicitor returned the nod.

"That's Frank O'Neill," said Farrelly. "Am I right or am I wrong?"

"Having a good time?" said O'Neill.

"Time," said Farrelly, glancing slowly round the room. "Time, gentlemen, time. Where is that whisky the swindler of the poor ordered for me?"

"Referring to me?" said the solicitor. "I didn't order any whisky for you."

"No," said Farrelly. "You're too mean. It's information you were looking for. You have it now, then. But watch out for yourself. Ramon Mor'll soon settle you."

"I'll be going," said the solicitor, getting to his feet.

"What's it got to do with you," cried Farrelly, "where Mrs. Costello was last night?"

"So long, Larry," said the solicitor, making for the door.

"Hold on a minute," said O'Neill, standing in the solicitor's way.

"Yes, hold him," said Farrelly. "Was the priest drunk, says he? "What's it got to do with him? What's he prying for?"

"Why were you interfering with that man?" shouted O'Neill, trembling with anger and tapping the solicitor on the shoulder.

"What in the name of God is the matter?" cried Finnigan, coming forward.

"It's nothing, nothing," said the solicitor, avoiding O'Neill and going out.

"Say, Jack," said Finnigan, running out after the solicitor.

O'Neill sat down and looked at Farrelly.

"What was he after?" he said.

"Eh?" said Farrelly, staring at O'Neill drunkenly. "The boss doesn't like you. He's going to run you out of the town. Dan, says he to me, I'll give ye five quid if ye tie a tin can to that fellow's tail. I will, says I, but not to-day. What was he after? He's too clever, that lad. Ye see, last night the missus walked in her sleep. Not my missus, but the boss's missus. The parish priest found her in a faint down at Jack Geraghty's cottage. The priest was staggering about. Terrified he was. Skinny Jack wants to make a scandal about it. Walk in her sleep, says I, with the tinker of Ballycash, who carried a spare ball like a pawnbroker for use on special occasions."

O'Neill became deadly pale.

"Then what happened?" he whispered.

"Eh?" said Farrelly. "What happened when? Will ye buy me a drink? I told that fellow I'd give him my vote at the next election if he bought me one. Now I'll give it to whoever pays me. It's information you're looking for, said Tommy Hernon to the peeler. If anybody asks you, says he to me, mind you say that he was as sober as a judge. What has it got to do with skinny Jack where a woman spends the night? Don't disfigure me, said the schoolmaster to the blacksmith. Disfigured you'll be, said the blacksmith."

He staggered to his feet, swayed and waved his arms. O'Neill rose also. He was trembling.

"There was no scandal," said Farrelly. "She's lying in bed. The doctor was up there. I went up to him and asked him how she was, as he was coming back. She's all right, says he. We'll stick to our guns, said the Cumberland's crew. I'm going now."

"Wait a minute," said O'Neill. "Wait till you have a drink with me."

"Nothing has been discovered," he thought excitedly.

He began to laugh. Farrelly looked at him cunningly.

"Ha! My little lad," he stuttered. "Is that how it is?"

"What do you mean?" said O'Neill, suddenly looking anxious once more.

"Nothing," said Farrelly. "I'm going to the office."

"My God!" thought O'Neill. "I must see the doctor at once. Did she tell? "

"Where are you going, Dan?" said Finnigan, meeting Farrelly at the door.

"To the office," said Farrelly. "Make way for the admiral."

He went out.

"What did ye fly at Jack Fitz for?" said Finnigan, looking at O'Neill in amazement.

"I don't like him," said O'Neill angrily. "He has no right to pick at a drunken man like that, looking for information. He's always looking for information."

"But good God, man," said Finnigan. "It's not worth flying into a rage about it."

He watched O'Neill's pale, trembling face and changed his tone.

"I have no time for him no more than you have," he said. "I always distrust a man that doesn't drink or go with women. Let's have a drink. You look worried. What's the matter?"

"Yes, let's have a drink," said O'Neill, nervously rapping on the mulled glass of the little porthole.

"Two double whiskies, Jimmy," said Finnigan, as the waiter raised the slide.

"I don't feel well," said O'Neill, glancing at Finnigan furtively. "I'm going to clear out of here. My sister gave me dog's abuse just now. I'm a proper fool. I should be in America by now. However, I'm going to clear out."

"Where are you going?"

The waiter placed two glasses of whisky on the sill of the porthole.

"I'm sure to get caught," thought O'Neill. "It's so obvious."

He picked up his glass and clinked it against Finnigan's.

"It's going to be a miserable town for me when you go," said Finnigan.

Finnigan took his glass of whisky in one hand and a glass of water in the other. He made a wry face, swallowed the whisky, doubled up, gasped and then swallowed the tumbler full of water.

"Ugh!" he said. "I haven't got long to live. I'll follow my father shortly. Three more years if I'm lucky. Kidneys are gone."

O'Neill took a small sip and then put down his glass.

"I mustn't drink," he thought.

"I hate this town," he said.

"Who doesn't?" said Finnigan. "I declare to God only for the old woman I'd clear out myself. The town is dead. God I It makes me sick. One day the dead spit of the other. Nothing only gossip and drink and women. I'm sick of women. I've been doing my best these last two months to start a boxing club. Nobody will give any help. Honest to God, they're so much afraid of Ramon Mor that soon they'll stop breathing, for fear he'd charge them for stealing his air. The doctor has a lot of talk about getting the people to co-operate, but when I asked him to give us a hand with the boxing club, he said we should have a library instead. How are ye going to have a library, when Fr. Considine 'd come and burn the books? Not that I want a library. That man Ramon Mor has this town sucked dry. Along with taking the people's money, he has taken their hearts as well. You're damn right to clear out of it."

Finnigan put his fingers into the pockets of his waistcoat and mused for a moment. Then he suddenly became jolly, laughed and said:

"Let's make a night of it. What d'ye say? The Glen Tavern after the fair. I'll get the boys together. Will ye come?"

O'Neill started and said:

"After the fair? Yes, of course. I say. I'll be back in a minute. I must go to see the doctor. If anybody comes looking for me here, Larry, say I'll be back in a minute."

"Hold on," said Finnigan. "You've time enough. Have another drink. Ho ! See who's coming?"

Two Government officials entered the room.

"How do you feel after last night?" said one of them, an excise officer called Timmins.

"Don't ask me," said Finnigan. "How's the body, Sweeney?"

"Not bad," said Sweeney, the clerk of the district court.

"How are you, Frank? I was just talking to your father out there."

"Hello!" said O'Neill.

"My God ! " he thought. "They all despise me. I'm ruined."

The door opened and a man put in his head. He had a grey tweed cap pulled down over his eyes. He beckoned to O'Neill.

"Be sure to come back," said Finnigan to O'Neill, as the latter was going out hurriedly after the man in the tweed cap. "I've just ordered a drink for you."

"I'll be back in a moment," said O'Neill.

"Hey! Lads," said Finnigan. "Who's that bloke in the cap?"

"I don't know," said Sweeney, the excise officer. "I think I saw him last night at Tullyfarnan. He's a stranger."

Finnigan placed drinks on the table. The door opened again and McMenamin, the policeman, came into the room. He was in civilian clothes. He was an uncouth fellow, with an ape-like face; but he had shrewd eyes.

"Good day, gentlemen," he said in a drawling voice. "It's a nice way to be spending the Government's money."

The two officials laughed.

"Say, Mac," said Finnigan. "'Where's the old fellow with the horns taking you to-day?"

"What old fellow with the horns?"

"The old fellow with the horns. Sure, there's only one."

"I don't know any old fellow with horns."

"Haven't you read your catechism?"

"It's not in police regulations. There's no old fellow with horns wanted or under observation, for all I know. Maybe you're under observation yourself, my fine bucko. Who was that fellow in the tweed cap that went into the smoke-room with Frank O'Neill?"

"That's just what I was asking Timmins," said Finnigan.

"Yes," said Timmins. "I think I saw him in Tullyfarnan."

"He has the build of that fellow that was had up in Dublin for a bank robbery last year," said McMenamin.

"So you were in Tullyfarnan last night. What were you doing there?"

"Tail," said Finnigan. "Bottle of stout, Jimmy."

"What did you make Farrelly drunk for?" said McMenamin.

"You're asking too many questions," said Finnigan.

"Go and get married. No use trying otherwise."

"I think ye men are up to some devilment," said McMenamin.

"Fine time ye have. The doctor was down at the Big House this morning. Did ye hear anything about Mrs. Costello being sick? What was

Farrelly saying?"

"Shut up," said Finnigan. "You're like an income-tax form."

Tommy Derrane, the wild man from the islands, came into the snug. He had been drinking. He laughed in an insane manner and looked around at the company.

"Friends, Romans and blackguards," he said, "you're all together here."

"Next door," said Finnigan. "There's a cheque waiting for you at the post office."

Derrane suddenly became serious and began to strike his breast. "The innocent are holy," he cried, "and the well-mannered go quietly among their kind, but the ignorant man is like a mad dog. He bites friend and foe. Wars and revolutions are no concern of the wise man, nor of the just man, nor of the innocent. Let the highway robber go his way and let the plunderer wait for the day of judgment. Christ was crucified. But the Devil is sitting under a wall down there by the shore, and he is bellowing like a bull, because his tail has gone on fire."

He paused, spat and said to Finnigan in a low voice: "I'll buy that sow from you, Mr. Finnigan, if you want to part with her."

"You're wasting your breath," said Finnigan.

O'Neill entered the room.

"Good day to you, sir," said Derrane. "You have something on your conscience."

O'Neill turned towards Derrane angrily.

"Don't disturb yourself," said Derrane, stepping aside. "You have a bad conscience, and you'll go further with it on the wrong road. But there is no use talking to you. The devil's tail is on fire. I'm off. Good day to you all. You'll be sorry later, Mr. Finnigan, for not selling me that sow. For wars and revolutions are no concern of the wise man"-he went out the door-"nor of the just man"-they heard his voice growing fainter-" and let the highway robber and the murderer"-his voice died.

With a stupid expression on his face, McMenamin looked at O'Neill, whose face looked distraught. He said in a slow, drawling voice:

"They say madmen can read a man's character better than those that are supposed to be in their senses. Who was that lad with the tweed cap?"

"Hell to your soul," said O'Neill furiously.

He picked up his glass and drained it.

"See you again, Larry," he said, rushing out of the door.

"God Almighty! " said Finnigan. "What's come over that man?"

"It's not daft he is," said McMenamin. "That's certain."

"What then?" said Finnigan.

"Wild horses wouldn't save that man's neck from the rope," said the policeman slowly.

CHAPTER XIII

IN the smoke-room, which was still empty, O'Neill pulled out of the pocket of his raincoat a revolver which he had just received from the man in the tweed cap. He broke the gun and examined the chambers. They were all loaded. He put the gun back into his pocket. He left the hotel and turned to the left, down Railway Street.

That street was very short. The railway station stretched across the far end. On the left there were only two buildings, the technical schools and the town hall. On the right there were six dwelling-houses. Beyond the houses, a road led to the right, out into the open country. The houses all belonged to Government servants stationed in the town.

The doctor's house was the third. It was similar to the others a two storeyed-building with a stucco front. There was a' little garden in front, bound by iron railings. A cement path led from the gate to the door. The house looked unkempt. There was nothing growing in the garden except rank grass and weeds.

As he was walking up the path, the door opened and he saw the doctor's wife standing in the doorway.

"What do you want?" she said angrily.

She was a short, heavily built woman of thirty-seven, with black hair, red cheeks and a powerful face that looked very masculine. She had a faint, dark moustache on her upper lip. A little bunch of strong, black hairs grew from a pimple on her right cheek. She was dressed untidily in a black skirt and a yellow jumper. She wore her hair full length. It was in disorder.

"I want to see the doctor," said O'Neill.

"Clear out," she said. "How dare you show your face here again ! " Her voice was guttural. He advanced into the hall. She retreated before him and picked up an umbrella off the hall-stand.

"I must see him," said O'Neill. "He can't insult me without an explanation."

"Get out," she cried, brandishing the umbrella.

The doctor put his head out of a doorway on the left of the hall.

"Molly," he said nervously, "put down that umbrella. What do you want now, O'Neill?"

"I want to speak to you," said O'Neill. "What did you mean this morning by calling me a cur?"

Three children, all about the same size, appeared at the end of the hall.

"I told you not to leave the kitchen," said Mrs. Fitzgerald, running towards the children.

"Come in here a minute," said the doctor to O'Neill. "I'll explain, if you want an explanation."

"Don't let him in," said Mrs. Fitzgerald, picking up two of the children. "Turn him out."

"Molly," said the doctor, "please don't interfere. This is my business. Come along, O'Neill."

"I warn you," said Molly, going into the kitchen, "not to have anything more to do with him."

"My God !" said the doctor, putting his hands to his ears.

The children began to cry in the kitchen. A door banged. O'Neill followed the doctor into the room to the left of the hall.

This was the doctor's consulting-room and study. There was a smell of iodoform there. It was in great disorder. Books, medical instruments and pictures lay everywhere, on the furniture, on shelves, on the floor. There was a little hole burnt in the carpet, near the window. The wallpaper was torn in places.

The doctor swept a pile of newspapers and magazines off a chair and asked O'Neill to sit down. He himself sat on the elbow of an armchair in which there lay several ragged dolls and teddy-bears. He was now wearing a dressing-gown and bedroom slippers. He had just shaved, and there was a small clot o£ congealed blood near his right ear.

O'Neill was tapping the floor nervously with his left foot. He had his right hand in the pocket of his raincoat, clasping the revolver.

"Well?" said the doctor.

"What did you mean by saying that?" said O'Neill.

"What did I say?" said the doctor.

"You called me a cur in the presence of ... "

The doctor stood up and began to gesticulate.

"I don't usually lose my temper," he said, "but I must confess, I simply couldn't imagine, it was a coarse expression, no doubt ... "

"Oh! Hang that," said O'Neill. "I'm not worrying about the expression. What do I care what you call me? I want to know why you said it. That's all."

"Eh?" said the doctor, sitting down on top of the ragged toys.

He had been afraid that O'Neill was going to strike him. Seeing that O'Neill was not really angry, but anxious about something remote from the insult which he had received, the doctor became arrogant.

"I simply couldn't imagine," he said, "that any man, I mean to say, that a fellow whom I had, rather than, it's simply incredible, how the insane idea could have got into your head, to go and do a thing, I mean to say, after coming to me in the first place and asking me, I mean to say, it was your own idea."

He paused and glanced at O'Neill. O'Neill's face was drawn. His hand, holding the revolver, began to shake.

The doctor started.

"Can't you answer a simple question?" said O'Neill in a low voice. "I don't know what you are talking about. Do you want to irritate me?"

"Irritate you?" said the doctor. "You are very cool about it."

"About what?"

"Did you do it for money?"

"What are you talking about?" cried O'Neill, beginning to lose control of himself.

"You pretend not to know?" said the doctor. "I had it from his own lips that you, how could he get to know otherwise, I tell you that you have ruined me. It's so sordid."

"I tell you," shouted O'Neill, "that if you don't speak plainly I'll make you speak. What are you driving at? Out with it."

The doctor's wife came into the room.

"What's this?" she cried. "I told you not to let him in. Turn him out at once. Do you want to drive me homeless along the roads, begging for bread? "

O'Neill turned to her.

"Can you tell me?" he said. "I want to know what you have against me?"

The doctor jumped to his feet and began to make gestures.

"Sit down, Jim," she said. "Don't disgrace me. Look here, Frankie O'Neill. I'll give you a bit of my mind, so I will. You're a rogue and a scoundrel and a perverted, drunken waster and a braggart and a bounder, a Judas that bites the hand that feeds you. That's what you are."

"I won't have it," said O'Neill, jumping up.

"You will then," she said, sticking her fists into his face.

"It's the truth. You egged him on to write that article and then you went behind his back and informed on him for a few shillings."

"Be accurate," said the doctor. "We know nothing of, I mean to say, the question of whether he was paid or not doesn't enter the ... "

"You're a fool, Jim," she said. "Sit down and keep your mouth shut."

The doctor sat down, O'Neill began to laugh and sat down also.

"You laugh," cried the doctor. "You find it a laughing matter?"

"Excuse me," said O'Neill, taking a packet of cigarettes from his pocket. "You're quite wrong."

"Pitch him out," said Molly.

"No, no," said O'Neill, striking a match. " You're quite wrong. I'm very sorry he knows about the article but ... It's Ramon Mor you were referring to, wasn't it?"

"This is extraordinary," said the doctor.

"I give you my word of honour," said O'Neill, "that I never spoke a word to Ramon Mor for the past ten years, and I never had any dealings with him in any way whatsoever. You may take that from me. It's immaterial to me whether you believe me or not, but it's the truth. However, that's another matter. Mrs. Fitzgerald, you'll be sorry afterwards for turning on me like this. You're in the wrong."

"Well, then," said Molly, "who told him if you didn't?"

"He must have known all the time. My partner must have told him. I bet that's why the skunk cleared out to America."

"You were birds of a feather," said Molly. "You both sold the information. It's not the first information you sold. It has been your job hasn't it, a Government spy?"

"Why do you turn against me?" cried O'Neill passionately. "It's easy to find means of insulting a fool. You are comfortable. You have a position and a roof over your head. But I have nothing. I wasted my life fighting against oppression. People have made use of me and then thrown me aside. When you betray a man's ideals it's a mean thing to sneer at him when he's broken and gone under. I know you didn't do it, Mrs. Fitzgerald, but you're one of the crowd that profited by my foolishness. I admit I was in the C.I.D. What of it? I have been led astray, but I have always fought and risked my life, no matter for whom. With no benefit to myself. What have you done?" He pointed at the doctor. "You went to jail once, but you soon turned tail and signed the Government form to get out. You never had the courage of a man. That article was anonymous. He can do nothing to you."

"You've been trying to blackmail me for the past two months with threats about that article," said the doctor, "and now you say he can do nothing."

"There's many a thing a man'll do when he's desperate," said O'Neill.

"My curse on you," said Molly.

"Molly," said the doctor, "do leave us alone. Look after the children."

"You poor fish," she said to her husband scornfully. "If you looked after your children and not paid any heed to these disturbers of the peace, you'd be better off. Let this be a warning to you."

She left the room.

"Look here," said O'Neill. "Let's get to the bottom of this. I swear that I never told him. How did he come to tell you I told him?"

"He didn't tell me you told him."

"Well! I'll be damned," said O'Neill.

"But who else could have done it?" said the doctor waving his hands. '

"Look here, Jim," said O'Neill. "For God's sake, can't you talk sense?"

The doctor got to his feet and began to walk round the room.

"Maybe I've been a bit hasty with you," he said. "But ... I was so upset."

"Forget that," said O'Neill. "A man says many things on the spur of the moment."

"He knows nothing," he said to himself, watching the doctor intently. "I must find out what the fool does know, though."

"Listen, Frank," said the doctor. "I'm in an awful fix."

He went to the door and opened it to see was his wife listening. Then he closed the door and sat down again on the elbow of the armchair. His lips were twitching.

"What is it?" said O'Neill.

Suddenly the doctor began to speak at a great rate, describing all that happened at Ramon Mor's house that morning, his conversation with Nora, her accusations against the priest and against her husband, his meeting with Ramon and then the impossibility of doing anything about Nora's request for assistance because of his wife.

"When I came back and told her," he said, "she flew into a rage. Then she went into hysterics. What am I to do?"

O'Neill had listened, scarcely breathing. He sighed with relief when the doctor had finished. Then he got to his feet.

"Leave it to me," he said eagerly. "Keep quiet. Do nothing to-day."

The doctor got to his feet and said :

"You think that would be best?"

He became cheerful at hearing this approval of his cowardice from a man whom he knew to despise him as a coward.

"Yes " said O'Neill vehemently. "You might only get her into 'worse trouble. I'll go around and...see what can be done. Then I'll come and tell you."

"This fool must be stopped or he'll mess everything up," he said to himself.

The doctor now became very courageous, as he saw the necessity for taking action disappearing.

"I'll do my duty," he said in a low voice. "I mean to say, even the children won't prevent me from doing my duty. If priests attack women ... "

Just at that moment Molly threw open the door and came into the room.

"Shut up," she cried. "My God! What have you been saying?"

"It's all right, Molly," said O'Neill. "You needn't be afraid. I'll see to this. Good-bye, Jim."

He left the room. Molly threw herself into the armchair on top of the toys. She burst into tears.

"Molly," said the doctor, in a broken voice, kneeling before her. "Molly, I say. For God's sake, don't give way. You'll break my heart."

She sobbed for a long time, while he watched her with his hands clasped. Then she got up and went out without looking at him. Still on his knees, he stretched out his arms in a gesture of despair and said aloud :

"Now, where am I? What's to be done?"

He stood up, put his hands *in* the pockets of his dressing gown and stared at the wall.

Away, away beyond the reach of the imagination flows the great, red river of the human soul, wandering without banks among the wastes of chaos, guarded by an unknown spirit who makes strange experiments as he pours a drop into each womb where seed is germinating. Sometimes he joins to an uncouth and servile body an alien soul, whose dreams are a torment to the flesh that covers it.

So was this man a product of such discord. His body was fitted to be that of a servant. His soul strove after beautiful harmonies. Born of a poor peasant family, his sensitive nature had from his infancy made him conscious of the great suffering of the people about him, and he determined to be a doctor in order to help them. He paid for his own education, being a clever boy.

Then, at the moment when he became a doctor, the revolution broke out. He was carried along by the wave of popular enthusiasm, even though he was by nature opposed to all manner of violence. The revolutionaries, seeking something definite and concrete, stopped when they had attained their object. The doctor, dreaming of something neither definite nor concrete, continued to revolt with the other idealists. He was put in jail. Immediately, his coward's body took terror and he recanted. He signed the Government form, promising to take no further part in political agitation. They released him. He took ill and went to hospital. There he met his wife, who was then a nurse. She also was of peasant ancestry, but of a different mould. She married him after having nursed him back to health. Then she conceived of him and when their child was born, she terrified him by proper ideas of caring for their child into going still further in the denial of his convictions. After considerable effort and protestation of loyalty, he secured the post of medical officer for the Barra district.

But as soon as he found himself secure, he began to repent of having forsaken his idealistic dreams. He became unhappy. His wife became unpleasing to him. He realised that he did not love her and that he kept dreaming of meeting some unknown woman, who would contain in her body and soul the ideal companion that he sought. Yet he went on cohabiting with his wife and she bore him two more children, because he lacked the courage to leave her, or to tell her that he did not love her. His work became a horror to him. He hated the people of the town. He only associated with the very poor. Then Nora came and her coming inspired him with a strange exaltation that sent him preaching to the people of the ideal world which would one day come into being, when mankind should be free from superstition and the oppression of the greedy.

Now for the second time, his courage was placed on trial. since his return that morning, he had been trying to muster up courage to defend his convictions and to defend Nora against her husband and the priest, the representatives of the two forces which, he believed, kept mankind in bondage, greed and superstition. But the courage was not forthcoming.

Now he stared at the wall, stupefied. First, he was attacked by an acute shame, which laid his soul naked before his conscience, exposing all his failings. He realised that he loved Nora, that he desired her for himself, that it was for that reason he so eagerly wanted to defend her. He saw that he hated the people of the town and considered them barbarians, because his body was too delicate to appreciate their rough and cunning zest for life. He saw that he hated Ramon Mor through jealousy of that strong man's power. He saw that his wife had saved him from penury, had brought him back to health, had given him the joy of three children whom he loved, and that it was because of these many favours which she had bestowed upon him, out of the store of her simple strength, that he despised her love. He saw his ideal society as an impossible and ridiculous phantom, as ridiculous as the heaven of the priests and of the same psychological origin, born of conceit and selfishness. He opened his mouth to the full extent of his jaws and blew out his breath through his open gullet, as if to vomit his sordidness.

Then he shuddered and became angry. His conscience leaped and turned its back, upon which he saw written self-admiration. He became haughty and pitied himself.

He went into the kitchen to his wife. She was preparing dinner. Her eyes were wet with tears, but her strong face was calm and she was working hurriedly and efficiently as if nothing had happened. Through the window, he saw the three children playing in the back garden. The maid had gone to the fair with her people. He became still more angry at seeing his wife doing her normal work efficiently at such a moment, when his soul was suffering from a crisis.

"What am I to do?" he cried petulantly. "Can you give me no help, but just go on as you always do, hysterics and ... "

She looked at him coldly and said:

"Get dressed and go over to the dispensary."

"The dispensary!" he cried. "Damn the dispensary. All you can ever think of is your own interest. God ! How you have ruined my life! You stand in my way at every step. Have you no sense of what my duty really is?"

"Clear out," she said coldly. "Let me get the dinner ready. I'm tired."

"Some day," he cried in a fury, "I'll go out and won't come back."

"I wish you would," she cried, turning on him angrily." I'm tired of it too. I wish I had let you die when I found you on your back, without a friend to look after you. You were glad enough to have me then. You were ready to swear black was white for the sake of a word of comfort. But you're a coward, and, like every coward, you are insolent when you may and servile when you must. But as I have gone this far with you, I'll have to go farther for the children's sake. Go now and put on your clothes. Attend to your business. I'll get you out of this scrape too, when I have given the children their dinner and Cissy comes back. God have pity on me. You should have been at the dispensary this last two hours and the whole parish looking for you. There is somebody else at the door now."

The door-bell had rung. The doctor started when he heard it. His manner changed at once. He became craven.

"Go out and see who it is, Molly," he said timidly.

"Go yourself," she said.

"But ... " he began, waving his hands.

"Clear out," she cried, waving a spoon with which she had been stirring a pot. "You'll drive me out of my mind."

He left the kitchen. The hall door-bell rang again. He opened the door and found himself face to face with the parish priest.

He stepped back. His heart stopped beating. The priest entered the hall. He looked dazed. He took off his hat and placed it on the hall-stand. His dark hair was moist.

"I want to have a few minutes' talk with you," he said. The doctor did not reply for some time. Then he started forward.

"This way, please," he said. "Come this way."

He opened the door of the dining-room, which lay to the right of the hall, and stepped aside to let the priest enter. He followed the priest, leaving the door open. The priest looked at the door. The doctor closed it. The priest sat down at the table, on which the remains of the doctor's breakfast still remained. The room had not been cleaned that morning. A child's little shoe lay on the mantelpiece.

"Please sit down!," said the priest. "I want you to understand that I have come to you as a friend. I hope you'll understand that. It will make matters easier for you."

The doctor tried to speak, but his mouth was so dry that he could say nothing. He sat down, and although he tried to arrange his thoughts, so as to be able to combat whatever charge the priest was going to bring against him, he could think of nothing but of the shame of admitting the priest to such a slovenly room. This, he felt, was the cause of his feeling inferior to the priest, to whom he should really feel superior as to a man who followed a disgraceful profession and whose mind was in darkness. This, alas, he felt, was the cause of the strange fear he felt of the priest, the awakening of his childish awe of the mystical powers of the priesthood. He feared the priest's hands especially. They ·were stretched out upon the table, and the priest moved them after the manner that was habitual with him. Those hands fascinated the doctor, by their whiteness, by their thinness, by the length of their fingers, by their occult movements. They were, he felt, a priest's hands. He began to feel afraid of God, in whom he did not believe.

The priest's face bore an expression of deep melancholy.

The two men resembled one another, by the asceticism of their features, by the emaciation of their bodies, by their dreamers' eyes. They were unlike in their manner. The priest looked calm and dignified. The trembling of his limbs and the furtive look in his eyes, which, in the presence of Ramon Mor and (to a lesser extent) of Fr. Fogarty, had shown him to feel at a disadvantage, had now vanished. Now, it was he himself who felt in the presence of an inferior.

It was the doctor who was excited and who trembled. The doctor struggled against the feeling of inferiority in vain. Instead ·of overcoming it, his struggle against it only intensified it, by changing it into a mysterious affection for the priest. He wanted to kiss the priest's hands; not because he loved the priest, but through the instinct of self-protection, which impels individuals to try to make themselves similar with and friendly towards those whom they fear. This did not comfort him, because he refused to submit to it and kiss the priest's hands. On the contrary it aroused in him an irresistible temptation to be impudent.

"I am told," said the priest, "that Mrs. Costello made an astounding accusation against me this morning. I have also been told that you intend taking some steps about it. Is this true? "

Although the doctor had practically made up his mind to take no steps, he could not prevent himself from saying:

"That's true."

He was not really replying to what the priest had said, but denying the suggestion that he should kiss the priest's hands and submit himself.

"What steps do you intend taking?" said the priest.

The doctor did not reply at all to this question. He drew back and opened his mouth wide, just as he had done in the other room, when he had been overcome with shame. Now his shame was that he wanted to kiss the priest's hands.

"Shouldn't you, in the first place, take some steps to find out if the accusation is true?" said the priest calmly.

"The secrecy of the confessional means nothing to you, Fr. Considine," said the doctor irrelevantly.

The priest's hand stopped moving.

"What do you mean?" he said.

"I know what you are hinting at," said the doctor.

"Even though I outwardly conform, you know very well I don't believe, that I am hostile to the Church. You are hinting at that."

The priest stared.

"I go to Mass and to Confession," said the doctor, carried away by this train of thought, which he did not understand, "because of my wife and children, not because I am afraid of people knowing my opinions. When a man lives in the midst of bigoted ignorance he is forced to do shameful things."

"Shameful things," said the priest, staring intently at the doctor and trying to understand what the man was driving at.

"Yes," said the doctor. "It is shameful."

"Ha!" said the priest. "You mean that you seized on this as an excuse to show yourself in your true colours. Sir, were it not for the secrecy of the confessional to which you referred just now. I'd ... "

"You envy me," interrupted the doctor, suddenly encouraged, because he had forgotten his desire to kiss the priest's hands. "That is the truth. You envy me my contempt for Hell."

"Fool!" said the priest. "I pity you."

"That is untrue. You envy me. Even though I have been a hypocrite through necessity and have kneeled to you in the confessional, I have told you that I ... "

"Silence I" whispered the priest in a horrified voice.

"No," said the doctor. "I refuse to be silent. I have told you each time that I ... "

"Silence!"

"That I did not believe."

They became silent, staring at one another. The priest's eyes were fixed. The doctor's eyes were unsteady.

"I told you I came to you as a friend," said the priest. "You want to make me an enemy."

The doctor cracked his fingers and said :

"I don't want your friendship. I am a free man. My mind is free. From now on, I'm not going to be a hypocrite. There is no further necessity."

"I pitied your wife and children," said the priest. "Pity is going to restrain me no longer."

"She and her kind," said the doctor, "are the types you prey upon."

"The little finger of one of them," said the priest, "is worth your whole body and soul. It's not women of her kind you respect but sinners."

"What do you mean?"

"She had her reasons for choosing you as her defender. She knew very well that she had made you her victim."

"Is that what you call friendship?"

"I'm still prepared to be your friend, for I pity you, or any man that falls into that pit. Even yet, for the sake of your wife and children ... "

"Damn it I" cried the doctor, clenching his hands. "What am I talking about? I had been in doubt, but your impudence has made up my mind for me. I assure you now, Fr. Considine, that I am going to take steps at once."

He got to his feet.

"Sit down," said the priest. "I have something to tell you first. I think you should know this before you decide to ruin yourself. Sit down."

Suspicious of the priest's tone, the doctor sat down. His determination to take immediate action had not been very strong, produced, merely, by the courage that comes from hysteria.

"Did Mrs. Costello tell you," said the priest, "where she had been before she met me this morning?"

"She told me what I believe to be the truth," said the doctor "and that is that she had been driven out of her house through fear of her husband murdering her."

"And where did she go?"

"To the Black Cliff."

"Did she tell you with whom?"

"Eh?"

"Hal She didn't tell you who she went to meet."

"What are you hinting at?"

"I have discovered who was with her."

"You have what?"

"Of course she wouldn't tell you. Fool! Dupe! You are the man that scoffs at the Church and at the clergy as ignorant, superstitious people. You consider your intelligence greater than that of men who have made the study of the human soul their life-work. Fool! The meanest, poorest, most ignorant woman from a mountain village is more intelligent than you, whose eyes are blinded by the sham wisdom of science. Bah ! I tell you she went to meet her lover."

He took from his pocket the piece of crumpled paper, which Ramon's heel had trodden on the library floor. He pushed it across the table towards the doctor.

"I'll think you'll recognise this handwriting," he said.

The doctor, dazed, spread out the paper and read its message. In a flash he remembered O'Neill's laughter.

"Now I understand," he said, "why he laughed."

"I beg your pardon," said the priest.

The priest's voice was triumphant. It aggravated the doctor.

"What of it?" he said. "The founder of your Church forgave Magdalene. If she did go, she was driven to it. That she omitted to tell me this does not prove the other things she said to be false. I still feel compelled ... "

"In that case," said the priest hurriedly, getting to his feet, "I also am compelled. I'm going to denounce you from the altar. Mr. Costello may take his own measures, but ... " i

He stopped suddenly, stared at the wall and thought:

"No. I must prevent him from interfering with my duty. It must be done at once. He must not prevent me."

He walked out of the room. The doctor sighed. As soon as the priest left the room, his anger died, leaving him empty and helpless. He heard the priest walking towards the kitchen.

"He has gone to my wife," he thought. "Oh! God! There you are. I call on God. God! Oh! God! I wish there were a God of some sort. Nora! Why did you do it?"

Suddenly he hated Nora; and as a direct consequence he wildly loved his wife. Each of his children appeared before his mind, small, round, helpless, dependent. He felt their infant arms around his neck, begging for his protection. Tears came into his eyes. He shivered with emotion. He saw how beautiful it was to be a person without the instinct towards revolt, a meek acceptor, living a dull life. He saw the folly of being opposed to Ramon Mor and the priest. Now they appeared to be both good men. Nora, he now realised, was a dangerous woman, who had sneaked into his house to wreck it, to alienate him from his wife whom he loved, to send him wandering the roads as a beggar, to die of hunger and nakedness.

How good it was to feel like this! How good it was with this new mind, to think that God, after all, might exist, if not now, at least at some future time, when pride had been sufficiently overcome. Now it was a simple matter kissing the priest's hands.

He went to the door, opened it slightly and listened. He heard his wife sobbing in the kitchen. That sound smote his heart.

"Molly," he cried, rushing towards the kitchen. "Molly." His voice was broken. He entered the kitchen with his arms stretched out, ready to embrace his wife. But he paused at the door on seeing the priest. The priest was standing at the range, with his hands behind his back. Molly was rocking herself on a chair, with her apron to her eyes.

"This is awful," said the doctor. "Forgive me, Molly. My God! What a mess I have made! Fr. Considine, can you forgive me? Come. You must let me explain. You can't wreck a family's happiness, I mean to say, the whole point is, Fr. Considine, what a figure I cut, don't act rashly on the spur of the moment, even now you can hear their innocent laughter out there, if I could only ... "

He broke off and wrung his hands. His wife raised her head and said:

"Jim, darling, I forgive you. I love you. I can't help it. But you'll break my heart."

The priest looked from one to the other of them coldly. The deep melancholy now cast a still darker cloud over his countenance.

Molly jumped to her feet.

"Tell him, Jim," she cried, "that you didn't mean what you said."

The doctor now stared at the priest.

"Sit down, Molly," he said with sudden dignity. "Let me explain, Fr. Considine, if you will be so kind, the whole thing from my point of view. I mean to say, to get at the root of the whole question, in a sense, you must consider that my convictions, that's not the word, but the word religion is so ill-used as to mean nothing but fetish worship and ... "

"Jim," said Molly, sitting down heavily, "what are you saying? Are you gone out of your mind?"

The doctor cracked his fingers.

"My God!" he said. "Yes. I suppose I'm making a fool of myself. Fr. Considine, I started to apologise. I'm determined to apologise. I insist on doing so. But there are times, if you understand what I mean, living in a barbarous state of society, I hope you understand clearly what I mean, when one has a vision above the ordinary, when the very form of the human soul, to use now the expression and symbolism which passes for reality in your Church, excuse me, I mean to say ... "

Fr. Considine suddenly stepped forward and said:

"Fool! It's impossible for you. You are damned."

"Don't go," said the doctor. "Allow me a moment. I swear to you ..."

Molly ran out of the kitchen. The doctor threw himself in front of the priest and cried out:

"You are quite right. I admit it. She has been trying to ruin me, I mean what I say."

Then he lowered his voice in a whisper and said humbly:

"Father, can't you try to understand me? Don't you see it's shame that drives me to say things like that?" The priest drew back and stared at the doctor in wonder.

The doctor continued in a humble tone:

"I believe. I confess to you that I really believe. I ask your forgiveness."

"That will do for you," said the priest, raising his hand. He looked distraught. "God have mercy on us both."

He walked out of the kitchen. The doctor dropped into a chair.

"Coward ! " he muttered. "How I despise you. Coward ! Liar! Cheat! I've done it again."

He heard his wife talking to the priest in the hall.

"I hate her," he said to himself. "I hate my children too. I hate everybody. I'm a coward. I wish I had the courage to kill myself."

He heard the priest go out. His wife came into the kitchen. She did not look at him. Wiping her eyes, with a look of sombre joy on her face, she hurried to the range, where the dinner was cooking.

"These potatoes are cooked to a jelly," she muttered.

The children out in the garden were swinging and singing as they swung:

"See-saw. See-saw."

The doctor felt an irresistible desire to nag at his wife.

"He's gone," he said. "What did he say to you?"

"Don't let's talk about it," she said quietly.

"Why not?"

"It's better to forget about it."

"Why do you always say that? Can you discuss nothing?"

"Jim, don't begin an argument now. It's bad for your nerves."

"Oh! Damn my nerves. What has really ruined my nerves is the utter stupidity of my life. Here I have humiliated myself again, to that priest. I wish I had the necessary brutality and cunning to be a hypocrite. Not a hypocrite because I am one. Yet, here I am, tied to this abominable town, destined to end my days in misery and obscurity."

"Wait till I see her," cried Molly, striking the range with a ladle. "I'll tell her, so I will. I know what's worrying you. You can go, though, if you want to go. I have two hands, and I can earn my living with them. You can go where you like and when you like."

The doctor opened his mouth, sighed and felt exhausted. He thought he was going to get ill. Ill? He went up to his wife and touched her shoulder. Immediately, the angry look left her face and her tired eyes became full of love. He put his arm around her and said:

"Molly, I want to ... "

"Yes, darling."

"I want to ... "

He wanted to tell her that he loved her, but her body. was unpleasant to his touch and he bit his lip. Again he thought of Nora with hatred.

"The great thing in life," he said, stepping away from her, "is, after all, to live without passion, observing humanity with interest, doing one's duty. And what is duty? The true expression of one's personality. That can be expressed anywhere. If he has tried to injure me, that's no reason why I should let him die without giving him assistance."

She looked at him in amazement.

"What do you mean?" she said.

"Ramon Mor. I noticed him this morning. He is very ill. I must go to him. It is my duty. In his own way. perhaps, he is more perfect than she is."

"You stay quiet," said Molly. "I feel something bad is going to happen in this town. Don't you get mixed up in it. Get dressed now, have your dinner and go over to the dispensary. These people'll go and complain if you don't go soon. I always knew that woman would bring trouble on everybody. Curse her."

CHAPTER XIV

NORA slept. The sun shone through the window of her room, upon her face and upon her golden hair. Her beautiful hair glittered in the sunlight. Now that her yellow eyes were closed in sleep, her face looked innocent and gentle. It was like that of a child, without a line or a tremor to suggest that her mind still struggled with thoughts that sleep could not still. She looked content, beaming with happiness. Her body was appeased by love. Her mind, which was simply the servant of her beauty, was also at peace. For her, consumed by the terrible pride of a woman, to whom her beauty is her only God, life was a glorious tragedy, in which she acted as the heroine, always dogged by men who struggled for her caresses, men driven to despair, men exalted, men damned; while in the background, playing humble parts, stood the women whom she had conquered, women enraged with jealousy, women scorned. *So* she slept peacefully, contentedly, while all these men and women, whom she had burned in the fire of her beauty, were rushing towards their destruction, as if possessed by furies.

Suddenly, her face became disturbed. She smiled faintly. Her mouth became cruel. She heard a slight sound in her sleep. The sound was pleasant, without form or association with anything material, an idea which entered her mind, became a thought, which multiplied and then, with great splendour, formed a picture of herself, triumphant, dressed in glorious golden garments, standing above prostrate enemies, with a crown upon her head and an inconsequent lover by her side. The lover knelt on one knee and he had his right hand upon his heart and he said: "I have revenged you." Then she heard another sound and the picture vanished.

She wrinkled her forehead and opened her eyes slightly, without moving her body. Ramon's mother was in the room. She stood with her back to the door, sniffing, with her hands folded on her bosom. Nora raised her head.

The old woman, without speaking, came across the floor towards the bed. Her little mouth, like the head of a knotted sack, kept twitching. She stood beside the bed, staring at Nora malignantly. Her head was hooded in a little black shawl, through which her greedy eyes peeped angrily.

"You're still lying there," she said in a low voice.

Nora dropped her head to the pillow.

"I thought I'd have a word with you;' said the old woman, "now that the house is empty."

Nora smelt the rank odour of the old woman's body and became afraid, thinking of her own smooth, white body that lay hidden under the bed-clothes.

"Do you hear me?" continued the old woman. "I have a few words to say to you. Now is the time to say them. There is no one in the house."

Nora began to tremble with fear, but she stared at the old woman defiantly.

"It's not for your good I'm telling you," said the old . woman. "You have brought trouble into the house and you must go before you bring more. I'm telling you that. I won't let you carry on with your game until blood 'll be spilt. It's well I know your game. Be gone before they come. Now is your chance. There's no one to watch you. Steal out!"

"No," thought Nora. "I mustn't let her make me afraid. I mustn't let that hag defeat me."

"What are you muttering to yourself?" said the old woman. "I tell you to get out before he comes back and catches you here. He's gone for the priest."

"The priest!" cried Nora, sitting up in bed suddenly.

Now she was really terrified. The old woman's eyes gleamed.

"Ha!" she said, "I have you now."

"What do you mean?"

"He'll soon find out what devilment you were up to. I knew you were shamming. I knew it."

"I hate you," said Nora.

"Tit for tat, then," said the old woman. "It's only natural for the criminal to hate the law. I knew the very first minute I clapped eyes on you what sort you were, so I did. But you came into the wrong house to steal a fortune. It's his money you were after. But thank God. I prevented him from making too much of a fool of himself. You'd have wheedled every penny out of him only for me. Well I know it. You were sweet enough when you came here, but. when you saw that it was no use trying your little tricks, you showed yourself to be the snake you are. I have saved him so far from being robbed by you and now I have you. You'll clear out of here and never show your head in this house again. Otherwise you needn't look for help from me, if he was to tear the eyes out of your head and wring your neck."

"I hate you," cried Nora, beating the bed-clothes, like a hare, which, grappled by the belly, pats the air with its helpless paws. "You brutes! Peasants! Pigs! Witch! You have horns!"

The old woman was unmoved by this hysterical outburst.

"Yes," she continued imperturbably. "Put on your clothes and go. Thank your stars for getting the chance of getting away alive. There is a law in the land. Women have been hung for less. You tried your best to kill him. I know your game. But I'm giving you this chance, for I don't want blood spilt in the house. Be gone before he comes. And take care you don't come back. If you do ... "

Suddenly, the old woman shook with passion, stretched out her shaking, withered hands and whispered:

"If you come back here again, I'll choke you.I'll tear your eyes out! "

Nora gasped. Suddenly she became possessed by an uncontrollable terror that laid waste all her schemes, drowned her vanity and made life a real tragedy, in which she was no longer a sad and triumphant queen of beauty. Instead, she felt weak and helpless, powerless, defeated, ragged, spat upon, stoned.

"Yes," she screamed. "I'll go. Leave me alone. I'll go."

The old woman drew back. Nora decided that she would run at once to the doctor and hide in his house, She would make him bring O'Neill. Why did she not run away at once with O'Neill? Now she loved O'Neill with her whole soul, although she had not thought of him once since she left him; at least not as a lover, but merely as the instrument of her triumph.

"Don't make a noise," said the old woman. "Go quietly."

"Go away," gasped Nora. "Get out of my room."

"I'm going," said the old woman, moving towards the door. "Take care now to be gone before they come. He's gone for the priest."

The old woman left the room. Nora immediately jumped out of bed, muttering:

"Francis, Francis, where are you? Oh I God I What am I to do? Yes, I'll run to the doctor. Why didn't he come back? What's happening?"

She staggered when she reached the floor. A feeling of remorse took hold of her. She sank to her knees and began to pray; but she could not think of God. She kept seeing the mouth of the old woman, like a knotted bag. Instead of praying to God, she prayed to the doctor, asking him to get O'Neill for her. She got to her feet and began to dress herself. She fumbled with her clothes, unable to hold them properly. She took a long time trying to pull on her stockings. When she had them on she saw that they were torn. That reminded her of her meeting with the priest. She threw herself face downwards into the armchair and began to sob, remembering the priest's breath as he bent over her and the curious way he uttered her name. Then she got up, rigid and self-possessed, having overcome her hysteria. She went to the wardrobe and put on a grey tweed suit. She even washed her face, powdered herself, cleansed her teeth, tidied her hair and brushed her clothes, then she searched the room, collecting all the more valuable of her trinkets and stuffing them into her handbag. She was putting the small silver box from which Mary had taken the letter, into her bag, when she opened it to examine its contents. She had remembered that she had put O'Neill's note into it. It was gone. She dropped her hands to her sides, gasped and muttered:

"They know. Now what's going to happen? I'm lost. Quick! Quick ! I must go to the doctor. Oh ! God ! If he knows that he'll turn against me. No, No. I must find O'Neill. But they may have caught him already. No. They couldn't arrest for that. Oh! Lord ! What am I to do? What am I to do?"

She leaned against the mantelpiece and began to wave her hands. There was a slight knock at the door. She gasped and thought:

"Here he is. He'll kill me."

The door opened and Mary entered the room. Nora sighed.

"What do you want now?" she said haughtily, so relieved at the realisation that it was not her husband that she became quite calm.

Mary came forward slowly, carrying her hat in her hands, twirling it round and round, like an awkward boy holding his cap. Suddenly she threw herself on her knees and looked up pathetically at Nora.

"You can kill me if you like," she said. "I'd be happier if you would.

I'd be better off dead. You have damned my soul."

"What do you want now?" repeated Nora, still more haughtily.

"It was your own fault," said Mary.

Then she said slyly:

"I took a letter out of your little box and I went to the priest with it. I told him about you and O'Neill."

Nora's eyes narrowed. She clenched her fists.

"You can kill me if you like," continued Mary, changing to a pathetic tone. "I hate you now anyway. I don't care if you beat me to death. You should have thought of that before you turned on me this morning. I told you I'd stand by you if you were kind to me."

"So it was you did it."

Mary got to her feet.

"Don't come near me," said Nora, holding her handbag before her face.

Mary began to sob. "Don't go," she said. "I don't know what made me do it. It was your own fault."

"Get out of my way," whispered Nora.

Mary ran to the door and put her back to it.

"I won't let you go," she said. "You can't go now after damning my soul."

"I'll kill you," said Nora, "if you don't leave my way."

She looked around the room, looking for a weapon.

"I must get out of here," she thought. "He might have told her to keep me here until he comes."

"God!" cried Mary. "What have I done? I didn't mean to do it. What made me do it? You hate me now. That's terrible. I ruined myself. She's going to kill me."

Nora picked up a shoe horn.

"I was jealous of you," said Mary, opening the door.

"You can't go. I'll tell mother on you."

As Nora came forward with the shoe horn, Mary slipped out. Nora dropped the shoe horn. She heard Mary running along the corridor towards the back stairs, calling to her mother.

"I'll go out the front door," thought Nora, "and then around by the side gate. But is it too late?"

She. hurried out of the room. Going down the stairs, she heard the purring of a motor-car coming up the drive. She rushed into the drawing-room.

"I'm too late," she muttered. "He has caught me."

Then she thought that if she went on down and got out the door, O'Rourke might help her. So she left the drawing-room and dashed down into the hall. She opened the hall door and then stood still. The car had just halted at the base of the steps and Ramon was getting out of it.

"Wait there," he said to O'Rourke. "I'll be back in a few minutes."

He had not seen her. She thought of hiding behind the door, of letting him go past her into the hall and then of dashing out. She would jump into the car and tell O'Rourke to drive away at full speed. But she could not move, the sight of Ramon hypnotised her.

He came up the steps with his eyes on the ground until he reached the doorway. Then he saw her feet. He stood still. She saw him shudder.

"Where are you going?" he said in a low voice, without raising his head.

She could not answer him. But she was trying to make signs with her eyes to O'Rourke, who was looking towards her.

"I want to speak to you," he said softly. "Come into the house a minute. I have something to say to you."

Now she was certain that he was going to kill her. But she had lost all power of doing anything counter to his will. She followed him when he walked along the hall towards the stairs. She even tried to measure her steps by his long, heavy steps, so powerful was the control be held over her.

He walked like a helpless old man, slowly, uncertainly, stooping. He did not look at her once and he mounted the stairs in silence. He entered the drawing-room on the first floor.

"Shut the door," he said, as she followed him into the room. She did so. He sat down on a small chair in the middle of the room. He told her to bring a chair near him and to sit down. She obeyed. His voice was listless.

"Bring your chair nearer," he said, "I'm tired talking."

She brought her chair nearer.

"Nearer yet," he said.

She moved the chair closer. Now she could hear him breathe. The colour left her cheeks. He was staring in front of him. She thought the dazed look in his blurred eyes was a look of murder. She lost all hope.

"Nora," he said, still in the same listless voice, "they have been trying to turn me against you."

"Ha!" she thought. "What is he planning now?"

"But I wouldn't listen to them," he continued. "It's a plot they concocted. They showed me a letter. But I wouldn't believe them."

"How cunning he is," she thought. "His strength is gone, that's why. He has got somebody else to do it for him." '

"We have been making a mess of things," he continued. "But I'm going to put an end to that. We won't make a mess of things any longer. We were both in the wrong. Do you hear?"

He looked sideways at her feet and shuddered.

"Why don't you speak to me?" he continued. "Do you hate me that much?"

He looked at her face for the first time. She was so amazed by the look of despair that she saw in his eyes that she began to doubt. Was he in earnest? Was what he was saying true? Could she trust him? Had she been making a fool of herself by going against this wonderful man who thrilled her by the very hatred he inspired in her? Was it hatred that he inspired in her? While he looked into her eyes, his power conquered her completely.

"I don't hate you," she said, "but ... "

"But what?"

"I'm afraid."

His eyes grew tender; but an expression of tenderness seemed so alien to him that it resembled idiocy rather than tenderness. And as if he were ashamed of this dangerous and strange emotion of tenderness, he looked aside.

"Don't be afraid," he said. "Everything is going to be different now. You needn't be afraid. I'm going to change everything."

Suddenly his eyes became sharp and cat-like. She saw them thus and started:

"How cunning he is!" she thought. "I was almost deceived."

"I'm going to show this scum," he said with violence, "that they can't trick with me. I'm not beaten so easily. I assure them that they're going to find themselves mistaken. I'm going to strike. I've been waiting for this."

He began to mutter to himself. She glanced towards the door; it seemed a long way off. He noticed the movement of her eyes, although he had been looking away from her. He stretched out the hand that was nearest to her, fumbled for her body and touched her knee. Then his hand moved up along her thigh. She watched its movement, spell-bound. At last he reached her left hand and covered it with his own.

"Your hand is as cold as ice," he muttered in a thick voice. "Why is your hand so cold? It's a hot day, it shouldn't be cold. But it's like ice.

Listen to me. You never understood me, nor I you. I have gone the wrong way about things. It's because of the way I was brought up, struggling all the way, never any time to teach myself anything that's necessary for a man to know when he goes abroad into the world. I mean, apart from work. I put my trust in the wrong people. That's the fault, too, of the way I was brought up. I never had time to study, so he got around me that way. I mean Fr. Considine. How badly that man tricked me. I believed in him all along, no matter what he did. It's all his fault. I've been listening to that man's tricky notions for the past ten years thinking it was the word of God was coming from his lips, and all the time his mind was a cesspool. He very nearly ruined me. It was he who tried to turn me against you. It was he did it. I see that now. Now, though, I mean to do right by you. There was always something. I have nobody to help me. I must do everything myself. I always had to do everything myself. I never had any time for play. In things like this I'm no good. I never had time to study the ways of women. Still ... the intention was there, although I may be a hard man to understand. The way it is with me, if a person is overhand with me, I'm overhand, but if a person is underhand, then I'm underhand. Now everything is going to be different."

His hand was limp. Their hands slipped apart. He loosened his collar. He was perspiring. He several times opened his mouth to continue speaking, but he said nothing.

"It's very hot," he said at length.

Then he closed his eyes. They remained silent for a terribly long time. At least it seemed to her to be a terribly long time. She now hated him, almost contemptuously. That was because of the limpness of his hand. His strength was gone. Although his eyes were still terrible, his flesh was limp and disgusting. He was a shapeless mass without force. It even seemed easy to catch him by the throat and strangle him. She now thought of how O'Neill had crushed her in his arms and how his body felt as hard as iron when he lay upon her. Her eyes became blurred at this thought. As the thought faded away, her eyes cleared and she saw how big Ramon was, in spite of his limpness. Her fear of him returned.

She did not believe a word of what he had said.

At last he raised his head, sighed, and said in a weary voice:

"I want to explain what I have in my mind, but somehow I can't do it. I want you to understand, though, what I want to do. I have just left Fr. Considine. I'm done with him now, you can be sure of that. I want to drive all that out of my mind. I have big schemes. It's too tiresome, going on like this. It must come to an end. It would kill me. It must stop."

Now. he was breathing very loudly.

"I never meant to leave my will like that," he said. "I'll change it now. I want you to ... see if you could... even now ... give me your hand."

Again he fumbled for her body and took her hand without looking at her. Her hand lay lifelessly in his.

Again their hands slipped apart.

"Your hand is as cold as ice," he muttered. "You still hate me."

"I don't hate you," she cried out in a loud voice, carried away by her fear. "I don't hate you. I never hated you." They looked one another in the eyes. Her bosom heaved. Her cheeks were deep red. She felt a sensation that was very similar to the sensation of amorous desire, but that passed very quickly, when she saw his eyes also gleam with amorous passion. She instinctively guarded herself against falling a victim to the power of his eyes and submitting herself, bodily, to him at last. He had never been as cunning as this, she thought. She muttered to herself fiercely:

"I do hate him. I always hated him. He can't defeat me."

He looked away. Now his eyes had a look of cunning and of triumph.

"Ha ! " he said. "Now I'll show them what they are up against."

There was a long silence. Then he startled her by saying, sternly:

"Pride, nothing else. I have never turned aside. They can't do it. Come with me."

He got to his feet.

"Come," he said sternly. "There's no time to lose. I must be on the spot. Fr. Fogarty is plotting. I'll march straight into them. They think they have turned me against you, but I'll show them. Little they know what tricks I have up my sleeve."

She followed him out of the room.

"Come on," he kept saying to her. "There's no time to lose."

They went down the stairs. Now he walked quickly, but still unsteadily. She walked after him, in a stupor, completely in his power again as soon as he moved. They were going across the hall towards the door when the old woman came running towards them from the kitchen. O'Rourke started the car.

"Where are you going, Ramon?" said the old woman. Ramon halted and turned round. Nora stepped aside.

"Turn off that engine," shouted Ramon to O'Rourke.

"Time enough to begin to waste petrol when I'm in the car. You go on into the car, Nora. Mother, those ruffians are beginning their dirty work."

"Who?" said the old woman, glancing with hatred at Nora, who was going out.

"They're all at it," he said. "Fr. Fogarty and the whole lot of them. Even Fr. Considine has gone over to them. They're going to start a co-operative society against me. They're ... "

"Ramon," interrupted the old woman in a low, tense voice, "where are you going with her?"

She pointed dramatically at Nora, who was going down the steps. The engine stopped. Ramon glanced at Nora and then at his mother.

"Eh?" he said. "Amn't I after telling ye that they ....What's on your mind? What are you saying about her?"

"Let her off," said the old woman. "Don't get yourself into trouble. Don't interfere with her; let her go quietly."

"What are you hinting at?" he said solemnly. "Eh? Where do you think I'm going?"

They looked at one another and each became amazed at the other's expression. They read one another's minds quickly, with the intuition of mother and son.

"Great God!" he said. "You thought I ... "

"Son," she said, bursting into tears, "you're going straight to your doom."

"Little you know me," he cried, raising his clenched fist. "I wouldn't let a flea out of my grasp. I tell you I see farther than you and that I have a trick up my sleeve that at they never suspected."

"No, no, no," she wailed. "You're gone out of your mind. She'll be the death of you."

She caught his coat and whispered in a broken voice:

"Ramon, you're all I have. It's been a long life of struggle ... all the time ... trying ... just for you ... the apple of my eye ... and now ... "

"Let go of me," he said hoarsely .

She drew back. He looked at her, shuddered and then turned slowly towards the car, where he saw Nora sitting, with the sunlight full upon her face, radiantly beautiful. He shuddered again, turned to his mother and said, almost savagely:

"I'd bring my ship into port if the Devil were sitting on the bowsprit."

"Mother of God!" said the old woman in an awed tone.

"Your eyes have the banshee's look in them."

He started. She pointed towards the car.

"Look! Look!" she said. "Look at the witch. Look at her. She has you by the throat. Tell him to drive her away. Hide from her."

"I'd rather roast in Hell," he cried suddenly, rushing along the hall.

The old woman stretched out her two hands. He closed the door after him. The old woman threw herself on her knees and began to curse. The car drove off. Nora looked at the house and felt deliciously happy, certain now that she would never set foot in it again. Then the car swayed, rounding a corner. Ramon's great body hurtled against her and her fear returned. She was tempted to stoop forward, seize the wheel from O'Rourke's hands and run the car headlong against a tree, so as to put an end to her torture. Then Ramon turned towards her and whispered:

"I'm going to make another will. Don't be afraid. There's no need, though, to make a will. Things are going to be different from now on. I'll go back into politics. I have other schemes. There are things you can do. You must get to work. You must help me. We'll cut the ground from under their feet."

Now she did not understand what he was saying, but she felt sure that he was very cunning; and that the old woman had given him some sinister advice.

"You'll need clothes," he said. "You'll need to go away a bit. I have wanted these years to go and have a look at Paris and Monte Carlo."

O'Rourke glanced back rapidly, saw Ramon's face and opened his eyes in wonder. He stepped on the accelerator.

"We might make a pilgrimage to Lourdes," continued Ramon. "The Bishop would like that. He's a man to have on my side. He's more intelligent than these paltry little parish rascals. Anyway, he knows the meaning of money. Then Fr. Fogarty can go and whistle for himself. Maybe I'll buy a few race-horses and get up a race meeting for the town. There's nothing like a bit of sport for getting the people on your side. Who knows? I'll cut the ground from under their feet. They may be sure of that."

She looked at him sideways and saw that his eyes were very cunning. He seemed to be dreaming. Yet in spite of his cunning look, his words were foolish, like those of a boasting boy. She wondered where he was taking her and what he intended doing with her. His body heaved with every breath and he kept shaking his head spasmodically.

His flabby neck and the fringe of hair that stuck up at the back of his head inspired her with an especial loathing.

He became silent, but his lips still moved. Then, when the car approached the main gate, he raised his head and said to O'Rourke in a haughty tone:

"Drive slowly down the Main Street."

"Yes, sir."

The car entered the town and turned to the left. Now everything was quiet in this street. There were only the loafers, who still leaned against the same walls, against which they had been leaning all morning. But these loungers, who had seen the cattle and the peasants and the first appearance of Ramon that morning with apathy, now became interested. They were excited either by Ramon's expression or by Nora's marvellous beauty. Afterwards they all said that they felt something strange was going to happen. ·

Now Ramon saluted all these ragged people with the air of a king. He became very animated. Nora, on the other hand, crouched back in her seat, terrified by everything she saw, by the eyes of the loungers, by the dirty street by the glare of the sun, by the smell that the beasts had left behind them.

The car went slowly down Main Street through the throng, halting many times, as Ramon recognised a friend. Ramon became still more animated, shouting, laughing, clapping people on the back. And yet, the people stared in the same strange way that the loafers had stared, either awed by Nora's beauty, or by the strange conduct of Ramon whom no man had ever seen acting in this manner. These people also said afterwards, that they knew something strange was going to happen.

The car entered the square. Ramon ordered O'Rourke to stop in front of the bank. He got out of the car and then bent ostentatiously over his wife and pretended to whisper something very intimate into her ear, touching her on the shoulder as he spoke. But what he said was:

"These people don't know all the tricks I have up my sleeve."

Then he walked majestically up to the bank, nodding in a friendly manner to the two Civic Guards, who stood there, watching. They saluted him.

"Now is my chance," said Nora to herself.

She looked around her to see whether she could get a clear passage to run from the car to the doctor's house; but everywhere she looked she saw eyes staring in wonder at her. The eyes really paid homage to her beauty. But she saw hatred in every one of them. She sat still. Then her heart began to beat violently. She saw O'Neill. He was walking across Railway Street towards the Railway Hotel. She was on the point of shouting out to him, but she restrained herself. He halted outside the door of the hotel, put his hand to his head, looked around him and then entered the hotel hurriedly. She sighed deeply and closed her eyes.

Ramon came out of the bank and entered the car.

"Drive to the office," he said to O'Rourke.

Ramon talked to her in a loud voice as the car went slowly across the square. He touched her on the shoulder intimately and bent over her. She did not hear a word of what he said. There was a singing sound in her head. Now she was aware of only one desire: flight.

Once his face became morose; he stopped speaking and glared savagely at the people. His right cheek throbbed, as if little bubbles were bursting beneath the skin. Then again he laughed and began to talk.

In the Fish Market, people were packed so close together that a falling pin would not find room to reach the ground. Although nobody saluted him he raised his hat and held it for a Long time above his head.

"Drive in through the archway," he said to O'Rourke.

The car went through the archway into the courtyard of the shop. Here there were scores of carts, being loaded with flour, meal, groceries, farming tools, kitchen ware, furniture, hides, oil, wool, lime, dried fish, bacon, oats, salt, boots, clothes, blankets, ropes, roofing material, timber, cement, glass. The counters of the shop were open to the yard. The great shutters were drawn aside as in a busy port, where ships load and unload their bellies by a wharf, on which great sheds rise towering over the sea. There was a stench. The cobbled yard was foul. Horses neighed. People shouted. There was a cloud of dust.

"We'll go through the shop," he said to her proudly, when the car halted. "You never saw it on a fair day."

She looked at him and saw that his eyes were now brilliant. He kept licking his lips.

"I feel ill," she said. "I have a headache. I want to go to the chemist to get some aspirin tablets."

"Yes, yes," he said, waving his hand, as if he only vaguely understood what she was saying. "You want to visit the chemist. Look at it. There is business for you. They think they can rob me of this. The fools ! "

Then he turned towards her suddenly, his forehead furrowed, suspicion in his eyes.

"You go home," he said, "and wait for me there. O'Rourke'll drive you home. Wait for me there. I'll deal with these people. I'll explain everything to you this evening. Everything. Now I have no time. A man has to keep his shoulder to the wheel. Look at it. This'll be all yours."

He made a gesture and again glanced around the yard, with brilliant eyes, sniffing at the many smells, which to him were sweeter than the sweetest perfume.

He got out of the car, getting more and more excited, licking his lips.

Now avarice, that seething opiate, shut out the grave and the grinning devil, and the fellows with pointed ears who prowled in ambush with schemes for his overthrow. It shut out, too, her golden beauty, the anguish of her empty womb and of his supine limbs embracing her cold, unresisting loins. It brought bubbling through his veins wild ecstasies, the ravishing contemplation of money in mounds ascending.

"Go now," he said to her vaguely. "Go home. Wait for me there. I'm busy now."

Gold! He strode away across the yard. The golden sun was shining on the dust that rose, turning it to gold, turning the house to gold.

He wandered through the shop, from counter to counter, from floor to floor, examining everything, giving orders, talking to customers, reprimanding his assistants, directing, encouraging, measuring, weighing, counting with apparent calm and sanity. Yet everything he saw turned to gold before his eyes. The smells were perfumes. The walls were of mahogany. The floors were o£ marble. His veins were bursting with golden blood. His muscles were of gold. His intelligence was that of a god, omniscient.

He left the shop and went out into the Fish Market. Here also, everything had turned into gold. The sun shone on the rocks by the sea's edge, on the sea, on the wrecked ship, on the spike of stone protruding from the Black Cliff, on the masts of the fishing boats, standing like needles on end, upon the drunken men who were singing, upon the man who sat on a box at the pierhead playing an accordion, upon the couples who were dancing on the cemented platform where fish were cleaned, upon the groups of beasts that were being driven away, upon the rowing boats that were putting to sea towards the islands, upon the sheep that had fallen into the sea from a boat and was now snorting, trying to swim, with its wet wool afloat about it like a mat. Everything had turned into gold and had no other meaning for him than that the whole world had been turned into gold at his bidding.

People were murmuring excitedly outside the door of his office. Some were cursing and threatening the window of the office with their fists. Tommy Derrane had taken off his coat and was threatening to fight Peadar Mor, who was remonstrating with the people. All these things had no meaning except that even the very words became gold as soon as they reached the air.

When they saw him the people became silent. He walked through them, paying no heed, just raising his hat, like a king. He understood that their silence was caused by their wonder at seeing his clothes turned into gold. The hall was crowded with people and he had to push his way through them. Feeling their bodies against his, he understood that the world was becoming so full of gold that he ran a danger of being overwhelmed by it.

The oily-haired clerk asked him would he have his dinner in his office or upstairs in the manager's dining room. Ramon nodded his head. He entered his office, sat down and was pleased to see that his chair had turned into gold; so had the pen on the table in front of him. The papers as soon as he looked at them, changed colour and became golden. The walls of the room, when he looked at them also became golden; not plain, but adorned with wonderful carvings.

They brought his food and placed it in front of him. He ate it rapidly. It was delicious because it was made of gold and floated down his throat, molten and cool, into his stomach, which it turned into gold; then it flowed through all his veins and arteries, until it reached the farthest comers of his body. Then, with a thud, the golden mania vanished.

His brain became clear and he saw distinctly a swift, red arrow swooping in a zigzag course, like lightning, from a dark sky. He saw it only for a fraction of a moment, but that moment was equal to eternity. His imagination soared into eternity, where he heard a great buzzing sound. On approaching this sound, he found that an immense, an incalculable crowd of people had gathered in a Fish Market, outside a shop, over the door of which was written a name which he could not read. Underneath the name were the words "Merchant and Contractor." When he asked these people what was the meaning of the buzzing sound they were making, they all answered with one voice. He had even time to wonder at the extraordinary discipline of these people, because not a single voice broke the harmony, even though there were countless millions of them. He was deeply impressed by the way in which they all spoke together and felt that there must be something really in their grievance, since they had gone to such trouble to get a common voice for stating it. They said that God had just died without having set his affairs in order. They were all God's children and now, being left destitute, for the lawyers would gobble up whatever was left after the debts had been paid, they would very likely have to go to America, as common emigrants, in order to earn their living. They blamed a certain woman of suspicious antecedents for God's premature death. Then, deeply impressed by the manner in which they stated their case, with one voice, he told them, speaking very well indeed, that they need have no fear. Henceforth, there was no need for anybody to emigrate to America. He had various schemes in mind, schemes which he had been considering with great care for some years. Now he was going to strike. He was going to build a large hotel, a kelp factory and a ...

The red arrow struck him on the back of the neck with great violence.

CHAPTER XV

THE sun had passed the apex of its circuit. It was flying down the sky. Wearied of its heat and gorged by the moisture it had sucked, it hurried to its evening bath in the blood-red water by the water's edge. Now drunken laughter filled the by-streets and the whoring had begun; the mocking laughter of jackals as the caravans decamp into the desert, leaving refuse to be scattered by the wind. Again the cattle moaned, driven from the square to the railway station and out along the road into the plain. Horses were being hitched to carts. The square was becoming naked.

She dismissed O'Rourke at the chemist's shop, telling him that she preferred to walk home. Then she went into the shop and bought a packet of aspirin tablets. She left the shop (it was at the corner of the Main Street) and walked around the square towards Railway Street, going to the doctor's house. Drunken fellows leered at her and whispered as she passed. Ashamed of their glances, she kept her eyes on the ground and did not see the doctor, who came out of Railway Street and turned to the right towards his dispensary just as she approached Railway Street from the other side of the square.

She knocked at the doctor's door. The door opened. She hurried into the hall. Molly had opened the door. She stood with one hand on the door, wiping her other hand in her apron. She had just finished her meal. Her face was spotted with smut from the kitchen range. She as perspiring. She looked worried. Her hands were trembling. Her strong face, now devoid of its youthful, buxom beauty had become almost uncouth and brutal, when confronted with Nora's beauty. It was sullen.

"Oh! Molly!" said Nora, "I want to see Jim at once. Is he in? Where is he?"

Molly did not answer. She was looking at Nora's feet sullenly. She did not remove her hand from the door, as if waiting for Nora to go out again. Nora had not noticed Molly's attitude. She was in the habit of treating her with very scant attention, as a person of no consequence. Molly hardly ever had come into the study while the doctor was talking to Nora and the doctor had often told Nora, while pitying himself for having ruined his life, that Molly meant nothing to him, that he did not love her, that she did not understand him, that she was not interested in ideas, that she was a burden to him, that he simply could not leave her because she was dependent on him. For that reason Nora had always treated Molly with kindly contempt; never, even paying her the respect of treating her as a rival. In fact, she looked upon her as a servant.

Now, however, Molly had become a person of great importance; just as a rich man, finding himself in jail on a serious charge, suddenly regards the common jailor as a person of great consequence and is grateful when that coarse fellow pauses on his rounds to utter a trivial remark.

Now it was Nora who felt herself inferior.

"Molly," she repeated, "where is Jim? Why don't you speak to me?"

"He's not in," said Molly sullenly. "What do you want with him?" .

She closed the door, folded her arms on her bosom and looked at Nora.

"Could you give me a drink of water?" said Nora, leaning against the wall.

She felt weak and at the same time instinctively determined to appeal to Molly's pity. Molly watched her for a few moments. Then she thrust out her lower lip, furrowed her forehead and went to the dining-room door.

"Come in here," she said.

She opened the dining-room door. Nora, with her handkerchief to her mouth, staggered to the dining-room door and passed into the room. She threw herself into a chair, leaned forward over the table, laid her head on her arms and burst into tears.

Now the remains of the doctor's dinner lay on the table.

"I'll give you a cup of tea if you like," said Molly.

"Yes, do," mumbled Nora. "I have eaten nothing ...all day! Can't you tell me, though, where Jim has gone?"

"He's gone out," said Molly. "Wait till I bring you a cup of tea. Then I'll tell you ... he told me to tell you ... wait a minute. I won't be a second."

She went out, leaving the door open. Nora got to her feet and walked about the room, beating her palms together.

"He's hiding from me," she muttered. "He'll do nothing. Oh! What's going to happen ! I'll ask her to send a message to O'Neill."

She sat down again. Molly returned with a cup of tea on a tray.

"Would you like a mutton chop?" she said. "There's one left."

Nora took the cup of tea and drank it at once. Molly watched her. Now Molly's nostrils began to twitch.

"No," said Nora. "I couldn't eat. I'm ... "

She looked up. She saw Molly's nostrils were twitching and immediately realised that she could hope for no assistance from this woman.

"Oh! God!" she thought. "She hates me. Why? I have done nothing to her."

"I can't take food that's offered to me like that," she said, trying to speak in a dignified manner, but without success. Her voice was broken.

"What have you against me? What have I done to you?"

Molly flushed and laid her coarse palm on the table.

"I wouldn't save you this minute," she said hoarsely, "from the teeth of a mad dog."

"Oh! God!" said Nora, putting her hands to her mouth.

Then she stretched out her hands across the table and whispered:

"Have pity on me. Help me. Won't you have pity on me? They're going to kill me."

"Who?" said Molly sullenly. "Eh? Who's going to kill you?"

"I don't know," sobbed Nora. "My husband, I think. I'm terrified. His mother drove me out of the house."

"Then why do you come here?" cried Molly excitedly. "What brought you here?"

"Can't you tell me where Jim is? He promised to help me."

"Oh! Did he? He did, maybe. But he won't help you now. Now he knows all about you. He should have known long ago. I knew you long ago. What have I against you? It's only a selfish woman like you could ask a question like that, after what you've done."

Molly suddenly sat down and began to cry, with her arms hanging by her sides.

"What have you done? God! All the nights I spent alone in bed, crying my heart out, when you came into the house with your cunning and sent him out of his mind, so that he ... I won't tell you."

She stopped crying as suddenly as she had begun and her eyes flashed with hatred.

"I won't tell you," she muttered hoarsely. "I have kept him. I won."

"Who? Who? Who are you talking about?"

"You wanted to take him from me. You wanted my husband."

Nora laughed hysterically and got to her feet.

"I want your husband ! " She laughed again. "I! "

"Yes, you wanted him. Haven't you a husband of your own? Is it any wonder they'd drive you out of the house? Is it any wonder he'd kill you after what you've done?"

"I'm more particular than that," cried Nora furiously. "I wouldn't touch your leavings. I don't want your help."

"You can't have him," cried Molly, getting more excited as she felt that she could not hurt Nora as much as she wanted. "He knows all about you now. He told me to tell you if you came that ... "

"What?" gasped Nora, sitting down again. "What did he tell you?"

"Ha!" said Molly. "You tried to fool me between you, you and O'Neill. But you weren't clever enough."

Nora shuddered. She gasped for breath. A great black cloud suddenly seemed to fall upon her, smothering her.

"He told me to tell you," whispered Molly, "never to come here again.

"The parish priest came here and told him where you were last night. He showed us the letter that ... "

"I hate you," cried Nora.

"I'm glad you hate me," cried Molly. "What brought you here, looking for pity, from me that you treated like dirt under your feet? Why should you be pitied? You with fine clothes on your back, living in idleness, and I with three children to rear and ... "

"And ugly," said Nora in a tense whisper, getting to her feet. Molly opened her mouth, shuddered and said nothing. Nora rushed out of the room. Molly covered her face with her apron and burst into tears. Then she got up, went out into the kitchen and, still weeping, began to work.

"God forgive me," she said aloud, "if I have been hard on her, but ... I have to ... look after my children and ... what happiness is there in ... I'm ugly. I've got ugly. He'll never want me again."

She caught a plate off the dressers, raised it above her head and was about to smash it against the ground as a gesture of rage against life, but she paused, lowered her hands slowly, brushed the plate with her apron, put it back on the shelf, wiped her eyes, shrugged herself and continued her work.

Nora turned towards the square and halted on the pavement outside Mooney's shop. She looked into the window, opened her bag and began to powder her nose, in order to find time to collect her thoughts and decide what she should do now. But she was disturbed by seeing Mooney within the shop, watching her, with his spectacles on the tip of his nose and his head bent. When she saw him he raised his head and pushed his spectacles up on his forehead. She turned away from the window and moved to the corner of the street.

"He is in the hotel," she thought. "I must send in a message to him."

People were going past her. They all looked at her as they passed and then turned their heads to have another look at her after they had passed. They looked simply from curiosity, attracted by her beauty; but she thought the wonder in their eyes was hatred and she could not find courage to ask anybody to do her the favour of taking a message to O'Neill. After having stood there five minutes she crossed the street and then walked past the bar window, hoping to see O'Neill through the window. But she could see nothing through the window, except a cloud of tobacco smoke and the heaving bodies of drinkers who were now getting thoroughly soused. They were singing. She turned back, determined to enter the hotel and ask one of the maids to tell him. At the hotel entrance, she was jostled by a big cattle jobber who was coming out. Instead of apologising he laughed into her face and said something obscenely humorous. She turned back in disgust and walked rapidly down Railway Street.

After she had gone ten yards she halted and asked herself where she was going. Then she clearly saw the Black Cliff, the moonlight, the golden road upon the sea and O'Neill's face, exalted with love. She turned back again. There was a lump in her throat. Her legs shivered.

Again she halted, remembering her husband. She turned back and almost ran towards the railway station.

"But there is no train now," she thought.

She crossed the street and turned to the right, down the road that led out into the country. She stopped thinking. The road was level, curving gently to the right, stretching to the horizon out into the great central plain. She walked in the middle of the road. The dust came to her ankles. A little in front of her there was a drove of cattle. The drivers were singing and she could hear the clacking of the animals' hoofs. Crows were flying high above the road. They flew in silence, as if watching in the expectation that some animal might fall by the wayside, die and become carrion. She passed the outskirts of the town. Sounds became dulled. The drove of cattle became a cloud of dust in the distance. Smells became sweet. Larks were singing. Brooks gurgled by the roadside. A young colt stood up to his belly in a pond, in a field. He neighed when he saw her. She came to an open gate and turned into a field and lay down under the hedge. She closed her eyes and began to fall asleep. She sat up, took the bottle of aspirin tablets from her bag and swallowed several.

Over a low fence she saw the colt standing in the pond. Now his head drooped. He seemed to be falling asleep. She shuddered. She must not go to sleep. She got up and walked straight down the field, along a track made by the wheels of a cart. She passed into another field, through a gap between two bushes. Several rabbits scurried away at her appearance. Two curlews rose, flew around in a half circle, uttered one cry and then floated down to earth in a field farther away. She must not go that way. She turned to her right, attracted by the cooing of two doves that were hidden in a tall tree that stood alone in the middle of a field. They flew away when she came nearer. Exhausted, she lay down under the shade of the tree in which they had been cooing. Her teeth began to chatter.

"What am I looking for?" she said aloud. "I have nobody to help me."

Then she got up hurriedly and walked away, saying:

"No, no. I mustn't give in. I mustn't do that. He'll come. I'm certain he 'll come. "

She went back the way she had come, on to the road and turned back to the town: Farther on, she saw two drunken men coming towards her. Seeing her at a distance, one of. them waved his hat and called out in a loud voice something that made her flush. She turned to the left into a lane that led towards the church. She reached the church. The door was ajar. She entered. There was nobody there. She walked down towards the baptismal font at the rear, tried to sit down on the comer of a seat, became dizzy, staggered and fell on to the floor. The dizziness passed, she sighed, stretched herself and fell asleep.

She lay on a stone slab under which a priest was buried. Her body curved around the ornate cross that was graven on the head of the stone. Sunbeams, coming aslant through the stained windows of the church, shone upon her.

Settling her head against her outstretched right arm she dislodged her hat. Her golden hair was caught by the gilded sunbeams and became a fiery red.

Her face became golden.

CHAPTER XVI

"HOLY God ! Is the man going to come at all?" said Dan Clancy from Ballycamcrosach. "I declare to the jumping son of Lucifer that there's a pain in my guts that would kill a regiment of soldiers. I'll write a letter to the papers about that man."

"Sure, yer time enough," said Degatty, the fisherman. " It's always looking for trouble you are, a skinny little fellow like you. He's a good doctor. It's not often he's late. You're always making complaints. Ramon Mor should have been a warning to you."

"Yes, by ganeys," said Louisa, the rip, from Prochlochlais.

"You brought an action against him for hitting you a wallop on the skull with his ash-plant and he made a showboard of you for the town."

"I got five quid out of him," said Dan Clancy, scratching himself. "Five bloomin' quid." .

"What is five quid," says she, "compared to the disgrace he made of you? And he up before the court, says he, he stood on my big toe, says he, on a corn I had and without turning around, I thought it was a dog that bit me, says he, I hit him a wallop. *So* here's five quid, says he, he's worth no more. Ye'd get more for a strong jackass and your head in a sling with the ditch he cut in it."

"Faith," said Clancy, "it's not every man's head is worth five quid, for vermin is cheap."

"By the seven Jackersties," said a bearded fellow, "this is too much altogether, and the seven parishes waiting for him. It's about a piece of land I came into the court-house, but now that I'm here I might as well have a bottle of medicine for a pain my father has. He can't stir out."

"Aw!, Holy God!" said an old woman. "There's a hurricane blowing in my insides. Whist! Who do I see?"

"Yes, that's him. There he is now. He's coming."

"Here he is."

A great crowd had gathered in the hallway of the courthouse building, from the doorway of the dispensary room to the bottom of the steps that led up to the building. Most of them had nothing whatever the matter with them and had merely come for medicine because it was free. Some had come into the building to interview the Government official about their land, their rates or their rents. Others had come simply out of curiosity, hearing that something had happened at the Big House, that the parish priest was concerned in some scandal, that the doctor had been up to the Big House that morning, and that they might be able to get some information out of him. Peasants are really the most inquisitive types of human beings.

The doctor, arriving at the building, found great difficulty in pushing his way through. Everybody shouted that he or she had been there first. They began to fight. A policeman came and had to draw his baton and to threaten to blow his whistle for help. Then half the crowd went away, cursing and threatening to vote against the Government at. the next election. Those that stayed were lined up in a row. The doctor entered the dispensary and began to listen to the complaints of the people.

He had been working only about twenty minutes, when there was a great disturbance outside and a man came running into the dispensary, pushing the people out of his way. It was one of Ramon Mar's clerks. He was bareheaded.

"Quick, quick!" shouted the clerk. "Come at once. Mr. Costello is in a fit."

"God between us and harm," cried the people.

The doctor grew pale. He did not move.

"It's urgent, doctor," shouted the clerk, mopping his face. "He's unconscious. You're to bring something."

"Of course he is," said the doctor. "I know. I'm coming at once."

He picked up his bag, put some things into it and ran after the clerk. Most of the people ran out after them, except those who were really ill. These latter began to grumble, saying it did not seem to matter whether .they died or not, but that it was a different thing where the rich were concerned.

As they dashed across the square, a crowd followed them. Outside Ramon's office, the people were standing close together, peeping into the hall, in silence.

"Make way, make way," cried the clerk.

"It's the doctor," whispered the people. "Let him pass."

The doctor squeezed his way into the office.

"Clear everybody out of the passage," he said to the man at the door.

The main office was empty. All the clerks were in Ramon's private room, except one youth, who, apparently terrified of sickness, stood behind his desk, biting a pen nervously. The doctor entered the private office. He saw Ramon lying on the floor, with his head propped against coats. He lay on his back. They had taken off his collar and opened his shirt and waistcoat. His stomach was heaving. His right cheek was swollen. His eyes were dilated. His lower lip trembled.

"I thought so," said the doctor, going on his knees beside Ramon and beginning to open his bag. "Keep back from him. Throw open that window."

"I just happened to come in, doctor," said Peadar Mar, who knelt on one knee by Ramon's head. "I found him like as if he were dead, sitting in his chair."

"Eh ?" said the doctor, looking up.

Peadar Mar, in his excitement, spat on Ramon's extended arm.

"I ran over to him," he continued, "and I shook him. He rolled out of the chair. The best thing to do is to draw his blood. I thought I'd wait till you'd come."

"Eh?" said the doctor again, putting his hand on Ramon's chest.

Ramon moved as soon as the doctor's hand touched him. The doctor, still terrified of Ramon, although the man was helpless, withdrew his hand.

"Hal" said Peadar Mar. "There's life in him."

"Thank God! He's still alive," said Mrs. Feeney, the wife of Ramon's manager.

"Be quiet, woman," whispered her husband.

Ramon moaned. Then he opened his mouth, closed it again, gnashed his teeth, clenched his fists, raised his arms and growled. He looked around him slowly. Everybody drew back.

"A drop of brandy would be best, now, doctor," said Peadar Mar.

The doctor felt helpless. Because of the terror that Ramon Mor inspired in him, he felt unable to do anything. It seemed to him that Ramon Mor was even more menacing lying helpless in that manner than he was when in full possession of his strength. He looked more like an animal.

Suddenly Ramon spoke.

"What the devil are you all doing here?" he said in a hoarse voice.

Then he closed his eyes, shrugged himself and tried to rise.

"Astounding!" muttered the doctor, getting to his feet.

"The man's a giant." .

"Wait till I put a hand on your shoulder," said Peadar Mar.

"Is that you, Peadar " said Ramon. "I thought it was you."

"You're all right now," said Peadar Mor. "It's the heat."

Their voices were tender. Blood to blood. Root to root. The others drew back still farther.

"You better stay quiet a minute," said Peadar Mor.

"The doctor is here now."

"Who?" said Ramon. "Who is here? Ha! There you are. Who sent for that man?"

"It was I sent for him, sir," said Mr. Feeney, the manager. "I thought that we should ... "

"Silence. Get back to work all of you. What are you all doing here? This is not a holiday. God Almighty! Give me a hand, Peadar."

Supported by his cousin, he got to his feet, staggered to his chair and sat down. His face was yellowish, with purple spots here and there on his cheeks. His mouth lay half open. He was breathing in rapid gusts. Everybody left the room except Peadar Mor and the doctor.

"Take a drop of this," said Peadar Mar, bringing over a bottle of brandy which a messenger had handed in at the door.

"Just a moment," said the doctor.

"Just what?" said Ramon, turning towards the doctor.

His throat shook as he moved his head. Now he was rapidly recovering his strength. His face seemed to expand and contract. His body twisted, as if he were drawing out a reserve of strength from an inner store, in order to face this fresh attack upon his life.

The doctor trembled. He was thrilled, in spite of his fear, by the man's wonderful courage and endurance.

"I want to tell you," he began, "that you ... "

"Tell me nothing," said Ramon, putting the bottle to his head.

"Good God!" said the doctor.

Ramon took a long drink. He put down the bottle.

"Look after the office," he said to Peadar Mor. "See is everything all right there."

Peadar Mor went out.

"He has left the door open again," said Ramon. "Shut that door."

Somebody shut the door.

"What have you got to tell me?" said Ramon to the doctor. "What brought you here? Did you think I was done for?"

He looked slyly at the doctor.

"He is a monster," thought the doctor.

"I was sent for," he said aloud. "That's why I came, although, allow me to tell you that I, at least I had made up my mind, although, perhaps, considering what has happened, I might have refrained at the last moment, through weakness, from ... "

"Why do you always talk like a fool?" said Ramon sarcastically. "Can't you talk properly? You're a fine man to be a doctor in a place like this. I might have died from want of help if I had been really sick. It's a dangerous thing to have a man like you in this town. You must resign at once."

He chuckled and sucked his lips. He seemed to be in very high spirits and to be enjoying himself immensely.

"I won't resign," said the doctor, raising his voice.

"Oh! You're not going to resign," said Ramon. "Eh?"

He chuckled.

"Oh! Boys!" he continued. "Won't I give you fellows a surprise when I set to work! A nice plot you had hatched between you. You will resign. I say it. I! Do you hear? I didn't see my way properly this morning. Now, though, I see my way. I'm going to enjoy this."

While Ramon had been speaking, the doctor had begun to gesticulate. He began to speak before Ramon finished.

"Let me tell you," he said, "that your present frame of mind is a common delusion or hallucination consequent Of your illness, and that it means, that is, almost should I on at least I am quite convinced, although your disease is phenomenal and purely individual as far as I can gather, without a proper examination .... After all, science is in its infancy and we know next to nothing, except what we can deduce under the circumstances from cases already examined. But this much I do know. You are in a desperate position, and if you don't allow yourself to be taken in hand at once ... Why should I tell you this? But the fact remains that I had a serious argument with myself and I felt that it was my duty. I would have come in any case if not just now, at least later on."

The doctor had said all this in one breath. When he paused for breath, Ramon said:

"Now I see. It was you plotted the whole thing. Poor Nora! I was'nt blaming you unjustly."

"I don't care what you do," continued the doctor, "now that I have told you and have come to you with the fullest, I mean the most generous, not generous but with the strictest intentions of doing my duty, even though, from a special point of view, I must admit it, I consider you are a monster and an evil influence. I consider that you are even more than the typical result of a vicious form of society, for Nature gave you talents that she denies to most, and you used them, I say you used them, allow me to tell you, but should I allow sentimental reasons, seeing you helpless just now, I say my heart softened towards you when you lay there, but when you moved, apart from my admiration of your diabolical courage, even though you are ill and dying, yes, dying, no sentiment should prevent me from denouncing you in the name of the hungry and of the oppressed, those that you have destroyed body and soul by your greed, when you might have made a more beautiful heaven than that of Jesus Christ, because more human, I mean to say and yet, why did I come? I tell you I didn't come to say this."

"Hand me my hat," said Ramon.

"Your hat?" said the doctor in amazement.

"Yes," said Ramon, pointing towards a hook at the back of the door. He had taken off his hat to eat and the clerk had hung it up on the back of the door. The doctor looked at the hat and then looked at Ramon. Ramon was grinning.

"Do you hear me?" said Ramon. "Hand me that hat, I say."

The doctor opened his mouth to say something.

"Be quick," said Ramon.

The doctor went slowly to the door, turning back several times to look at Ramon's grinning face.

"Ha!" said Ramon. "Fine doctor you are. Ha!"

He stopped grinning, thrust out his lower lip and scowled. The doctor returned with the hat and threw it on the table.

"Is it any pleasure for you to humiliate me?" he said.

"Put it on my head," said Ramon.

The doctor did not move.

"Do what I tell you," growled Ramon.

Then he suddenly grinned again and said:

"Is that how you treat a patient?"

Trembling, the doctor caught up the hat and was placing it on Ramon's head, but Ramon snatched the hat and said:

"Damn you!"

He clapped the hat on to his skull.

"I'm not your servant," said the doctor, stepping back and striking his chest.

Ramon began to snuffle as he fixed his hat on properly, turning the rim up behind and pulling it down in front over his eyes.

"Yes, of course," said the doctor to himself. "He's seriously ill. If he dies, perhaps, I wonder should I warn, the situation might be difficult. I have been here alone with him."

"What are you muttering about now?" said Ramon.

"I beg of you for the last time," said the doctor, stretching out his hand beseechingly, "to let me take you in hand. I want you to understand that I have done nothing intentionally mean. It's not yet too late. You accuse me of propaganda against you, but it's untrue, because I merely spoke generally to the people, about the anarchy of their social life, when it really should be a co-operative effort ..."

"Eh?" whispered Ramon, starting, when he heard the word "co-operative."

"And religion," continued the doctor, "should be the sum total of the people's ... "

'"None of that," cried Ramon, trembling.

"Cultural achievements. I told them, in a sense, what I have told you here now, that no man has a right to prey' upon his fellows, because the negative passions of greed and hatred ... "

"Enough of that," cried Ramon, striking the table.

"Yes, yes," said the doctor, lowering his voice to a whisper. "I should admit to you, why do I forget things, that I have discovered to-day, from Fr. Considine, something that shows me I was led astray to a certain extent, and that I acted under her influence and that your wife ... "

"Yes!" growled Ramon. "My wife ! Now we are at the bottom of it. It was your work. It was you turned her against me. You were all in the plot."

"That's untrue," said the doctor. "I thought your wife was unhappy and I tried to comfort her. I swear to you that there was never anything else between us. You are following the wrong track. I never discussed you with her, except once or twice, when she asked me about your health and I told her you were in danger of, of course, I must tell you ..."

He stopped for a moment, leaned over the table and whispered:

"For God's sake, Mr. Costello, listen to me. You are on the verge of death unless you ... "

"So you have changed your tune," said Ramon. "You have changed your tune since this morning. What about these threats you made to my face this morning? What are you going to do about that? Ach! "

He rubbed his hands along his cheeks and sighed wearily.

"Have you no pity?" cried the doctor, breaking down completely.

"I came here genuinely to help you and you insist on my ruin. Death is staring you in the face and you only think of revenge. I have a wife and children, and you ... "

"What about me?" cried Ramon, with despair in his voice. He spoke indistinctly, hoarsely, as if his voice were smothered in his throat by a load of anguish that came rushing from his heart, smothering him.

"Have I not got a wife? Does your wife mean as much to you as mine does to me? Curse you ! You ! You come to cure me after having poisoned my life."

The doctor stood erect. Ramon's face had become transformed by an expression that made it pitiful instead of terrifying. The ferocity and strength were gone, giving place to a sort of uncouth tenderness. Uncouth, because, whereas the weak wear the cloak of tenderness and meekness as their most fitting apparel, the strong wear it awkwardly, in pain.

Then he shook himself and said:

"I despise your philosophy. I don't want your help. I'll die when my time comes, as I have lived, fighting, without help. I despise you. I despise all cowards and failures. I'm going to go on till I drop, in my own way. But I'll defend my own. I'll hold what I have. And the people will follow me, too, because I am of their blood, do you hear? And because I am a man. A man. Not a rat, like you and Fr. Fogarty and the rest of you schemers. Take that from me. I don't want your help. I never took help from any man. No man is going to get the upper hand of me as long as I live. If any man tries, let him look out. I'll wring his neck. That's my philosophy. I didn't get it out of books, either, but out of my own guts. You'll go. You'll resign. Clear out. I'm busy. What are you standing there for?"

The doctor's face was deadly pale.

"Mr. Costello," he said, "I don't care what happens to me but my wife and children ... "

There was a knock at the door.

"Come in," said Ramon.

The door opened and Fr. Considine entered the room.

"What has happened?" he said excitedly.

Seeing Ramon sitting in his chair, apparently in full possession of his strength, he started and said:

"I was told you were ... "

"You were told a lie," said Ramon. "You're still here, Dr. Fitzgerald. I told you to leave my sight."

"I'm glad," said the priest, mopping his face with a handkerchief.

"Fr. Considine," said the doctor, "would you kindly explain to Mr. Costello what we were saying, I mean, he still insists ... "

"Get out of my house at once," said Ramon.

"Yes," said the priest, "I'll explain."

"Then I'll go," said the doctor, hurrying to the door. "I have patients at the ... "

He went out. The priest came forward, staring at Ramon in a dazed manner. From his expression, it was obvious that he was at one and the same time very anxious about Ramon and utterly indifferent to him. One part of his consciousness paid heed to what was present. The other, more important part contemplated what was absent and as yet merely an idea. His anxiety was caused by the fear that any untoward event in the actual world, like Ramon's illness, might prevent the idea from becoming, in turn, the actual world. He no longer looked distraught. He had become completely insane.

"Yes," he said, " I went to the doctor. He'll keep quiet. What happened to you?"

He spoke very hurriedly, glancing in all directions as he spoke, as if he were in a hurry to get away.

"It's no concern of yours, Fr. Considine," said Ramon.

"What?" said the priest. "What are you saying? Why did they send for me? I rushed at once."

He took out his watch and looked at it.

"I don't want any more of your meddling," said Ramon.

"I didn't ask you to go to the doctor. It has nothing to do with you. I'm done with you."

"You don't know what you're saying," said the priest, glancing towards the door, as if afraid that somebody was going to come behind him and prevent his getting away.

"I see it was a waste of time my coming here. You are all right, aren't you?"

He appeared to pay very little attention to what Ramon was saying, satisfied by seeing Ramon sitting there, apparently all right, that the actual world was not going to interfere with his idea.

"I'm done with you," said Ramon, also so immersed in his own schemes, which were almost equally fanatical, that he did not notice the priest's absorption and indifference.

"You'll have to mend your ways. No more drinking or gambling, do you hear? I don't want any more scandals in my town. You had better keep away from that cottage, too. I'll buy it from you. I'm going to give you no more money. I don't see why you should have a good time at my expense."

Suddenly the priest became rigid. He listened for a moment with his head turned aside. Then he looked at Ramon and opened his mouth. His eyes moved from side to side. His idea had become disturbed.

"I can pray for myself," said Ramon. "I have a better chance of getting heard than you have. You've been trying to make a fool of me. I may tell you that I found you out just in time."

He struck the table, looked at the priest, started, became furious and said :

"You don't like that. You may take your medicine, though. I have my schemes ready. None of your whisperings to me any more. I'm going back into politics. I'll start a few companies here. I'm going to build a big hotel and a golf course. I'll set this town humming. See that? I have seen my wife. Now there is nothing worrying me on that score. We have at least come to an understanding. I warn you not to interfere with her any more. Do you hear ?"

He held out his right hand, closed his fingers and twisted his wrist.

"Understand?" he said in a menacing voice.

The priest whispered:

"I'm carrying the Blessed Sacrament."

Ramon pushed back his chair and crouched, as if he had been told that a snake was about to jump at him.

"What did you say?" he muttered hoarsely.

"I mean," said the priest in a fanatical voice, "that I have been consecrated as God's representative on this earth and that it is my duty to cast out devils and to crush the viper that spat upon God's face in the garden of Eden. To-day I have been spat upon and the whole town is whispering blasphemies against my name. They have come to my house to tell my servant of this scandal that is being whispered. But as I have always struck, wherever the demon of lust and concupiscence has shown its head, so I must strike now. I see my way and I must follow it. The hand of God will guide me. Vengeance is Thine."

He looked at Ramon, muttered something and left the room.

"What does he mean?" said Ramon.

For a few moments, his courage failed him. His reason began to probe into the events of the past few hours. That was painful. He shuddered and turned away his thoughts. He rehearsed his projects, the factory, the hotel, the race-course, the fleet of steam trawlers, the trip to the Continent, his return to politics. He pictured himself absorbing the whole country, conquering it.

The mania of power passed from his mind to his body. He rose from his chair and went out into the main office. Seeing him, the people looked in wonder, knowing that, a little while ago, he had lain stretched upon the floor like a corpse.

He hustled the clerks. He went behind the counter and greedily looked at the piles of money that lay in the tills. An old woman was arguing with a clerk, trying to persuade him to accept two pounds less than he demanded as payment of her debt.

"Listen," said Ramon. "If I let you keep that two pounds, your husband'll drink it and if he doesn't you'll spend it foolishly, anyway. Don't be afraid. You'll get everything you need. What? You want to send the money to your daughter. What? She's in hospital in Dublin. Why didn't you come to me and tell me that? They wouldn't let you in. Who wouldn't let you in? I'll give you the money out of my own pocket. Listen to me, all of you."

He raised his voice and addressed not only those in the office but those that crowded in the hall-way trying to come in.

"I'm going to set things going here, if ye have patience with me and not listen to those that are plotting against me. I know all that's happening. I'll stand by you, if you stand by me. There's going to be lashings of work for all of you. I'm going to start work in the town. There'll be work for everybody. I'm going to set things humming. I'm going to start a kelp factory, a saw-mills, a big hotel. There are mines up in the mountains. I'm going to get experts over from England to have a look at them. Provided you stand by me. If you don't, if you listen to the scoundrels that are plotting against me, there'll be another story. That's my word for you."

He came from behind the counter and advanced upon the people, towering above them. Almost immediately they began to murmur in praise of him. He went out of the office into the Fish Market and went among the people, talking cunningly about the schemes he had in mind, inventing new schemes as he went along. The people became excited. They began to talk of the great times that were coming, saying that the seven lean years had passed and the prophecy was going to come true. For it was said by the ancients .that the son of a man from Inismuineach would become king of Barra and pave the streets with gold.

"I'd rather put my trust in him than in a stranger," said one. "He's of our blood."

"He's a changed man to-day," said another. "God has whispered in his ear."

Ramon, with his hat over his eyes, enormous, gathered their money into his tills and whispered cunning words into their ears, while the sun flew westwards and the town grew full of drunkards and Nora slept upon a priest's tomb before the baptismal font.

What is time? One moment in eternity, when the forked lightning swoops from the sky upon the aged oak and the roots concealed for many centuries rise with a crash into the naked air.

CHAPTER XVII

"DO you fellows know what I'm going to tell you?" said Finnigan. "It's not proper to spread stories like that about a priest. Even if it's true, it's not right to talk about it. By the hammers of Hell, that woman would tempt many a man. Still, it's not the thing to talk about it."

"You're right there, Larry," said Connors, the cattlejobber. " If a man fancies a woman, he has a right to try and get her, if she's willing. A priest is another thing. The less talk there is about priests the better. There's many a thing a priest does that the ordinary man can't understand. It's not right to be talking about him."

Billy Danvers, the degenerate, startled everybody in the snug by saying:

"Priests ministering to women under like circumstances are beyond the pale of reason and beyond the judgment of humanity, for theirs is not flesh and blood but the fire of the Holy Ghost."

He wore a shabby raincoat to conceal his lack of a shirt. His pointed nose was red. His weak eyes were running water. He looked around at the company, giggled and added:

"I bet there isn't one of you with enough intelligence to understand that."

Although they were all startled by his blasphemous remark, they were too muddled with drink to know exactly what to do about it. O'Neill, who sat gloomily in the corner beside the man in the tweed cap, pointed a finger at Danvers, the degenerate.

"Who's that fellow?" he lisped drunkenly, nudging the man in the tweed cap.

The man in the tweed cap leaned towards O'Neill and muttered:

"Take no notice of him. Sit still. We'll soon have to be moving out of here."

"Begob," said Tynan, the farmer, "it would be easy to have as much intelligence as you, anyway, Billy Danvers."

Tynan, the farmer, lurched forward. Then he lurched backward. Then he fell straight down to the floor against the wall, with his legs crossed under him like a Turk.

"Don't spill your pint, Tynan," said Mr. Matthews, the engineer.

"Devil a drop I spilt," said Tynan, the farmer, looking proudly at the pint measure which he still held upright in his hand. "I don't know how I did it, but it's done now. There you are. Now, Billy Danvers, you fool, do you think you have enough sense to fall straight down on your arse out of your standing without spilling your pint? What?"

Danvers, the degenerate, blinked his watery eyes, giggled and sniffed through his pointed, red nose. He shook himself within his shabby raincoat. He stamped on the floor, first with one foot, whose shoe had no heel, and then with the other foot, whose shoe had only half a sole.

"I'm the only man in this town," he said, still giggling, "that has any intelligence."

"You have intelligence enough," said Finnigan, "never to pay for your own drinks."

"Or for anybody else's," said Doyle, the commercial traveller.

"That's Doyle," said Sweeney, the clerk of the district court.

Did you eat your chop yet, Doyle?" said Timmins, the excise officer.

"Yes, by cripes," said Dooley, the schoolmaster. "Mutton chop and is it that time? That's all you can get out of him·"

"What I want to know is this," said Conners, the cattlejobber. "What has a mutton chop to do with the question at hand? The question is ... "

"Allow me to interpose," interrupted Danvers, the degenerate, "in order to say that the question is, did he or didn't he?"

"Who? Ye dirty little ferret, who are you talking about?" said Tynan, the farmer, from the floor.

"The Holy Ghost!" said Danvers, the degenerate.

"Jesus ! " said Finnigan. "That smells to me like blasphemy."

"You let it yourself, if it does," said Danvers, the degenerate.

"Larry, what about that half-gallon?" cried Timoney, the cattle-jobber, appearing at the door and putting his two great paws on the shoulders of two men, who were separated by another man.

"Come and take it," said Finnigan.

"There's no room here for that savage," said Conners, a rival cattle-jobber.

"Matt, ye dirty scut," said Timoney, "ye tricked me to-day by paying that price for Ramon Mor's cattle. Farrelly would have given them to me for less."

"Ask himself," said Connors. "Farrelly is here. Farrelly, where are you? Speak up and say would you have given them to him for less. Where is Farrelly?"

"Where? Oh! Where are the days of yore?" said Danvers, the degenerate.

"He's fallen like a gentleman," said Doyle, the commercial traveller.

"He's fallen like a pig," said Finnigan. "Look. In the name o' God, Farrelly, what d'ye mean by spewing all over the floor?"

"Blast him," said Dooley, the schoolmaster. "He has dirtied my shoe."

"Leave him there under the table," said Tynan, the farmer, from the floor. "He's all right there under the table. It was the thirty-first of April, the fiftieth of July, I met a farmer's daughter and I prodded her in the thigh, Killooleeioo, Killooleeiay."

"Hey!" said O'Neill, suddenly getting to his feet in the corner. "What did that man say about the Holy Ghost? Who's that man there in the bowler hat? Who is he, Larry?"

The man in the tweed cap jerked O'Neill, who sat down just in the same way that Tynan, the farmer, had sat down.

"Allow me," said Danvers,. the degenerate, "to answer the inquiry of my intoxicated friend in the corner, as politely as the situation will permit. Mr. O'Neill, you should know me very well, and the principal cause of the failure of your recent literary venture---"

"Listen, lads," said Timmins, the excise officer. "Listen to Billy."

"---was," continued Danvers, the degenerate, "the strange obstin-obstina-obsinisy with which you consistently refused to avail yourself of my collaboration. I, sir, am a man of letters. A provincial, no doubt, but I am proud of the provinces. But I am known, too ... "

"Where, ye dirty little race-course tout?" cried Tynan, the farmer, from the floor. "Where are you known? I gave you a job looking after my cattle and you wouldn't ... "

"Don't interrupt, Tynan," said Finnigan. "Drink your pint."

"Yes," said Mr. Matthews, the engineer. "Go ahead, Danvers."

"I'm going to bash that fellow," whispered O'Neill to the man in the tweed cap.

"You sit still," said the man in the tweed cap. "This is no time to get a fighting jag on you. We'll soon have to move."

"But I am also known," continued Danvers, the degenerate, "in the metropolis .I have the honour to be an habitue of Mr. David Byrne's public-house, and I have the entree to the circle o£ metropolitan litterati, among whom I claimed as a friend the late Padraig O'Conaire, God rest his soul, who is now among the immortals on Mount Olympus, the favoured of Jove, on the right hand of Homer and Sappho, not to mention the ancients."

"More power to you," said Dooley, the schoolmaster.

"I have also acted," continued Danvers, the degenerate, "as the Barra special correspondent of the *Western Eagle,* the most cultured provincial organ in the whole country, and my contributions have ceased, not through lack of appreciation by my public, but because of a difference of principle as between the editor and myself."

"Listen to the liar," said Tynan, the farmer, from the floor. "He was sacked on account of a poem he composed about Ramon Mor. He was sacked for drunkenness from every job he ever held."

"Throw Tynan out," said Sweeney, the clerk of the district court.

"There's not a man in Barra can do it," said Tynan, the farmer, from the floor.

" Be quiet, Tynan," said Finnigan. "Go ahead, blear eyes."

"Hey! Hey!" said Timoney, the cattle-jobber. "Don't call the poor bastard names. Go ahead, Billy. Pass along that half-gallon."

Danvers, the degenerate, now overwrought with emotion, trembled from head to foot.

"Mr. O'Neill," he continued, "I offered you a poem for publication in your paper, a poem which I consider a *magnum opus,* and which you refused. I have since recited it in various taverns and public places with great success, and with the favour of the company I now propose to recite it here, in order to enliven the proceedings with a dash of the Hellenic fire."

"Begob, yes," said Timoney, the cattle-jobber, receiving his half-gallon. "I heard him sing that in Tullyfarnan. It's good. Out with it."

"That fellow is trying to insult me," said O'Neill. "I'll bash him."

"You'll do nothing of the kind," said the man in the tweed cap. "Come along. Let's get out of here."

"It's in free verse," said Danvers, the degenerate, "written in accordance with the most modern canons of the art of poetry. It goes as follows, and it was originally inspired by the marriage of Mr. Costello and by ... "

"What did I tell ye," said Tynan, the farmer, from the floor. "It's on account of that poem he was sacked."

"Hold your tongue," said Finnigan.

"With the later additions," said Danvers, the degenerate, "including a final canto inspired just now by current rumours, it will go down in history, perhaps, I may modestly say, as The Song of the Golden Woman of Barra. Here it is."

"I'm going to stand a drink for the house," said Tynan, the farmer, from the floor.

"Wait till we hear the song," said Dooley, the schoolmaster.

"Let's have the song," said Doyle, the commercial traveller.

"To hell with the song," said Tynan, the farmer, from the floor. "I know the one. It's no good. That dirty little drunkard, I took pity on him, but he wouldn't look after my cattle."

"Shut up Tynan," said Connors, the cattle-jobber. "Go ahead, Danvers. After all, even though he's a shot out of a gun, his father was reputed to be a gentleman."

"You are very coarse, sir," said Danvers, the degenerate. "I won't recite it at all now."

"Recite the blasted thing, or we'll murder you," said Timoney, the rival cattle-jobber, raising his half-gallon measure to his lips.

"What are you getting cocky about?" he added, lowering his half-gallon measure in order to spit.

O'Neill got to his feet and began to argue drunkenly with the man in the tweed cap. Danvers, the degenerate, grew agitated on seeing O'Neill rise. He said in a loud voice:

"I'll recite it for your benefit, Mr. O'Neill, in order to prove to you that what you rejected would have brought fame and emolument to your paper."

He looked at the ceiling, and put his right hand, which lay in the pocket of his shabby raincoat across his abdomen, and his left hand on his hip.

He began:

"Who are you? Whence have you come? Golden Head!
To this city by the sea, led by the valiant son

Of Michael, the Pedlar, a famous man in his day.
No other than Great Ramon found you
In the cities of the East, when all others
Had failed by their blandishments to rouse the giant's passion.
Enamoured of his name and the prowess of his mighty arms,
You saw in him the conqueror foretold in ancient song,
Who would bring wild horsemen galloping
From the mountains to the fat plains, naked of foot,
With foam on their white flanks, without bridle.
And lo! When you set foot within this town and all the press
Of admiring' eyes fell upon your golden hair
And saw your limbs fairer than those of Helen
And your eyes in which the stars had drowned their brightness
Within the flame of a greater fire,
A passion was unbound which boded a menace to the town.
Gold to gold comes running as moths come to the flame
And lust's dark anger does stain love's holy face."

The poet paused, looked about him excitedly and wiped his watery eyes with a wretched handkerchief.

"That's extraordinary," he said. "Those last two lines were just added on the spur of the moment, and I think they have a very deep philosophical meaning and an epic quality."

"Aw!" said Tynan, the farmer, from the floor. "Bladkerskite and rotten herrings I Why can't ye sing us a decent song? I want to stand a drink for the house."

"Throw Danvers out," said Mr. Matthews, the engineer. "My ears won't stand doggerel."

"Continue, Billy," said Timoney, the cattle-jobber. "I don't know what you're talking about, but go ahead, all the same. Watch me, lads, swallowing this half-gallon without drawing breath."

"I won't allow her name to be insulted in a public house," said O'Neill, trying to break away from the man in the tweed cap. "I'll let daylight through that fellow's head."

A great roar of laughter issued from the drunkards' throats, as the half-gallon measure, poised at an angle before the mouth of Timoney, spilt its porter down the open throat of Timoney, who stood with his elbow raised and his abdomen at ease, full-bellied, drinking. He emptied it and said:

"Ha-a-a-aw!"

"This is the second verse," said Danvers, the degenerate.

He began again to recite, although nobody listened to him.

"He imprisoned her, or so the people said.
A great dog he chained in his back yard,
He retired from politics.
The blackguards of the town made fun of him.
For no midwife came when the course had run,
Which brings merry childish prattle to the humblest home.
Among the gold and ornaments of that great house
She remained as empty as a ... "

Suddenly O'Neill cried out like one possessed and rushed from the arms of the man in the tweed cap. He bad his hands stretched out towards Danvers, the degenerate. He knocked aside several men who stood in his way. He was tripped by the foot of one of the men who staggered aside. He hurtled forward, knocking the pint measure out of Tynan's hand. The measure broke upon the floor. He fell on the broken glass. At once blood spouted from his wrist. He struggled to his feet. His wrist was belching blood.

"Hold him," they cried, rushing at him. "He's got a fighting jag on him. Hold him."

They held him. He still screamed. Then gradually his voice died down, he shuddered and became silent.

"Take him to the doctor at once," said Finnigan. "Go on, lads, keep talking. Don't let the police come in. It's nothing."

"I'm bleeding," said O'Neill. "Look at the blood." The man in the tweed cap tied a handkerchief quickly about the bleeding wrist and pushed O'Neill towards the door.

Danvers, the degenerate, heedless of the disturbance, had continued to recite. He was now saying:

"What ultimate destruction in the ratio
Of man's inhumanity to the finer passion
Shall be encompassed by this betrayal
Of fair beauty's charms.
I'm damned if I know.

But this much I do know.
Several are after her,
With foam on their white flanks, without bridle.
God alone knows what's going to happen,
But it's sure to be her nemesis,
For the crime of desecrating God's tabernacle
With the flames of lust."

"You're the cause of that man's wrist being cut," said Tynan, the farmer, from the floor. "He spilt my pint on account of you."

"Throw him out," said Sweeney, the clerk of the district court.

"Gentlemen," said Danvers, the degenerate, imperturbably, "if you will kindly allow me to add the verse I have just composed, inspired by the rumours that were inadvertently set moving on their pernicious rounds by Farrelly, who is now lying incontinently drunk under the table, after having fouled the premises, I think I could ... "

"Take him by the seat of the trousers," said Timoney, the cattle-jobber, replete with porter, "and drop him in the gutter. He's getting impudent."

"Clear out," said Timmins, the excise officer.

"Get out of here," said Mr. Matthews, the engineer.

"Foet! Foet!" said Finnigan. "Phew!"

They threw him out. He went into the public bar and joined in a ballad which was being sung by a crowd of peasants and fishermen, who had joined hands in a circle and were stamping on the floor, howling out of tune:

"When first I came into this
Coun-ter-e-e-e-e,
It was for to view
The green flowers ga-a-a-ay."

"I don't want to be seen going across the square with you," said the man in the tweed cap to O'Neill in the smoke-room. "You go ahead. Get this fixed and come back here at once. It's your right hand, blast it. I told you not to drink."

"I couldn't help it, Jack," said O'Neill. "I'm a ruined man. I couldn't let him insult her. I'd give my life for her, Jack. I'm telling you straight. I'm ruined, all the same."

The man in the tweed cap swore.

"Chuck her, Frank," he said. "Have no more to do with her. We'll carry this out and then you'll come along with us. There's no danger, anyway, seeing O'Rourke is standing in with us. As soon as Jimmy moves off with the car we'll go up the lane and put on our masks. You can fire with your left hand if necessary. Hurry on, blast it, there's no time. Wait a minute till I put your gun in your left pocket. There you are. Don't be a fool. She'd only make a fool of you. Let her look after herself. Take no chances. The superintendent has an eye on you. You come along with us afterwards."

O'Neill left the hotel. He met a party of young girls outside the door. They were dressed for tennis. They had rackets and balls. They were going to play tennis on the new court that had been made by the curate, who had organised a public subscription in aid of a tennis club, for the sons and daughters of the shopkeepers who wanted to become refined.

The girls saw the blood on O'Neill's clothes. They gasped, clutched one another, and passed by, looking at him very haughtily, since he was a notorious character and the curate had called him a "professional seducer."

He crossed the square unnoticed because two dogs were fighting outside the bank. They stood in silence throat to throat. A crowd was rapidly gathering to watch them, including two young men who came out of the Foresters' Hall with billiard cues in their hands. Near the dispensary, O'Neill passed a group of men from his own village. They were running awkwardly across the square towards the dog fight and they did not see him. He entered the dispensary.

It was now empty, except for one old man, a pensioner of the Royal Navy, who had spent most of his life at sea and in whose philosophy the doctor was interested.

"My God!" said the doctor, on seeing O'Neill enter the room. "What has happened to you?"

"Quick!" said O'Neill. "I cut my wrist. Bandage it up for me."

The doctor set to work bandaging the wrist. The old man, taking no notice of O'Neill nor of the bloody wrist, continued what he had been talking about before O'Neill entered.

"I was wandering by the shore," he said, "and I saw something shining in the shore grass, above the Long Beach. I went towards it and found it was a human skull. The sea is eating into the land at that place. A battle was fought there long ago. I sat down by the skull and meditated for hours. It once contained a brain that thought itself immortal. Now it was scoured and bleached and empty, leaving no trace of the brain, and I thought how the brain thinks of almost every part of the human body with interest except of the skull that covers it. Yet when all is gone to dust the skull alone remains. I came to the conclusion that man has a long way to go yet before he reaches the use of reason, which is a proper sense of proportion. But you'll be coming to see me soon, doctor, I hope."

He got to his feet.

"Yes," said the doctor, "I'll come to see you."

"It's the only pleasure I have," said the old man, "talking to you. Good day to you."

He went out.

"It's a bad cut," said the doctor, tying up the bandage. "Use the hand as little as possible."

"Right," said O'Neill. "Thanks."

He was rushing away as soon as the bandage was tied.

"Wait," said the doctor.

"What do you want?" said O'Neill.

The doctor caught the lobe of his right ear and pulled it.

"I found out why you laughed this morning," he said.

"You have?" said O'Neill. "I don't know what you're talking about."

"I might have saved that soul from unhappiness," said the doctor, "if you hadn't turned up like a demon and dragged her down again. I wish your throat were cut instead of your wrist."

"I have no time," said O'Neill, dashing out. "I'll settle with you later."

The doctor sat down and put his head between his hands. As if the cup of his skull had been emptied and scoured, he sat without thought, listening to the sounds of life outside. These sounds had no meaning individually and the rumbling of a cart was identical with the musical sounds drawn from his accordion by the blind man who stood outside the post office. The squealing of the dog that limped away with a broken leg from its enemy outside the bank was identical with the neighing of the horse that drew the rumbling cart. But altogether, the sounds had a very interesting meaning, other than their actual meaning, to his brain, which had left his polished skull, forsaking in disgust its human habitation, where there was only sorrow and disillusion. It soared away into that vague place, where the mind always soars when it contemplates the universe. Thence it looked down, listened, heard the sounds of life and strained with all its powers to understand their meaning. They became amorphous. They lost comparison. Pain became identical with pleasure, sorrow with joy, anger with love. Then they lost the attributes of time and space. The whole of existence became a sound, undulating in a beautiful harmony, good and evil balanced to maintain beauty on its throne.

He shook his head and said to himself:

"What I need is passion. I should have loved her like an animal."

The sounds then became real. He got up and went to the window. A motor lorry was coming into the square from the direction of Main Street. There were banners floating over it and there were men sitting on a seat at the rear, playing brass instruments. He recognised, among those sitting in front, Fr. Fogarty, Mr. Fitzpatrick, and Mr. Costigan, the Chairman of the County Council. There were others whom he did not recognise. A crowd was gathering from all directions.

"No," he said. "There is no sense in it. None whatsoever. I wonder what's going to happen to her now?"

There was a spider's web on the top, left-hand corner of the window. The spider, within his web, was fighting some sort of an insect that had crawled into the web. The insect was a reptile of some sort. The doctor leaned against the window-sill and watched the fight. The spider was dashing about in a frenzied fashion, running back and forth among the alley-ways of his web, attacking the reptile on the flank and being continually routed: at least, so it seemed. The reptile always joined the ends of its body when the spider approached. Then it straightened itself, with the reverse action of a bow shooting an arrow.

The doctor tried to determine whether the spider was trying to drive away the reptile or to capture it and whether the reptile had been trapped by the web or had come in deliberately to attack the spider. He also wondered whether the reptile was more powerful than the spider, since it pursued, apparently, more powerful defensive tactics, and was definitely advancing for the apparent purpose of driving the spider into a corner. But then, he took into consideration that the spider was noted for its cunning. It might be deliberately feigning retreat, defeat and hysterical movement, in order to decoy the reptile into an assailable position. These meditations were astonishingly interesting. He lost all interest in the motor lorry which had now halted in the middle of the square.

The music ceased. The crowd gathered round. A group of horsemen came from High Street into the square. A policeman halted them and told them that they could not come on horseback to the meeting. The horses might stampede in case of trouble. The horsemen galloped away, down a side-street, into the yard of a Temperance Hotel. The chairman o£ the meeting, Mr. Costigan, stood up on the lorry and took off his wide-brimmed, black hat.

He mopped his face with a red handkerchief. He was a short, portly man, dressed in a blue serge suit, that shone at the seat. A gold medal glistened on his watch chain.

"Men and women of Barra," he began in a squeaky voice, "and of the surrounding districts. We are gathered here to-day to launch a campaign that may become a clarion call to our distracted country."

His voice carried all over the square. As soon as he commenced to speak, faces appeared at upper windows. Groups of people came from doorways towards the lorry.

"It's astonishing," thought the doctor, "with what savage enthusiasm and obstinacy the most, apparently, superfluous forms of life do their duty. Purely by instinct, I suppose. The spider looks like winning, whatever its purpose may be."

With all its legs stretched out, the spider now made curious movements, expanding and contracting, causing the whole fabric of the web to shake. The reptile became tied in a knot. Its wriggling grew less imposing. Suddenly both the spider and the reptile became motionless.

The doctor raised his head and looked out upon the square, where the lorry was now surrounded by a dense crowd. The people's heads were raised. The sun shone on their red, healthy faces. The doctor felt a thrill of pleasure. He realised how beautiful the human body was.

Mr. Costigan had his left hand raised above his head. He twirled his raised hand several times, twisting his body and shaking his head like a dog throttling a rat. Then he brought down his hand with tremendous force, looked about him and blew his nose. The people on the lorry clapped their hands. A man in the crowd yelled. Several people laughed, either at the yell or at Mr. Costigan.

All this appeared to be very vague to the doctor, as the spider and the reptile remained perfectly still, apparently in a swoon, either contemplating some fresh ruse, or fulfilling a mysterious ritual of insect war. His mind became interested in the contemplation of the folly of his own life. Pursuit and conquest, he thought, if one were to judge correctly that both the spider and the reptile had really been hysterical in their movements prior to becoming motionless, were really worthless compared to the subtle pleasure of understanding. Now both the spider and the reptile appeared to be defeated, since they lay motionless, either exhausted by their efforts or in doubt as to their further actions. Yet, he himself, being passive, had just experienced a great pleasure. He had become aware of the beauty of the human body.

Now he became interested in what was taking place in the square, but from an extraordinary angle. Seeing that nearly every mouth was open and that every eye looked towards the performers on the lorry, it became manifest to him that the desire to appreciate the full sensuous and mental pleasure to be derived from a phenomenon, by means of wonder, was probably the main instinct in life. That was probably why the spider, if it had won, as was very likely, was wasting time in watching the crippled reptile.

The solicitor, who had arisen to speak, was now the phenomenon in the square, as far as the crowd was concerned. But the doctor, looking through the window and standing apart, being gifted with the power of universal observation and being indifferent to the actions of the phenomenon and to the object of his activities, was able to appreciate not only the phenomenon of the solicitor, erect and about to speak, but also the phenomenon of the people, who were watching and trying to appreciate the phenomenon of the standing solicitor.

Striking his narrow chest and twisting sideways the upper part of his body, like a man going to strike a hopping handball in a handball court, Mr. Fitzpatrick, the solicitor, said:

"The hour has struck, when the people of Barra and the surrounding district and of the whole country," waving his arms, "must root out the cancer that is eating into the heart of their social life. I refer to the curse of usury, the curse of the middle-man, the stranglehold on the life of the community by the greed and oppression of men all over the country, who, by their ... "

"He can't talk for tripes," said Finnigan to Mr. Matthews, the engineer, as they both issued, unsteadily, followed by their cronies, from the hotel into the square.

"Aren't you a middle-man yourself?" cried Bob Finnerty, the labour union organiser. "It's not people like you is going to free the people from oppression. It's up to the working" class to ... "

"Soup ! " yelled a big man, who strolled into the square from High Street. "Soup! A bowl of soup!"

The big man was dressed in grey frieze trousers and in a blue jersey. His cap was on the side of his head. He had long, fair moustaches. He had a beautifully muscular body. He swayed as he walked.

Still the spider and the reptile remained motionless. The doctor, looking at them, thought that, even though they remained motionless, they were more interesting in their immobility than the people in the square, whose actions and words seemed to deteriorate in importance owing to their anarchy and their detachment from their natural environment. Then he thought that the creative faculty, especially in a human organism that was too weak to give it expression, was a great menace to the true understanding and enjoyment of life. He understood, as a consequence, that his life hitherto had been confused and anarchical and detached from its natural environment because he had endeavoured, without just reason, to lead a creative life, in the sphere of idealising the social relationships of human beings, with emphasis on the cultural and artistic results of the life he had in view. In that he had failed. His failure had perverted his judgment of ordinary phenomena. Now it became obvious to him that he was really equipped for leading an analytical life, for accepting reality and for influencing his fellow-creatures towards the pursuit of beauty by moving inwards on his own soul, just as the spider had done, instead of trying to move his own soul outwards into the souls of others, after the manner of the solicitor and the reptile; the solicitor, of course, being, at the moment, merely the representative of the whole class of men, obviously the most ridiculous kind of proselytisers, who entered other people's webs, under the pretence of trying to improve them.

In that case it was false and unjust to have tried to remedy the disharmony in Nora's life. It was equally false to have sided with the people against Ramon Mor, or to have adopted any attitude towards Ramon Mor, other than that of intellectual and sensuous interest. It was still more false to have suggested to the people that they were under the influence of priestly superstitions, since all priests, gods and religions owed their reality and existence to the existence in the minds of the people of a desire for mystical exaltation. Finally, it was false to be led by envy and fear into antagonism to an individual like Ramon Mor, who by his movements and the manifestation of the creative impulse in him, following a definite purpose, purely by instinct, in all directions, variously, gave pleasure to the contemplative mind.

As for Nora, his attitude towards her henceforth must be one of simple admiration, being aware of her existence and seeing in her, purely in thought, the beauty, to a superlative degree, of all well-formed bodies.

He flushed. Although the spider now moved, running hither and thither through its web, weaving, growing less, spinning the substance of its belly-bag, he noticed the insect no longer and took no interest in its movements. The beauties of life rose before his mind in wonderful harmony. Mr. Fitzpatrick, the solicitor, continued to talk strenuously. He said that the people must rouse themselves from their apathy, take their courage in both hands, organise, put faith in their leaders, whom they saw before them there that day on the lorry, and march forward. Where? A hubbub prevented the people from learning where they were expected to march. The big man in the gansey kept calling out the word "soup" in a loud voice. Tommy Derrane, the insane man from the islands, began to address a portion of the crowd. Bob Finnerty, the labour union organiser, who had been arguing with two farmers, was touched on the shoulder by a policeman and ordered to move away.

"What do I care what people say I am?" cried Finnerty, as he was pushed away. "I'll tell you if you want to know. I'm a Communist."

"My good man," said Mr. Hennessy, the district superintendent of police, who passed just then, going the rounds of his men, "nobody cares a dog's flea what you are. Can't you be quiet and not make trouble for everybody?"

Looking at the reptile which was now obviously dead and tightly imprisoned in countless sticky strands of the web, the doctor regarded the future with enthusiasm. He saw his children growing up about him, each one beautiful. Be watched their growth, feeling the delicious tenderness which birth and growth and innocence always inspired in him. His irritation against injustice would now become a sense of proportion, which was, of course, reason, inasmuch as it would measure correctly and balance, not individually but by taking all cases collectively, the beauty of growth against the struggle for existence, with its attendant cruelties. Even old age would be equally beautiful, though less resplendent, since it completes the harmony of a perfect circle, by contrasting the dignity of experience with the passionate energy of youth. Henceforth, he would truly appreciate his wife, no longer seeking in her all the qualities which the folly of idealism seeks in one individual, instead of observing them with pleasure in various individuals, without aiming at possession. He would be henceforth indifferent to fame, to the opinions of his enemies, to the irritations of society. Henceforth he would see that life was good and beautiful in all its manifestations, when absorbed by the senses without fear and judged by an unprejudiced intellect. Henceforth evil would cease to have a meaning, since even fog, rain and hail were really useful contrasts to the sun's heat and light, and therefore a measure of the sun's beauty. Existence itself in its simplest form, the act of inhaling air into the lungs, would be as beautiful as its most complex manifestation, the act of love, fully enjoyed both physically and mentally. All human beings became beautiful and lovable, each after its kind, one by the beauty of its body, another by its wit, another by its gentleness, another by its courage, another by its ferocity; others acting as contrasts by their cruelty, ugliness, stupidity, by being diseased, criminal, insane, perverted. All their activities became beautiful, their marriages, their drinking, their dancing, their sowing, their reaping, their dying, their birth, their wailing, their laughter, their games, their love their hatred, their wars; all the many-formed movement of their collective life. After them came the animals, the birds, the insects, the earth itself, the sea, the firmament with its countless worlds and its milky way, where the spawn of unborn worlds float in space, waiting for the spark of life. From whom? That did not matter now, to his mind, ruminating on beauty, right to the dissolution of his existence, his disembodiment, his decay, his return to the earth, the earth's bursting, becoming spawn, which, in its turn, floats in space, waiting for the spark of life. From nobody. A circle has no beginning once it is completed.

"Obviously," he said aloud, thrusting his thin hands into the pockets of his shabby trousers, "the best thing that could happen is that he should die this very day, at least as far as I am concerned. He's done for. I can see that. Let him die. In any case, it would be merely rank hypocrisy to suggest to him, or even to my own conscience, that I could save him now. He has gone too far. Then, in the name of common sense, why should I not want him to die at once before he has me dismissed from my job? Tut, tut. Very often, I am inclined to think, duty and conscience are just other names for sentimentality. Why should I worry about him or about her, either? She is obviously the sort of woman who ruins every man that comes under her influence. No, thanks. I am very well rid of her. Every man for himself. I'll go home. It looks as if there is going to be trouble here. Silly fellow, that Fitzpatrick. I rather think, though, that Fr. Fogarty is not entirely a bad fellow."

He put on his hat and left the room. As he was walking around the square, going homewards, he glanced at the lorry and saw that Fr. Fogarty was now addressing the people. He paused to listen for a few seconds. He noticed that the people were paying great attention to what Fr. Fogarty was saying. There were frequent murmurs of approval.

He thought that it might be useful to make amends with Fr. Fogarty and even conform outwardly, insofar as religion was concerned, not only by attending the services and receiving the sacrament, but also by word of mouth. Fr. Fogarty was very likely to succeed Ramon Mor should the latter die, as the chief man in the district. That would make life more pleasant, as Fr. Fogarty had ideas above the ordinary in the matter of culture. Would it really benefit the people? He shrugged his shoulders, continued his journey, passed out of the square into Railway Street, and out of Railway Street into his home, disappearing, utterly indifferent to the welfare of the town, to the welfare of the people, to the welfare of humanity, to justice, and really, if the truth were known, to beauty itself.

"That's a rotten, cowardly fellow, that doctor," said Tynan, the farmer, who had seen the doctor pass.

"Yes," said Mr. Matthews, the engineer, casually, "he's a bit of a funk. Hello! What's going to happen now?"

A crowd of peasants, islanders and fishermen appeared in High Street, coming towards the square. From the raised ground on which they stood outside the bar-room window of the hotel, Finnigan and his friends saw this fresh crowd approach, over the heads of the crowd that surrounded the lorry. Being drunk and having no social consciousness, Finnigan, the hotel-keeper, Tynan, the farmer, Mr. Matthews, the engineer, Dooley, the schoolmaster, Sweeney, the clerk of the district court, Timmins, the excise officer, Connors and Timoney, rival cattle-jobbers, Doyle, the commercial traveller, and Danvers, the degenerate, who had crawled back into the company, began to giggle and to nudge one another, realising that there was going to be a riot.

The people on the lorry, facing the hotel and the sun, did not see the crowd that was approaching from the sea.

"Friends," said Fr. Fogarty, standing elegantly, with his right, well-manicured hand on his hip and his left hand holding out his silver-topped cane in gesture, "you quite understand how difficult it has been for me to thrust myself thus forcibly into public life and to face a task which I would gladly place on other shoulders. You understand I trust, that it was not through motives of self-interest that I chose to throw down the gauntlet in defence of the people and to attack a system of..."

"No, no," cried the people, now enthusiastic, carried away by the honey of his words.

"A system," he continued, "that is so bound up with the personality of one man, that it becomes identical with that man, that I am forced to the conclusion that that man must be brought to heel before ... "

"Hurrah! Hurrah for Ramon Mor! " cried the crowd that now debouched into the square from the Fish Market.

Fr. Fogarty started, stopped speaking and looked behind him. All the people on the lorry looked behind them. For a moment there was dead silence in the audience. Then a murmur passed from end to end of the multitude, there was a shuffling of feet, as the name rang out again:

"Ramon Mor! Hurrah for Ramon Mor!"

When two clouds, big with rain, clash in the firmament and the shock of their bursting shakes the earth beneath and the echoes roll afar in the thunder, even the insects shudder in the grass. So now this name struck terror into those that had been on the point of rising in revolt against its possessor.

"Hurrah! Hurrah for Ramon Mor!"

"Costello! Costello! "

The rival crowd advanced, shouting. The audience drew back from the lorry. Fr. Fogarty commenced to speak once more, but now he spoke jauntily and his voice had lost its persuasiveness. The people no longer listened to him.

Then Ramon Mor appeared in the wake of his followers, followed himself by another crowd.

"Costello! Hurrah for Ramon Mor!"

He was mounted on a dray-horse which carried neither saddle nor bridle. It was the first thing that came to his hand when he got news of the meeting. He had been in the courtyard of his shop, settling a dispute about some oats which a party of peasants from a distant village wished to purchase in common. The dray-horse stood nearby. It had just been taken from its cart to feed. He mounted it and rode out into the market-place. There he harangued the islanders, fishermen and peasants. They advanced into the square. He followed, when he had rallied a sufficient number to make his appearance impressive.

The horse had enormous feet and just a wisp of a tail, like a stuffed sock. But its majestic size, the depth of its great chest, its neck that was like a slanting tower, its enormous haunches, its flanks that glistened when it moved, rippling its powerful muscles, its grooved, broad back, suited the giant that sat astride it, with one hand grasping the ribboned mane. Its colour was a dappled grey. Ramon was dressed in grey, with a face that was blood-red with anger.

Men walked on either side of the horse's head.

There was dead silence in the square. All watched the strange spectacle in wonder. Those that had watched from windows now came from their houses. Tradesmen left their shops. The barber came in his apron. The whole town gathered. The square became full to its pavements.

The stolid horse advanced straight to the motor lorry, striking the ground majestically with its heavy hoofs. Ramon Mor sat motionless upon its back, his left hand on his thigh, his right hand grasping the mane. His head was crouched.

Fr. Fogarty turned to face his enemy.

Mr. Hennessy, the district superintendent of police, followed by his men, pushed his way through the crowd to the lorry and towards Ramon Mor, who had almost reached the lorry. People on the outskirts of the crowd dashed to the pavements; but they rushed back again almost at once, unable to tear themselves away, although they feared a riot. Ramon told his men to hold the horse's head. The horse halted.

Then Ramon stretched out his right hand towards the lorry, made a semicircular sweep with his left hand and cried out in a loud voice, that carried far beyond the square:

"I'm here now to defend myself. If they have anything against me, let them say it to my face. I'm listening."

There was dead silence. The superintendent of police had now reached the lorry.

"Superintendent Hennessy," said Fr. Fogarty, in a calm almost contemptuous voice, "I ask you to maintain order at my meeting. Otherwise I can't ... "

"Your meeting ! " shouted Ramon Mor. "Your meeting, is it?"

He sat erect on his horse and threw out his two arms to their full length. He held them out for a few moments, rigid. Youth seemed to possess him. For his body appeared lithe and mobile. The gross swellings of age were concealed by the great force of his gesture, stretching his limbs, as if to rend his enemies.

Now he looked away from the people on the lorry. He withdrew his arms. He bent his head and swung himself, first to the right, then to the left, swinging his hands on the axes of his elbows, as if to touch each member of the multitude.

Mr. Hennessy raised his hat to Fr. Fogarty, shook his head and then climbed nimbly into the lorry.

"Men and women of Barra," cried Ramon, "I am a proud man because I come of a proud stock that never bent the knee nor asked for favour from friend or foe. For a long time I have known that lies and scandalous rumours have been spread far and wide in this town and countryside about me. But I took no notice. I never opened my mouth in the market-place nor at the chapel gate to defend myself. Because I never turn on a cur, nor on a worm, nor on a sneaking scandalmonger. But the time has come when I must speak and defend myself, when a conspiracy has been set on foot to make me a beggar and an outcast." He stretched out his two hands towards the lorry.

"Choose now," he cried, "between them."

He struck his chest with both hands and added :

"And me."

He paused. He glanced around him slowly. There was dead silence. The superintendent was whispering to Mr. Fitzpatrick, who appeared to be in a state of extreme fear.

"If you choose to follow them," cried Ramon, shaking his clenched fist above his head, "take the consequences."

He lowered his fist slowly and looked about him fiercely.
Then he continued;

"I ask for no mercy, and I give none. Let them start their co-operative societies. Let them make me a pariah among my people. Let them pull the roof from over my head. Let them send me to my grave. Let them send my old mother begging her bread. Let them desecrate the grave of my ancestors. Let it be said from end to end of the country that the people of Barra bit the hand that fed them. Let it be said that they made war on their own flesh and blood. Let it be said that they became the tools of the cunning lawyer and of the ambitious priest and of the corrupt politician and of the bankrupt shopkeeper and of all the cut-throat brigands and ne'er-do-well fanatics that have plotted against me and have organised this meeting and have even sneaked into my home .... "

Suddenly his voice rose almost to a shriek and he clutched his chest as if to tear the clothes of it and cried :

"They have even sneaked into my home with their poison."

He paused, drew back and then pointed sideways, with one hand, open, horizontal on his chest, the other, open and horizontal, stretched out full length towards the lorry. A great murmur rose among the people and feet shuffled.

"But if you choose to follow me," he continued suddenly, striking his chest and lowering his head, "I'll do what I was going to do, when you listened to the whisperings of my enemies and turned against me. For two years now ... "

His voice became pathetic.

"My life has been a misery to me. I felt a gap between me and those of my own flesh and blood."

He raised his right hand, threw out his chest and his voice became triumphant.

"But that gap is going to remain no longer between me and my people, for I'm going to come and open my heart to the people, and I'm going to tell them what it's in my heart. Men and women of Barra, I'm going to throw every penny I possess at your feet. If you work with me and help me ... "

He paused, brought down his raised hand heavily into his left palm and said:

"There won't be a poor man within twenty miles of this square."

There was a roar. The crowd rocked. Hats and caps were thrown into the air. Before the cheering ceased, Ramon Mor cunningly goaded their enthusiasm towards greater transports, by shouting louder than the cheers:

"I'm going to put a fleet of trawlers on the bay."

"Hurrah for Ramon Mor!"

"I'm going to build a big hotel."

"Costello ! Costello ! "

"I'm going to build a kelp factory."

"King of Barra ! Your ancestors were kings."

"I have other schemes in my mind that I won't go into here, but I swear to you, by my father's grave, that I won't stop, while God leaves breath in my body, until I have made this town, this countryside and this people the envy of the land."

The shout that greeted his last words drowned the report of a revolver shot. Another shot rang out. The people heard it. They stopped cheering. There was still another shot. The police began to run out of the crowd. Everybody began to talk excitedly. Mr. Fitzpatrick lay down on the floor of the lorry. Mr. Hennessy jumped to the ground. Fr. Fogarty, still calm and almost contemptuous, raised his cane and said:

"Keep calm. There's no danger."

Ramon Mor, so carried away by his speech that he did not hear the shots, was about to continue, when he heard a cry:

"Robbers! Robbers! Stop them." The voice came from the direction of the Fish Market. The people all looked that way. A Ford motor-car, with the hood raised, white with dust, came into the square from High Street, turned sharply to the right, almost striking the lamp-post at the corner, and went at full speed towards Main Street.

"Stop them. Stop them. Robbers."

A bare-headed man came running up High Street, shouting and waving his arms. Policemen ran towards him. Three more shots were fired from the Ford car as it turned into Main Street.

"Commandeer a car," shouted the superintendent of police. "Take every car you find."

"Get after them," shouted everybody.

"What's up now?" whispered Ramon stupidly to the man that held his horse's head.

Suddenly the illusion of youth had left his body. He became lax, bloated and powerless.

"I don't know," said the man. "Whist! Here's Mr. Feeney."

The bare-headed man was Ramon Mor's manager. As he approached Ramon, he threw his arms above his head and began to stammer :

"They ... they robbed us and we ... and we taking the money to the bank. They took ... they, they, they ... they took it all."

Ramon shuddered.

"Who?" he said. "What are you saying?" "Three ... three men in a car, just as we .. . they came up ... point-blank ... masked and . .. it was so sudden ... "

"They robbed ... "

"All. Every penny."

"All?"

"They grabbed the bag. O'Rourke just ... "

"Robbed!"

Ramon raised his clenched fists to his ears and cried out in a voice that was like that of a wounded animal:

"I've been robbed. Robbed! In my own town! Robbed! Plundered! I'm disgraced. Ruined! Oh! God Almighty! Before my eyes ! I'm stabbed to the heart."

He shook his trembling hands at the motor lorry, which was now hooting and trying to move off through the dense crowd.

"They did it," he cried. "It was they did it. It's their work. My money! No insult could be worse. In my own town! They have torn out my heart. My curse on them! "

He was now a pitiable sight, repulsive, his face distorted. He crawled off his horse, moving his limbs helplessly, palsied like a decrepit old man. There was a wandering look in his eyes. His fingers were turned in upon his palms. His shoulders were drawn up.

People began to threaten those on the lorry with their fists. Fr. Fogarty, feeling that, for the present at least, he was in the wrong camp, stepped off the lorry. The people began to shout.

"It's Fitzpatrick's work. The crooked lawyer."

"Look at Costigan. That wicked old scoundrel."

"It was them spread the lies about Fr. Considine, too."

"The blasphemers."

"They've been at their dirty work all along."

"Let's pull them off the lorry and beat hell out of them."

"See? The priest has left them. Pull them off the lorry."

"Down with Skinny Jack!"

"Costigan, the ward heeler! "

"He sold his country."

"Soup ! " yelled the big man in the blue jersey. "I want to fight. Let me at Skinny Jack. His grandfather changed his religion for a bowl of soup. I want to fight."

People ran after the moving lorry. They jumped up at the back. They seized the musical instruments and smashed them. They threw the musicians off the lorry. They seized Fitzpatrick and Costigan. Police drew their batons. The lorry stopped as the driver was dragged from his seat by the scruff of the neck. Somebody threw a stone. A woman screamed.

In a flash, rioting began. Everybody struck at his neighbour. Peasants called out the names of their villages as battle-cries.

The dray-horse stampeded.

Supported by his friends, Ramon staggered over to the post office, dazed, trembling, muttering :

"Robbed! They have torn the heart out of me. Get me my money!"

They put him sitting on a chair in the post office and a man went to fetch some brandy.

The superintendent of police came in and said to Ramon:

"The telephone wires have been cut, sir, but we'll get them all the same. Don't worry, Mr. Costello. I'll have both the men and the money before morning."

He dashed out again.

"Morning I" mumbled Ramon. "What morning?"

They brought him the brandy. He drank a little. Then he got to his feet and shouted :

"Where is my wife? Eh? Where is my wife? Bring me my car."

"It's gone, sir," said a clerk. "The police took it." "Get me a horse, then, a cart, anything. I want to see my wife. Quick, blast it. Quick!"

PART III
NEMESIS

CHAPTER XVIII

HE had seen her in the church when he had gone to fetch the Host from the tabernacle. The messenger had told him that Ramon Mor was dying, and he had come prepared to administer the last sacraments.

That was why he had kept looking behind him furtively while he was talking to Ramon. He was afraid she might escape him, and that somebody might prevent him from returning to her in the church.

Yet, when he left Ramon's office, he did not return by the shortest route, which lay by High Street into the square, across the square into Main Street, to the right through Prior's Lane, past the ruins of the Cistercian Monastery into Monastery Place. The church lay at the far end of Monastery Place, in front of the cemetery, which lay beyond, on the outskirts of the town, overlooking a green meadow.

Although he was not conscious of returning to the church with a purpose that would necessitate secrecy, he chose a roundabout route, going across the Fish Market on to the Lower Quay, then up by the coal-yard, then by Cross Street to the Junction of Main Street and New Street, as if he were going to his own home. In fact, he was not conscious of his movements and never answered the salutations of the groups of idle fishermen, who still loafed on the quay wall watching the tide, which had again begun to ebb. A violent whispering was going on in his mind. It was quite unintelligible, except for an occasional phrase that detached itself from the mass of nonsense.

When he came to the cross-roads he halted. His mind cleared, and he was surprised to find himself glancing all round cautiously, lest he might be noticed. Then he vaguely realised why he was returning to the church and was horrified at the idea. He even tried to force himself to the right along the road that led to his own house. But a voice which he did not recognise as his own called out brutally, without making any sound:

"Come on. This is not the time to argue about it."

He trembled and hurried across the yard. He walked a little way up New Street, towards the gate of Ramon Mor's demesne. Then he turned sharply to the left, into a lane called Railway Cottages. That lane led to the church. Ragged children scurried away as he passed. He reached the church and entered the sacristy. He hung his hat behind the door.

There was an odour o£ incense there. He sniffed at it. The embroidered hem of an alb protruded from a drawer of the tall-boy that contained his vestments. He went over to the tall-boy and fondled the hem of the alb. Then he glanced to the right, towards the door that led into the church from the sacristy. It lay slightly ajar. Was she still there?

He shuddered. Wetting his lips with his tongue, he sank down on his knees, put the hem of the alb to his face and began to kiss it. Then he dropped the alb, leaned back, and put his hands to his face, as if shielding himself from somebody that threatened him. Still with his hands to his face, he got to his feet, slowly took away his hands and looked at the ceiling.

"Yes, yes," he whispered. "I obey. I obey. Have mercy on me."

Then he breathed deeply, stood erect, thrust out his chest, joined his fingers in front of his chest and marched to the door of the sacristy. His face became stern. The whispering, which had begun once more in his brain while he was kissing the hem of the alb, now ceased. His eyes became extraordinarily brilliant. His blood itched.

He cautiously pushed the door wide open and advanced into the church. There was complete silence there. It was speckled with coloured shadows, caused by the sunbeams that came slant-wise through the stained-glass window.

The long windows with curved heads reproduced themselves on opposite walls, intermingling slant-wise. Christ, with His cross, on fourteen mural tablets, crowned with thorns, lashed, bleeding, macabre, shone yellowishly.

He walked slowly along the narrow strip of carpet straight ahead for seven paces, then sharply to the left for six paces. He halted, turned to the altar, paused, genuflected, rose, turned to the baptismal font, walked three paces to the communion rails, leaned his hands against the white communion cloth and shuddered. He saw her, stretched out, asleep, on the priest's tomb. He contemplated her for a long time, perfectly motionless, thoughtless, as if he were dead. Then he pushed aside the wicket gently, passed into the aisle and closed the wicket behind him. He twisted his head suddenly towards the altar, stooped with his head twisted, dropped his lower lip and closed his right eye. His forehead wrinkled and tremors passed along his cheeks. Then he turned his head to the baptismal font, closed his lips tightly and advanced slowly on tiptoe, making no sound.

When he was within a foot of her outstretched hand he halted. Trembling, he stooped, stretching down his right hand, until his fingers were within a few inches of her hand. He raised his hand and shook it as if he had put it too near a flame. He breathed on his fingers. Still stooping, holding his breath, he glanced over her body eagerly. Her wrist was bare. Her sleeve was drawn upwards by the position in which she lay. There was a watch on her wrist. A lace frill protruded from her sleeve.

He rose hurriedly, glancing at her heaving white throat as he rose. Then he was attracted by her bust. He withdrew his eyes hurriedly, but as he raised them to avoid seeing her bust, they saw her golden hair shimmering in the fading sunrays. He angrily lowered his eyes, turning his head slightly; but his eyes saw the beautiful boles of her legs and he could not prevent them from pausing to admire their beautiful roundness, their curves, their silken clothing.

With his head turned away, he bent down several times, with his hands stretched out to touch her, but he withdrew his hand each time when he was within a few inches of her. He shook his head and walked around her on tiptoe. He went to the confessional box that stood to the right of the baptismal font. He opened the door of the box, entered, closed the door, sat down, uncovered the grille and watched her. She still slept, breathing softly. The sunbeams faded. It grew chilly in the church. She began to shudder in her sleep. She moved. She awoke, raised her head, listened, looked around and said in a whisper:

"Where am I? Good God I In the church. How horrible! Look! I'm lying on a grave. How did I get here? Where is my bag? Heavens! I must go at once. What time is it? The train is going. But I have no money. No. No. He'll come. Oh! Aunt, why didn't I write to you? I must hurry."

She got to her feet, picking up her hat and her handbag. He

became very excited and experienced great difficulty in preventing himself from stretching out his hands to fondle the nape of her neck, which was within four feet of him when she stood up. She walked away hurriedly towards the door.

Suddenly he became exalted. The blood rushed to his head. Whirling lights appeared before his eyes. He tried to rise, in order to rush upon her, but his muscles refused to act. Perspiration poured down his face. She passed out of the church. He became rigid. His face became cold. His toes itched. His muscles acted. He opened the door of the box, stepped out and ran towards the church door on tiptoe, careless of the sound he made. When he reached the door and looked out, he saw her walking towards Railway Cottages. He waited until she had entered the lane. Then, as if he was about to follow her, he started looked back towards the baptismal font and examined the ground where she had lain. There was nothing there.

Good!

Then he closed the church door and hurried towards the lane. It was getting dusk. He kept her in sight, at a distance. She kept looking anxiously from side to side, but she never looked back. Sometimes he lost sight of her for a moment. Every time he lost sight of her he became possessed by a terrible fury. As soon as he caught sight of her again, he grew calm. His mind was absolutely devoid of thought. At a distance of about fifty yards he followed her into New Street. He started when he saw her pass the entrance to Ramon Mor's demesne and continue along the road that led towards the mountains. He smiled faintly and then wetted his lips with his tongue. His forehead began to twitch.

People were returning to the mountains, in carts, on horseback and on foot. Dusk hid the dust of their passage, and in an undertone, to the raucous overtones of their singing, the tramping of their weary feet, the rumbling of their carts, the trotting of their horses, mingled with the sounds of falling night; falling among the shadows from the heights on to the plain and to the darkening town the evening echoes came, of asses braying, of cows lowing, of blackbirds singing, of curlews crying wildly to the night, returning from their marshes to the sea-rocks, whence they had arisen at dawn to hail the rising sun.

She passed unnoticed, walking on the grass by the roadside, her golden hair now colourless in the dusk. Their weary eyes were careless of her beauty. And he, following her, also passed unnoticed, the dusk concealing his blackness, as it concealed her golden glory.

The road ascended. Lights began to glimmer on the hillsides. There were lights upon the sea, from boats returning to the islands. There, too, upon the flat white bay, was the sound of rolling song, a laughing shriek, thole-pins being struck, the creaking sound of a sail being raised. Upon the plain, a train rumbled over its winding road, and shrieked, departing.

Shrieking, whistling, singing, calling to the night, the fair vanished.

He crept closer, fearing he might lose her in the darkness. She turned to the right into the lane that led to the yellow strand by the far wall of the demesne. He crept still closer to her on entering the lane. Now he could not see her. It was almost pitch-dark in the lane. But he could hear the sound of her footsteps. Thick bushes lined the lane on the left. On the right rose the wall of the demesne, tall, covered with ivy. Birds, startled by her passage, came flying into his face. There were bats. A frog croaked by a pool The murmur of the sea became distinct. The air became salty. Suddenly the bushes disappeared and the lane was bound on the left by a stone wall. He saw the great shadow of the Black Cliff above, with its protruding snout of stone. He halted until she passed the cottage and turned to the left to climb the cliff-path. He followed her, stooping, along the wall. He also began to climb the cliff path. He could see her above him, ascending, a round, black spot among the rocks. There was hardly any light. The sound of the sea became louder. Rock-birds were croaking on their ledges. Seagulls swooped over him. He could hear her panting quite near him. She had reached the summit. She began to speak. No. She was crying. No. Yes. She was crying and talking also. He came a little nearer and threw himself flat on the rock to listen to her.

"Francis!" she said. "Where are you? Are you here? Francis!"

He turned his head to the right. The edge of the cliff was within a foot of his face. Without seeing it actually, he saw, in his mind, the face of the precipice stretching down steeply to the dark sea, that heaved back and forth, licking the black rocks. He smelt the emptiness and thought how rapidly a thing fell, whirling, down into the sea, that swept it westwards on the ebbing tide into the ocean, between waters, to the depths where sharks upturned their pale bellies, opened their jaws and snapped at their prey. The sea did not always deliver up her dead; not as it fell, but in sand; or mummified, it was found by hewers, embodied in rocks, unrecognisable.

Then he crawled forward on his hands and knees. A. seagull rustled its great wings, swooping inquisitively.

"Francis ! " she whispered. "Is that you?"

He raised his head. She had seen him. It was less dark now. He was at the summit. He could see her quite distinctly, against the horizon of the sea that stretched away to the west. He saw the spike of stone to her right. On her left was the stone wall and beyond it, the craggy field. The crag was covered with rows of splintered rocks, like teeth, lying flat, creeping to the cliff. The mountains lay behind. The sky was growing clear. His head alone was visible to her. Then he got to his feet. She gasped.

With his hands hidden behind his back he moved towards her slowly. She did not move her feet as he approached, but she leaned back, stretching out her hands. A hoarse voice began to scream in his head, and he saw a hunchback, with one eye in the centre of his forehead, dashing through a lane, with a child, which was screaming for its mother. The screaming became louder and louder, as a flock of sea-birds, startled by the moaning of a seal, flew from their ledge and whirled round and round. He opened his mouth wide and the screaming ceased. He took his hands from behind his back. She gasped and put her hands to her breasts, dropping her handbag as she did so. He saw her eyes watching his hands. He was within a few inches of her. He looked down for a moment at his hands and saw them rising up. Then he said:

"Ha!"

He drew in his breath through his clenched teeth and then saw golden snakes as thin as hairs, passing back and forth through his teeth, that bit at them, tearing their heads off, until their bodies became limp and swayed backwards, and he lowered his hands to encircle them about the waist and savagely kissed them on the open lips and then flung them from him and became rigid as he saw them fall and disappear, creating by their disappearance a vision of a palace among the clouds, of a myriad of women, waiting in wanton postures for their lovers, who became one and identical with himself, armed with the amorous qualities of countless men, which qualities, towards all the women, he simultaneously squandered, thus abolishing by one enormous effort the will to love.

CHAPTER XIX

"COME on. Stop the car and let me get out. I'm not coming with you. I don't care what you say. I gave her my word of honour. I'm not going to break my word. Stop the car."

"You're drunk. Stay where you are."

"Stop the car, curse you, or I'll ... "

"All right. Go and be damned. Stop the car, Jimmy."

The car stopped, braked so suddenly that it skidded sideways and then came to a standstill, with a wisp of smoke rising from the radiator. The man in the tweed cap caught O'Neill by the shoulders and shook him.

"Wake up," he said, "you're drunk. Pull yourself together. It's a certainty that they'll catch you if you go back there."

"All right, Jack," said O'Neill. "I don't care. Give me some money. I promised her some money."

"What's all de lousy argument about?" said the driver excitedly. "Chuck him 'is stuff, and let's beat it. Chuck it at 'im."

"No ill feeling," said O'Neill.

The driver straightened out the car. The man in the tweed cap slashed with a knife the leather bag, plunged in his hands through the slit, grasped two handfulls of banknotes and began to count hurriedly.

"Doesn't matter," said O'Neill. "Hurry up. A few hundred is all she needs."

"In bundles of a hundred, I think," said the man in the tweed cap. "There's seven. You can rely on me, later if more is coming to you.

O'Rourke comes in on this too; ye see."

"Put it into my pocket," said O'Neill. "Doesn't matter." "Holy God!" said the man in the tweed cap. "We shouldn't leave him, Jimmy. He's stocious."

"Give 'im de bird, quick," said the driver. "Let's get out of here."

The man in the tweed cap stuffed the notes into O'Neill's breast pockets.

"For God's sake, Frank," he began ...

"Take 'is gun," said the driver. "That's my gat 'e's got."

"Gimme that, Frank," said the man in the tweed cap.

"Take it out of my pocket," said O'Neill. "I don't want it. I'll just go straight to her and give her this and say: 'Look here, I'm a ruined man, but I gave you my word of honour. That's the sort of fellow I am."

He staggered to his feet and fell on the road as he got out of the car.

"Leave her go to hell," cried the man in the tweed cap, preparing to jump out and drag O'Neill back into the car.

"Dat be damned," cried the driver, setting the car forward with a jerk.

O'Neill got to his feet, waved his hand at the car, which was already hidden by a cloud of dust and then turned backwards towards the Glen Tavern. He began to talk to himself.

"I'll go straight up there and wait for her," he said. "Then I'll give her this money and I'll tell her ... never mind. I'll just tell her that I love her but that ... God ! How I love you, golden head ! How I love you! They can hang me, but I'll still love you. I'll still love you, golden head, dead or alive. Nothing else matters. I'll give you this money. I robbed it for you, to put jewels in your golden hair. What does it matter if I became a robber on account of you? Sure, I'd do murder for you, if you asked me."

He walked in the centre of the road unsteadily, swinging his bandaged arm. The bandage had become bloody. there were stains of blood on his raincoat. His cap was at the back of his head. His dark curls hung down over his forehead. His eyes were bloodshot. He walked at a fast pace, thinking of her. He would go straight to the cliff, lie down and sleep, waiting for her to come. She would awaken him with her kisses. He would be sober then. She would take him by the hand and lead him away to some quiet place, where they would live together and start life afresh. Some day they would have a little child.

Tears flowed from his eyes. Yet, when he reached the cross-roads and saw the Glen Tavern facing him, instead of turning to the left along the mountain road by which he had come down that morning from the Black Cliff, he walked straight towards the tavern, without thinking of where he was going.

Two carts were in the yard. There were two women on one cart and a woman with two small children on the other. A white mare was harnessed to one cart, and a bay horse was harnessed to the other. The mare neighed, with her head raised, looking towards the mountains where she had left her foal that morning. Milk was coming from her taut udder, along the insides of her thighs. The bay horse had his head stretched out towards the mare, sniffing and wondering why she was neighing, because he smelt nothing on the air, towards the mountains, whither she was looking. The women were talking about the fair in plaintive voices. The children were eating candy, which had left its brown rime on their mouths. They all glanced at O'Neill and wrinkled their foreheads when they saw the blood-stained bandage.

There were two doors to the tavern. The door on the left led into the common bar, where peasants drank. The door on the right led into a porch. To the left of the porch there was a large kitchen. To the right there was a parlour, rather gaudily furnished, with naughty pictures on the walls and a piano which a pretty young woman was playing.

As soon as O'Neill entered the porch, the young woman stopped playing the piano and rushed towards him, crying :

"Hello! Frank, did you come to take me to the dance?"

O'Neill started when he saw her and realised where he had come, and that he should not be there. He turned about with the intention of leaving the house at once. But the girl threw her arms about his neck and whispered :

"Take me to the dance."

"Let me go," he said angrily. "What dance?"

"The dance at the town hall. You promised to take me. Have you been drinking? How horrid! Come in and sit down. God! You're tight."

"Let me alone," said O'Neill, angrily thrusting the girl away from him. "I'm in a hurry."

"Well, a mac, where is your hurry taking you?" said a fat old woman with a terribly dirty face, approaching him from the kitchen, with a tray, on which there was a bottle and four glasses.

"Good evening, Mother Stokes," said O'Neill. "I must be going. I'm in a hurry."

The old woman's sinful, ugly face creased as she laughed silently.

"Ha!" she said, winking at him slyly. "Was it you I saw in that Ford car that went by a minute ago? Some little bird ye picked up in Barra, was it?"

"Eh?" said O'Neill, shaking himself in order to overcome his drunkenness.

"I better stay here now," he thought. " I must explain. What must I explain?"

"Can you tell me the time?" he said. "I really came in to find out the time. My watch is stopped."

"Hurrah! there is no such thing as time," said the old woman, "as long as there's drink and women in the world."

"I think I can tell you the time," said a fat, bald-headed man, who was sitting in the parlour beside a girl with a painted face.

O'Neill went into the parlour towards the man who had spoken. The man was just taking his watch out of his waistcoat pocket when O'Neill said angrily:

"I don't want to know the time."

The man looked up in amazement and dropped his watch into his waistcoat pocket.

"Damn the time," said O'Neill.

"Look," said the painted girl. "He is covered with blood."

"Shut up," cried O'Neill. "What has it got to do with you?"

The bald-headed man, who had a face like a eunuch, looked around him gloomily, brushed his forehead with the tips of his fingers and said:

"This young lady is in my company."

"Be quiet now," said Mother Stokes, putting the tray on the table. "Lydia, pass around these drinks while I attend to the bar."

"Take no notice of that fellow," whispered Lydia in O'Neill's ear.

"I don't want to have anything to do with him," said O'Neill. "He insulted me, though."

"How have I insulted you?" said the bald -headed man, getting to his feet. "Your manners, sir, allow me to tell you, are those of a brute."

"I see," said O'Neill furiously. "I'm not wanted here. I'm going."

He really was not angry at all, but picked this quarrel with the other man in order to have an excuse for leaving the place at once without attracting too much attention.

"You had better," said the bald-headed man, "or otherwise I'll throw you out."

"Never in your natural life," said O'Neill, getting really angry and throwing his cap on the floor.

The bald-headed man changed his mind as soon as he saw O'Neill was getting ready to fight. He picked up his hat, walked hurriedly to the door and called out:

"Let me have my bill at once."

"Oh! I say," cried O'Neill. "Look here. I didn't want that. I'll go. You stay here."

"Let me have my bill," shouted the other man.

He went out into the porch and closed the parlour door behind him.

O'Neill dropped on to a couch, put his head in his hands and began to cry. The girl, called Lydia, came over and sat beside him.

"What's the matter, Frank?" she said. "How did you cut yourself? "

"Let me alone," moaned O'Neill. "I'm a ruined man. I'm in love."

He raised his head, beat his forehead with his clenched fists and cried out:

"I'm ruined. Why am I here? Why am I drunk? I'm ruined. Curse it. I curse God. I hate this world."

"Lord! He's in the jigs," said the painted girl, running out of the room.

Lydia left the couch and stood by the piano, looking at him nervously :

"What do you want?" said O'Neill to her savagely. "What are you grinning at?"

Mother Stokes returned to the room, followed by the painted girl.

"What's the matter with you, sonny?" she said to O'Neill. "Take a little drop of whisky. Maybe you were having some fun in the car and it unsettled your stomach."

O'Neill looked at the old woman pathetically.

"I'm a ruined man, Mother Stokes," he said. "I'm in love. I had no right to get drunk. I was told not to touch a drop. It's that damn doctor. I hate that man. It's no use trying, though. I can't pull myself together. I shouldn't be here. There's some witchery attached to this. Everybody is insulting me and I can't leave people alone. First it was Danvers and I cut my wrist. Now it's this fellow."

"Don't mind that fellow, Frank," said Lydia, coming over again, as she saw that O'Neill had become quieter.

"Nobody here likes him. He's only down on a holiday from the city. I think he's a shocking man."

She sat down on the couch and put her fingers in O'Neill's curls.

"Don't touch me," he said angrily.

She moved away a little.

"Leave him alone," said Mother Stokes. "Here, drink this. It will settle your stomach."

She poured out a glass of whisky from the bottle on the tray. It had been purchased by the fat man, who had gone away.

"Yes," said the painted girl. "He is a shocking man.

He brought two young fellows with him the first time he came and he watched them. Then he began to get ideas into his head himself. Mr. Matthews, the engineer, told me that he was a ... "

"Gossip," said the old woman. "Wash your face and plaster your tongue with the dirt. What nonsense are you saying? He's a prominent man and he gave a thousand pounds to the Vincent de Paul Society, for the poor people. Drink this."

O'Neill swallowed the glass of whisky the old woman had brought him. Then he began to sob once more.

"I'm a ruined man now," he said. "No matter what happens I'm done for. I deserted my old father and I shamed my sister, but there was always a chance of getting on my feet again. Now there is none. I'm in love. Do you know what love is? I tell you it's driven me mad. But I got to go."

He stood up. A motor-car went past in the road outside.

"Sit down and take a rest," said the old woman.

A young woman with a light shawl over her shoulders dashed into the room.

"What happened in the town?" she said excitedly. "First I saw a car covered with dust going past as I was talking to Mrs. Magee, at the cottage there below; then as I was coming along here just now, I slopped to say a word to Mrs. Rogers and a big car, I think it was Ramon Mor's car, only O'Rourke wasn't in it, it was Guard Luttrell was driving it, full of police, it came up from Barra, stopped, they had revolvers in their hands, and asked me did I see a car go by."

She paused for breath. O'Neill sat down and opened his mouth. The old woman looked at him shrewdly.

"So I says," continued the new-comer, "that a car, covered with dust, went towards Tullyfarnan and off they went like mad. I wonder what happened."

"Go out to the bar, Lydia," said the old woman coldly, "and see what those men want."

"Mother Stokes," called out a loud voice in the common bar.

O'Neill looked cautiously at the old woman, who followed Lydia out of the room. The painted girl and the new-comer went into a corner and began to whisper. O'Neill began to perspire. He tried to rise and go away, but the last glass of whisky had made him completely incapable of movement or of thought.

The old woman came back again. She had been whispering to Lydia in the kitchen. A peasant, wearing kneebreeches and leggings, with a pock-marked nose, appeared at the door of the parlour behind her.

"Go and lie down on the bed," she said to O'Neill. "Rest for a little while."

O'Neill looked at her.

"I hate this place," he said savagely. "I hate all this sin. You are all damned."

The peasant sidled into the parlour and began to light a cigarette.

"Play the piano," said the old woman to the painted girl. "Let's have some music."

O'Neill staggered to his feet, stared at the old woman and said: "Who are you?"

"Be quiet now," said the peasant, sidling over. "Don't start a row."

O'Neill sat down again on the couch. Suddenly there was a great uproar on the road outside and two motorcars drew up.

"Hello!" said the painted girl, rushing from the piano.

"That's Mr. Finnigan's voice."

She and the other woman ran out to the porch. Finnigan, Matthews, Tynan, Sweeney, Dooley, Timmins, Connors, Timoney, Doyle, Danvers and some others, who had later joined the company, all singing and shouting, carrying Farrelly, now came towards the tavern door.

"I must leave now," said O'Neill, getting to his feet.

"Take your time, and have a drink with the lads," said the old woman.

Suddenly O'Neill's head cleared and he saw that the old woman was trying to hold him until the police came. He moved towards the door.

The crowd of drunkards, entering, prevented his going out.

"Ho! Ho! My merry lads," cried Connors. "Look at what we've got."

"The lassie from the Clyde," said Tynan.

"And will ye look at Julia?" said Finnigan. "The taximan's wife! Where did ye leave your husband?"

Danvers, the degenerate, raised his voice and cried:

"We enter now the portals of concupiscence.

Let lust array her blandishments
And Bacchus cast aside the last restraint."

"What will we do with Farrelly?" cried Doyle.

"Leave him by the fire in the kitchen," said Sweeney. "Keep the parlour clean."

"Drink, drink," cried Timoney. "Gallons of it."

"Drink," cried Farrelly, being dragged, with his toes scraping the ground.

"Drink, said the fishwife to the magistrate, has brought me to this. Drink."

"Lydia is mine," said Matthews.

"Ha!" cried Finnigan. "Look at Frank. Here's where he got to. First come, first served. Come on, you codalogical codfish, we'll make a night of it."

"Let me go, Larry," said O'Neill "I'm in a hurry."

"The devil a go," said Connors. "No man must leave this house till morning."

They all rushed into the parlour, carrying O'Neill before them, except Farrelly, whom the pock-marked peasant stretched upon a form by the kitchen fire.

"Here I am," cried Tynan, hurtling lop-heavy to the floor. "The die is cast and now I go, a lonely soldier 'to face the foe."

Danvers, the degenerate, pointing at O'Neill, cried out:

"Where is she now? Where shines her golden head?"

"Light the lamps," cried Connors.

"Wait till I tell you," cried Finnigan, grasping O'Neill by the coat. "You lost it. Skinny Jack got codded at his meeting. You never saw the likes of it. Ramon Mor came ... "

"Mounted on a dray-horse," said Dooley.

"Who fired the shots?" cried Timoney.

"Every penny is gone," said Sweeney. "They've torn the heart out of me. Christ! He nearly fell off his horse."

"They'll catch them," said Matthews. "The law must be upheld!"

"Wait till I tell ye," said Finnigan. "You should see him going off on the baker's cart."

"Aye," said Doyle. "One minute he was sitting there like this, poof, with his cheeks swelled out and then he jumps to his feet."

"I want my wife, says he," cried Timmins.

"Who feeds among the lilies now?" cried Danvers, the degenerate.

"He went off on the baker's cart," cried Finnigan, "galloping like mad."

They all began to talk at once.

"They'll get them all right."

"O'Rourke is arrested."

"Not money. The wound lies deeper still."

"And when they sentenced him to die, the judge and jury ..."

"He! Hey! Hey I Don't let in those goats."

A herd of goats came bleating to the porch and thrust their heads into the kitchen, wanting to be milked. In the excitement nobody prevented them from entering the kitchen and they entered, filling the house with their stench.

And the drunkards tried to rush out into the kitchen to expel the goats. Some of them fell on the parlour floor and were unable to rise again. Tynan struck at Danvers, missed him and hit Timoney instead, who, returning the blow, felled Tynan like a log. O'Neill was pushed out into the kitchen with Finnigan, Matthews, Connors and Sweeney, who seized the goats and began to tussle with them. Farrelly rolled off his form, caught a goat by the hind leg and tried to suck her teat. O'Neill ran out of the house, followed by the pock-marked peasant who had been watching him all the time.

Outside the door, two peasants were mounting a springcart to which a skittish mare was harnessed. They were both very drunk. O'Neill asked them in which direction they were going.

"Jump up," they cried.

He jumped on to the hay that lay in the back of the cart. The two peasants sat on a board in front. They shook the reins. Snorting, the mare set off at a gallop.

"They're from Rossnacaorach, aren't they?" said the pock-marked fellow to a bystander.

"They are if they get there," said the bystander.

"Right," said the pock-marked peasant, returning to the tavern.

People shouted after the galloping horse. The two drunken peasants each took a rein and swaying from side to side, tugged at the mare in turns. Their hats fell off. Their coats dangled behind them. The mare, maddened by the disorderly driving, hurtled from side to side of the road. They began to climb the mountain.

"Hey!" cried O'Neill. "Let me down at the next turning."

They yelled at him in answer. The road twisted. The wheels of the cart grazed the walls as the horse bounded hither and thither. O'Neill stood up.

"Stop!" he cried. "Let me out."

"Hurrah ! " they shouted.

He leaned forward, seized one rein and tugged at it with all his might. The mare jerked aside. The wheel struck a stone in the wall. The cart was thrown violently to the opposite side of the road. It struck the wall, upturning the mare. O'Neill and the two peasants were thrown right over the low wall on to a mound in the field beyond. The mare began to moan. The three men lay dazed for a few minutes, then O'Neill got to his feet.

"What time is it?" he said.

Then he staggered across the field towards the Black Cliff.

One peasant shook himself and began to laugh.

"Hey! Nick," he said, "what happened to us?"

"Can't you see I'm speechless?" said the other, rolling about.

"Where's that young fellow going?" cried the first peasant, seeing O'Neill running away towards the cliff.

"Hey! Where are you going?"

O'Neill disappeared. Then the two peasants, hearing the moaning of the mare, remembered what had happened and became a little more sober. They crawled on to the road, saw the mare lying in the ditch, with the cart smashed and one of the wheels lying in the middle of the road. They examined the mare. Her two hind legs were broken. They sat down on the road and began to curse. They cursed one another at first and then they began to curse O'Neill.

A motor-car came towards them. It halted, lighting up the peasants, the wheel, the wrecked cart and the dying horse, with its headlights, McMenamin and another policeman got out of the car and came forward. They had revolvers in their hands.

"Who are you? Where are you from?"

The peasants did not answer.

"Speak up. Where are you from?"

"We're drunk," said one peasant. "Will you pay me for my mare? That's what I want to know."

"'Where do you come from?"

"Glen Tavern," said the other peasant.

"Where's the man who was with you?"

"It was he did it, blast his soul," said the first peasant. "He jumped up and caught the reins out of my hand, and ... "

"Where is he? Be quick."

"He did it on purpose," said the other peasant.

"Where is he? Quick. Do you want to get arrested?"

"Are you going to pay me for the mare? He ran off through that field. You go and catch him and make him pay for it. I'll bring an action against him."

"Through that field."

"Yes. Off that way. I called after him, but he ... "

"Come on, Mullaly," said McMenamin. "Luttrell, you stay here with the car. Don't let these two men go away." McMenamin and Mullaly jumped over the wall into the field, separated and moved towards the cliff, searching.

The moon appeared.

"Is he armed?" whispered Mullaly.

"I don't know," said McMenamin. "In any case... whist! What's that? Do you hear a voice?"

The two policemen drew close together and listened.

"Yes," whispered Mullaly. "It's a voice all right. No. It's a seal."

"A seal?" said McMenamin. "That's not the moaning of a seal. It's a man's voice. He's crying like a woman."

"God Almighty," said Mullaly. "It's like nothing that I ever heard. It sends a shiver through me."

They moved forward a few paces cautiously.

"Look!" whispered McMenamin, grasping Mullaly by the arm. "What's that thing there sticking out?"

"That's only the spike of the Black Cliff," said Mullaly. "It's like a ... "

" It's the moon that makes it look so queer. Hush! There's that bloody voice again."

"Great God! It's a man's voice. Do you hear?"

"Hush! It's he. I know the voice. Listen."

They were now abreast of the stone wall that bound the cliff top. They heard a voice coming from beyond the wall. At first it seemed to come from a great distance, a low moaning sound that gradually became louder and more distinct, forming a word which, for a long time, was unintelligible to them. At last the voice rose to a shriek and the word rang out distinctly, sharp, a heart-rending cry :

"Nora!"

Then the voice again became a moan.

"At him quick," cried McMenamin, rushing at the wall and jumping over it.

"Hands up," he cried, pointing his revolver at O'Neill.

O'Neill lay on his face, with his arms and legs stretched out sideways. In his right hand he held the handbag which Nora had dropped as the priest approached her. In his left hand he clutched a lock of her golden hair.

He raised his head and looked at McMenamin. His face had become distorted. His mouth was twisted. With an idiot's grin, he said:

"She's dead."

The policemen looked at one another.

"Who?" said McMenamin, going on one knee.

"Nora," whispered O'Neill. "She's dead."

"Nora!" gasped McMenamin. "You mean ... "

"Look ! " said O'Neill, again grinning like an idiot. "Look at her hair. Her lovely hair !"

He opened the hand in which he held a golden tress. The two policemen crossed themselves. They looked at the handbag and then at the rock, on which more golden hair was scattered.

McMenamin took the handbag, opened it and then closed it again, suddenly. He put it in his pocket.

"Where is she?" he said to O'Neill.

Suddenly O'Neill screamed and pointed towards the brink of the cliff.

"Don't look down there," he shrieked. " Her blood is on the edge, Nora!"

"I warn you," said McMenamin, "that anything you say will be used as evidence against you."

O'Neill gaped at the policeman. Then he grinned again like an idiot, and began to moan, uttering the one word :

"Nora!"

They had to carry him away like a cripple.

CHAPTER XX

IN the excitement, they had not sent word to the old woman of her son's seizure at his office. Since Nora's departure with Ramon, the old woman had remained in her kitchen, knitting and waiting. She never uttered a word. Several times Mary had tried to talk to her, to find out what had happened to Nora, but the old woman cut short Mary's questions by pursing up her lips and stabbing the air with a knitting needle.

Mary wandered back and forth through the house, going into Nora's room, into the drawing-room, into her own room, out on to the lawn and then back again to the kitchen.

"Mother, she hasn't come yet. Where can she be?"

The old woman would look up suddenly, knit her lips and stab the air with her needle.

When Tom Patch came in and stammered something about the stallion, the old woman looked at him in the same manner, knit her lips and stabbed the air with her needle.

It was customary, on fair days, for relatives to come in the afternoon to pay their respects to the old woman. On that day nobody came.

Then suddenly, Ramon Mor himself came driving into the yard on the baker's cart, shouting. The horse halted at the back door, slipping up on his haunches. Ramon threw away the reins and jumped down. The horse panted, shook himself, stood erect and then trotted away, with the reins dangling.

The old woman got to her feet and folded up her knitting. Ramon Mor came into the kitchen, staggering. When he saw his mother, he stretched out his two hands and muttered :

"I've been robbed."

"Robbed," said she. "Who by?"

"Give me a drink of water," he said, dropping on to a chair.

Mary was at the range, stirring a pot, in which porridge was being cooked for supper. She ran to fetch him some water. When she brought it to him he looked at her fiercely and said:

"Remember what I'm saying. From now on watch yourself."

"Ramon," said the old woman, "what has happened? Where is your shirt front and your tie?"

He opened his eyes in wonder and put his hand to his throat. He had not put on his front and necktie after they had been removed in the office during his fit.

"I kept silent too long," he cried, getting to his feet and taking the glass of water from Mary's hand. " I was too late." He raised the glass of water to his lips, but instead of drinking it, he hurled the glass to the floor.

"You too," he roared, raising his hand over his mother. "You too led me astray. I was surrounded with enemies. Even my own flesh and blood was plotting against me. You went to the priest, you, with your stories. You tried to drive her out of the house. Even O'Rourke was in league with the robbers. A plot!"

He struck his chest.

"I was too late," he cried. "But there is still time unless ... "

He looked at his mother savagely. Then his big lower lip trembled and he licked it with his tongue.

"Watch out for yourself now," he said. She burst into tears.

"Ramon," she said, "why don't you tell me ... ?"

"Ga, ga, Mr. Costello,': cried Tom Patch, appearing at the door. "You came just in time. The stallion is dead."

Ramon turned towards the man and stared.

"Ga, ga, sir, will I skin him now or will I ... ?"

"Clear out," said Ramon hoarsely.

The man started, fondled his beard, backed out of the kitchen and then ran across the yard, crossing himself and muttering:

"Jesus, Mary and Joseph!"

"Ramon," said the old woman, "what has happened to you?"

Looking at her, he muttered to himself for a few moments and then he raised his head, listening.

"It's not too late yet," he said. "Yes, yes. What did you say? Yes. They held a meeting. Then, when I thought I had them beaten, suddenly ... God!"

He raised his hands and cried:

"They tore the heart out of me. Robbed!"

He turned to the door and staggered out of the kitchen.

The old woman followed him :

"Where are you going?" she said.

Mary followed them.

"What do you want?" Ramon shouted at them, as he turned to mount the stairs. He waited until the old woman reached him.

"You must tell me about this, son," she said, glancing at him anxiously.

"I must see my wife first," he whispered, moving up the stairs.

She let him advance ten steps and then she called out:

"No use going up there looking for her."

Ramon halted, shuddered and grasped the banister violently with his left hand. He did not turn round.

"She's not up there," said the old woman. "She's not in the house."

The banister shook. He turned his head. Both Mary and the old woman drew back, terrified by his eyes that shone in the dusk like a cat's.

"She didn't come back, Ramon," cried Mary. "Something must have happened to her."

"Shut up, you," screamed the old woman.

But she caught her daughter by the waist and embraced her; and Mary leaned her head on the old woman's shoulder and burst into tears.

Muttering, Ramon turned around and came down the stairs, pausing after each step, with his head swaying on his neck. When he reached the floor, he whispered:

"What did you say?"

"I'm telling you the truth," cried the old woman. " She didn't come back."

There was a terrible silence.

Then they heard Ramon sucking his tongue. "After all," he said, "it's too late. No. No. I can't endure this." Then he roared, beating his breast, with his head thrown back:

"God ! I can't endure this. This is too much. I warn you, God, that my patience is exhausted. I warn you."

He stretched himself to his full height, with his hands raised above his head. They heard his muscles crack. He seemed to be trying to burst. Then they heard him say in a quiet tone that was even more terrifying than his roar :

"I must go."

He moved towards the door.

"Mother," he said, in the same strange tone, when he was at the door.

"Mother, speak to him," whispered Mary. "Don't let him out."

The old woman's little shrivelled body suddenly became limp in Mary's arms.

"Ramon, Mother has fainted," cried Mary.

Ramon groaned and opened the door.

"Ramon," cried Mary. "Where are you going?" His shapeless figure swayed in the doorway, darker than the gloom about him. Then he staggered down the steps becoming darker. '

The old woman recovered from her swoon, started looked at Ramon's retreating figure and then caught her daughter fiercely.

"Stop him," she gasped. "Go after him."

"I'm afraid, mother," gasped Mary. "I ... I can't move."

They both began to call after him, but they did not move. He turned around when he reached the bottom of the steps and they saw his arms rise above his head and they heard his voice crying hoarsely :

"I must find her."

Then they began to wail.

He passed into the darkness among the trees, whispering:

"Nora! Where are you? Come to me. I'm getting blind. I can't see. Nora! Speak to me."

He groped with his hands, passing over the lawn among the trees, feeling their trunks with his thick fingers.

"Quick! Quick!" he muttered. "I'm freezing. I've something to tell you. Nora!"

Then he stood, with drooping head, in an open space, dropped his arms limply and muttered:

"I can't speak. I'm choking." ,

He felt the extremities of his limbs becoming numb. His joints ached. The nape of his neck seemed to be turning into stone. His heart beat with great violence. It seemed a great fire was burning there. The flames were rising in his throat. His head was trying to rise from his body. He opened his mouth and tried to shout. He made no sound, but the shock of the effort loosed his muscles, restored his energy, set his brain thinking and he saw, all together, the two priests, the meeting, the letter crumpled on the floor, the empty cold bed, her golden hair, the red arrow, the doctor stammering, and lastly, the mad look in the priest's eyes as he dashed out of the office.

He rushed through the trees, stumbling against their trunks, rustling their branches with his arms, crunching the gravel on the drive, with fire before his eyes. Now his whole body ached, and there was a burning tube reaching to his heart that writhed with love for her.

Farrelly's wife was standing in the gateway, before her lodge, with a child in her arms.

"God bless us," she said. "Mr. Costello, did you see my husband?" He paused and looked at her.

"I heard somebody singing," she said, "and I went down the road thinking it was Dan, coming along drunk, and it's somebody else singing down there in Jack Geraghty's cottage ... God save us from harm! Where is he, sir? He's gone since dawn."

"Singing," said Ramon, dashing out into the road.

"Singing," he repeated, running to the left along the sandy road.

The woman ran out into the road after him. Then she ran back, past the lodge, up to Ramon's house. The moon appeared and shone upon the earth and sea. It gleamed on the yellow sand about his feet, on the shoregrass, on the falling beach, on the weeds that rolled in the foaming wash of the sea's edge, on the white walls of the cottage, on the rocks that rose in rising walls to the cliff, upon whose summit the spike of stone stood out over the sea, beneath the towering mountains, whose peaks were in the clouds.

Above the murmur of the sea he heard a voice chanting.

He halted.

"That's he," he muttered.

Then he advanced, slowly now, towards the cottage. When he was moving over the rocks at the gable, he heard a shriek from afar. The chanting ceased. He listened and raised his face to the sky. The shriek re-echoed many times on the silent air. He heard it. It was her name that had been shrieked. Then he rushed forward, stumbling against the gable, round the corner, to the window of the cottage, through which he saw a light gleaming. He thrust his face against the window. He saw the priest within, sitting motionless at a table, with his head turned to one side, listening.

The door was wide open. The walls of the room were white. The floor was brown. There was no furniture except the table and the chair upon which the priest sat. Both the table and the chair were white. There was nothing on the table except a candle in a white candlestick and the priest's hands, which looked yellowish in the moonlight. The priest sat close to the table, erect in his chair, with his head turned to one side, listening. Ramon could only see one eye, looking away. The stock of the priest's collar lay over his left shoulder and one end of the collar stuck up over his ear. His waistcoat was in disorder. Some of the upper buttons were missing. There was a rent in the right sleeve of his black coat near the shoulder. His forehead was scratched in several places. His black hair was tousled.

Then he slowly turned his head and looked at Ramon's face, which lay against the window. He withdrew his hands from the table. His face showed no emotion. His eyes were fixed.

Ramon moved towards the door, stumbling along the wall, groping with his hands. He entered the room. He straightened himself against the wall, between the window and the door. He stared at the priest. Neither spoke. The priest hunched up his shoulders, sniffed and put his hands on the table.

A moth appeared near the candle. It whirled round and round the light.

They were both disturbed by the noise of the moth's wings.

"Where is she?" whispered Ramon.

The priest's hands began to move. Ramon looked down at them. He thrust forward his right foot.

"Don't move," said the priest sharply.

"Ha!" said Ramon.

He looked around him, sucking his tongue.

"Where is she?" he repeated.

The priest did not reply.

Ramon looked again at the priest, to find that the priest's face was now shining.

"What have you done with her?" he whispered, taking another pace forward.

"I hate you," cried the priest with great force. "I have hated you for years. She's dead now. It was you I hated, not her."

Ramon staggered back against the wall, with his arms stretched out. He shivered from head to foot and muttered:

"Dead! She's dead?"

"She's dead," said the priest in an extraordinary voice, waving his hands. "She's dead. Dead. You know who is dead."

Then he looked towards the door and said in a still stranger voice :

"By now she's miles from here."

"Nora dead !" gasped Ramon. "My Nora ! Do you mean my Nora?"

The priest began to scratch the table and muttered :

"Quem advocatum sum venturus ... "

"Nora dead!" cried Ramon, throwing back his head and raising his arms. "God! I say! God! Do you hear me? Is Nora dead?"

He staggered forward and then became motionless, with his head thrown back and his hands raised above his head. Then his body sagged at the knees. His head fell forward on his chest. He seemed to be about to crumble up on the floor. But suddenly, as he was falling, his shoulders stiffened, his eyes grew narrow, his hands clenched, he lowered them and cried with great force:

"Now, neither God nor devil can stop me."

The priest uttered a low cry, pushed back his chair and upset the table. The candle was quenched as it fell. A yellow stream of moonlight lay across the floor, between Ramon and the priest, who ran to the far wall and crouched with his hands before his face.

Ramon stepped back and closed the door. The room became quite dark. There was only a narrow stream of moonlight shining through the window on to the wall on the left. The priest began to whisper.

"Speak up now," cried Ramon hoarsely, "and save yourself if you can. What did you do to her?"

"Passion of Christ, comfort me ! " whispered the priest. "Comfort me as I fight my way, safe to the haven of Thy Sacred Heart. Comfort me when every hope is lost, and when that last dread hour has sounded and my eyes are closing on this world of sin."

"Speak, devil. What have you done to her?"

"O! Passion of Christ. Lead me gently to Thy wounded sacred feet above. I have obeyed Thy voice."

Ramon was now close to the priest. He stretched out his hands. The priest stretched up his hands and whispered:

"Sweet Jesus ! Tell me now it was Thy voice that called me, that my hands crushed this serpent at Your bidding. Tell me before I perish."

"Ha!"

"Dies ir-r-r-r-rae ... "

"Ha! Ha! Ha!"

Then Ramon dropped the lifeless body to the floor.

CHAPTER XXI

THEY found him dragging himself along the yellow sandy road towards the lodge. He was moaning. He was using his right hand to claw the sand in front of him and his right leg to push himself against the crunching yellow sand behind. His left arm and his left hand hung limply. He lay still when they approached and stopped moaning.

Farrelly's wife, Peadar Mor, Tom Patch, Mary, a policeman and a crowd of peasant men and women, who had arrived at the house with news of the robbery and of the riot, were there.

One of his eyes was closed. The other was wide open and fixed. He did not see them. He was blind. Neither did he recognise their voices. Only a small fraction of his being was conscious, a little red spot somewhere in the centre of his body.

That spot was fixed on a mass of golden hair that floated high in a vacant place, where rain was falling from dark clouds, falling without sound upon the waving strands of golden hair that wove her name among the falling drops as they floated. All round the gleaming gold, the walls of eternity were closing slowly, creeping through the rain upon the waving hair.

"We caught the robbers, sir, two of them. Their car broke down."

He moved one side of his mouth, trying to mutter that it was her hair he saw. They caught him around the body and tried to lift him.

"Bring a chair out of the lodge. We'll put him on it."

With a sudden swoop, eternity joined its walls and blotted out the hair. Now the rain fell with a loud sound and there was nothing else in all the universe. The red spot grew dim. He began to writhe and to gasp for breath as they raised him to put him sitting on the chair.

"No. Get out a mattress. We can't carry him this way."

They brought out a mattress and put him on it. He lay like a corpse as they carried him, six of them. His right hand kept groping. Now he saw nothing and all his energy gathered round the spark, blowing at it, to keep it from extinguishing.

They carried him up the steps into the hall. They laid him down gently on the floor. His mother ran forward and threw herself on his chest. The peasant women knelt. The men took off their hats. The door was closed. They brought a lamp and placed it on the hall-stand above the· mattress. An old woman sprinkled holy water on him. His mother fumbled at his shirt, opened it, and put her withered hand over his heart.

The red spark disappeared. There was a rumbling sound in his throat. He thrust out his right hand and caught the leg of the hall-stand. He squeezed upon it, raised his chest off the ground and then as it fell with a thud upon the mattress, the leg of the hall-stand splintered and broke. His hand fell heavily to the ground, clutching a piece of the wood.

He lay perfectly still, with his mouth open.

The old woman shrieked and beat her face against his chest. The peasant women threw themselves on the ground and began to chant the death dirge. The men knelt and crossed themselves.

An old man went to the door and threw it wide open, to let out the departing spirit.

The moonlight poured into the hall upon the wailing women, upon the kneeling men, upon the old woman tearing her hair, upon Ramon Mor's enormous corpse, stretched stiff upon the mattress and upon his eye that stared, unblinking, at eternity.

THE END

ABOUT THE AUTHOR

Son of a Fenian father, Liam O'Flaherty (*Liam Ó Flaithearta*),1896 – 1984, was born in Inishmore, the biggest of the Aran Islands, off Ireland's Atlantic coast. He became one of the most distinguished and prolific writers, in Irish and English, of his generation and was one of the major figures of the Irish Literary Renaissance. Abandoning an early intention to join the priesthood, he joined the British Army, under his mother's surname and was wounded the Western Front. After the war, he travelled to South America, Turkey, Canada and the Soviet Union, holding a variety of jobs before entering the United States illegally in 1920. He joined the Communist Party there, a move that determined the politics he supported for most of his life. He returned to Ireland in 1921, at the height of the War of Independence. His ideas for Ireland's future differed radically from those of Sinn Féin. Two days following the foundation of the Irish Free State, he and some followers occupied and held for four days the Rotunda building in Dublin, flying the red flag in a failed attempt at socialist revolution. Shortly afterwards O'Flaherty made his way to London where he wrote short stories in Irish. However, this early work was badly received, prompting him to write henceforth mainly in English. His first novel, *The Neighbour's Wife*, was published in 1923 and was followed by a stream of novels, short stories, and poems. *The House of Gold* (1929) has the distinction of being the first of many literary works to be banned by the newly constituted Irish Censorship of Publications Board in 1929. Subsequent works of his were to suffer the same fate. His writing combines a graphic and striking naturalism, acute psychological analysis, poetry and biting satire together with an abiding sympathy for the common man and anger against injustice. The powerful ideological substratum of the writings of this lifetime Marxist is seldom noted or commented upon. Liam O'Flaherty died on 7 September 1984, aged 88, in Dublin. A memorial garden in his native village of Gort na gCapall, Inishmore, commemorates the life and work of this literary giant.

CPSIA information can be obtained at www.ICGtesting.com
Printed in the USA
BVOW03s2159091213

338666BV00012B/467/P

9 781484 097496